LAW MAKING
IN THE LATER
ROMAN REPUBLIC

LAW MAKING
IN THE LATER
ROMAN REPUBLIC

BY

ALAN WATSON

OXFORD
AT THE CLARENDON PRESS
1974

Oxford University Press, Ely House, London W. 1

GLASGOW NEW YORK TORONTO MELBOURNE WELLINGTON
CAPE TOWN IBADAN NAIROBI DAR ES SALAAM LUSAKA ADDIS ABABA
DELHI BOMBAY CALCUTTA MADRAS KARACHI LAHORE DACCA
KUALA LUMPUR SINGAPORE HONG KONG TOKYO

ISBN 0 19 825326 5

© *Oxford University Press 1974*

*Printed in Great Britain
at the University Press, Oxford
by Vivian Ridler
Printer to the University*

FOR
LISL AND HERBERT HAUSMANINGER
SIGHILD AND FRITZ RABER

PREFACE

In this book I am concerned with the contributions of what might very loosely be called the 'sources' of private law in the last two centuries of the Roman Republic. More than most others, these two hundred years form a historical unity, different from what preceded and what came after, and without doubt they constitute the period of the world's greatest legal development. Yet the law of the later Republic and its making have been the object of remarkably little independent systematic study. It is this which accounts for two possibly unfortunate features of the present book: first the frequent references to my own researches, in particular to the four volumes on the substantive law of the later Republic; secondly the predominance of detailed argument to establish what contributed, and when and how, to the growth of the law. The book takes the place of a volume originally promised under the title 'Legal Science in the Later Roman Republic': the name was changed when I discovered that neither I nor most of the friends whom I consulted had any clear notion of what 'legal science' meant. But the search for a satisfactory title made me more aware of what ought to go into the book and, in the result, its scope is wider, not narrower, than what is often comprehended in the term 'legal science'. Most of Chapter 3 reproduces an article of the same name first published in the *Journal of Roman Studies* 60 (1970) and I must thank the Society for the Promotion of Roman Studies for their generous permission to re-use the article in this form. Four friends—Professor A. M. Honoré and Professor Reuven Yaron, both lawyers, Professor Francis Cairns, a Latinist, and Mr. Robin Seager, an ancient historian—read the whole typescript and gave me the benefit of their criticism and experience. Others, in particular Professor Giuliano Crifò and Professor

Barry Nicholas, permitted me to make use of their work before publication. To all of them I am very grateful.

Apart from final revisions the writing of this book was complete by October 1972.

ALAN WATSON

Edinburgh
January 1973

CONTENTS

THE DEVELOPMENT OF THE LAW

ABBREVIATIONS

BIDR	*Bullettino dell'Istituto di Diritto Romano.*
Bremer, *Iurisprudentiae* i	Bremer, *Iurisprudentiae Antehadrianae quae supersunt*, i (Leipzig, 1896).
Broughton, *Magistrates* i, ii	Broughton, *The Magistrates of the Roman Republic*, i (New York, 1951), ii (1952).
Bruns, *Fontes*	Bruns, *Fontes Iuris Romani*, 7th edit. by Gradenwitz (Tübingen, 1909).
Buckland, *Textbook*	Buckland, *A Textbook of Roman Law*, 3rd edit., revised by Stein (Cambridge, 1963).
CIL	*Corpus Inscriptionum Latinarum* (Berlin, 1863–).
Daube, *Forms*	Daube, *Forms of Roman Legislation* (Oxford, 1956).
FIRA i, ii, iii	*Fontes Iuris Romani Antejustiniani*, 2nd edit., i (Florence, 1941), ii (1940), iii (1950).
Horak, *Rationes* i	Horak, *Rationes decidendi*, i (Aalen, 1969).
Index Itp.	*Index Interpolationum quae in Iustiniani Digestis inesse dicuntur*, i, ii, iii, and *Supplementum* (Weimar, 1929–35).
Jolowicz and Nicholas, *Introduction*	Jolowicz and Nicholas, *Historical Introduction to the Study of Roman Law*, 3rd edit., (Cambridge, 1972).
JRS	*Journal of Roman Studies.*
Kaser	Kaser
RPR i	*Das römische Privatrecht*, i, 2nd edit. (Munich, 1971).
ZPR	*Das römische Zivilprozessrecht* (Munich, 1966).
Kunkel, *Herkunft*	Kunkel, *Herkunft und soziale Stellung der römischen Juristen*, 2nd edit. (Graz, Vienna, Cologne, 1967).
Lenel	Lenel
Edictum	*Das Edictum Perpetuum*, 3rd edit. (Leipzig, 1927).
Pal. i, ii	*Palingenesia Iuris Civilis*, i, ii (Leipzig, 1889).
Mommsen, *Staatsrecht* i, ii, iii	Mommsen, *Römisches Staatsrecht*, i, ii, 3rd edit. (Leipzig, 1887), iii, 1st edit. (Leipzig, 1888).

RE	Pauly–Wissowa, *Real-Encyclopädie der classischen Altertumswissenschaft* (Stuttgart, 1873–).
RIDA	*Revue internationale des droits de l'antiquité.*
Rotondi, *Leges*	Rotondi, *Leges publicae populi romani* (Milan, 1912).
Schulz, *Legal Science*	Schulz, *History of Roman Legal Science* (Oxford, 1946).
SDHI	*Studia et Documenta Historiae et Iuris.*
TLL	*Thesaurus Linguae Latinae* (Leipzig, 1900–).
TvR	*Tijdschrift voor Rechtsgeschiedenis.*
Watson	Alan Watson
Obligations	*The Law of Obligations in the Later Roman Republic* (Oxford, 1965).
Persons	*The Law of Persons in the Later Roman Republic* (Oxford, 1967).
Private Law	*Roman Private Law around 200 B.C.* (Edinburgh, 1971).
Property	*The Law of Property in the Later Roman Republic* (Oxford, 1965).
Succession	*The Law of Succession in the Later Roman Republic* (Oxford, 1971).
ZSS	*Zeitschrift der Savigny-Stiftung (Romanistische Abteilung).*

INTRODUCTION

THE subject of this book is the making of private law, that is the forces which shaped the development of private law, in the later Roman Republic. The rules of private law will not be discussed for their own sake but only in so far as they illuminate the general development.

The period surveyed will be from the Second Punic War at the end of the third century B.C. to the establishment of the Principate by Octavian in 27 B.C. The reign of Augustus is no arbitrary date. Though the Republic was restored in theory, the law-making factors were in practice profoundly modified: the Praetor's Edict virtually ceased to introduce new edicts; legislation at the request of the Princeps became important; the influential jurists were to some extent controlled by the obscure *ius respondendi* and the likelihood of public office at the pleasure of the Princeps.

No such clear break is apparent to set the beginning of the period, but the choice of the time of the Second Punic War is easily defended. There is a vast difference between law and legal science—and history, literature, religion, and society—at the beginning and at the end of the Republic. The most natural division for law, as for other things, between the early Republic and the late Republic falls near the end of the third century and the beginning of the second century B.C. Thus, at that time there were more statutes important for private law than in any other corresponding period in the Republic: the *lex Atilia de tutore dando* probably of 210, the *lex Cincia de donis et muneribus* of 204, the *lex Laetoria* (or *Plaetoria*) of 193 or 192, and, very likely, the *lex Furia testamentaria*. The earliest known praetorian edict dates from 213 B.C.[1], though it has little significance for the development of private law. While it was not until late in the second century B.C. that the Praetor's Edict modified the substance of private

---

[1] Livy 25. 1. 12; cf. *infra*, p. 45.

law, the measure of damages was being changed by edict in the
last quarter of the third century B.C.: the *edictum generale* for
iniuria is probably the work of an urban praetor of that period.[1]
The curule aediles were issuing edicts by 189 at the latest.[2] The
first jurist of whom we have any record who did not hold a priestly
office was Sextus Aelius Paetus Catus who was consul in 198
and censor in 196.[3] He was also the author of a book of a new type,
the *tripertita*, whose significance can scarcely be exaggerated.[4]
A more prosaic reason for beginning this book around 200 B.C.
would be that evidence of legal science in earlier days is too sparing
to permit of continuous exposition.

Politically the victory over the Carthaginians in 202 B.C. meant
that Rome was the most powerful force in the Mediterranean,
while the wars which followed gave Rome an economy based on
conquest and slaves. The conquest of Greece in the next few years
not only increased her power but left her open much more than
before, in major and minor ways, to the influence of Hellenism.
The *early* Republic had seen the introduction in great measure of
Greek religious ritual and Greek gods. The last step in this process
in the Roman state religion was in 205, a time of intense religious
excitement, when the Phrygian *Magna Mater* was brought to
Rome.[5] Thereafter during the Republic the state religion declined.
But in other matters such as literature, philosophy, and the
visual arts, the later Republic was the main period of Greek
influence.

It was during the two centuries covered by this book that
Roman law became what it was essentially to be right up to
Justinian's codification. But we must not forget that the period of
change had really begun about a century earlier. Thus the archaic
nexum disappeared as a result of the *lex Poetilia* of about 326 or,
as I think, 313.[6] The earliest recorded juristic book, which may
or may not be imaginary, was *de usurpationibus* by Appius Claudius

---

[1] Cf. *infra*, pp. 45 ff.
[2] Plautus, *Cap*. 803 ff.; cf. Watson, 'The Imperatives of the Aedilician Edict',
TvR 39 (1971), 73 ff. at p. 82.
[3] Cf. Kunkel, *Herkunft*, p. 8.   [4] Cf. *infra*, pp. 112 ff.
[5] Livy 29. 10–14; Varro, *de ling. lat.* 6. 15.
[6] Cf. *infra*, pp. 9 ff.

Caecus, censor in 312, consul in 307.[1] The forms of the *legis actiones* were published, it is said, by his scribe Gnaeus Flavius not later than 304.[2] This *ius civile Flavianum* was followed, not many years afterwards, by a second collection of the *legis actiones*, the *ius Aelianum*, by an otherwise unknown Sextus Aelius.[3] *Plebiscita* came to have the force of law by the passing of the *lex Hortensia* in 287. The *lex Aquilia* of 287 became the basis of the law of damage to property. *Formulae* were introduced[4] for some types of case, even when both parties were Roman citizens,[5] so was the earliest *bonae fidei* action, the *actio tutelae*,[6] and, in my view, at least the two most important of the revolutionary consensual contracts, *emptio venditio* and *locatio conductio*.[7] In the circumstances I hope readers will forgive the frequent backward glances.

The scope of this book owes much to Cicero, *top*. 5. 28, where that writer seeks to illustrate definition by enumeration: 'If one were to say that the civil law consists of statutes, decrees of the Senate, previous court decisions, the authority of the jurists, the edicts of the magistrates, custom and equity.'[8] Tempting though it might be, one cannot take this enumeration of the parts of the civil law as a list of the sources of the civil law in the time of Cicero.[9] When he proceeds to make plainer the difference between

[1] The most recent detailed analysis of the evidence for this book is by Mayer-Maly, 'Roms älteste Juristenschrift', *Mnemosynon Bizoukides* (Thessalonike, 1960), 221 ff.
[2] The sources conflict as to whether he published the actions in 304 when he was curule aedile or earlier: D. 1. 2. 2. 7 (Pomponius, *sing. enchirid.*); Livy 10. 46. 5; Cicero, *pro Murena*, 11. 25; *ad Att.* 6. 1. 8; *de orat.* 1. 41. 186; Pliny, *N.H.* 33. 6. 17.
[3] Not, I think, Sextus Aelius Paetus Catus, consul of 198. On all this see Watson, '*Ius Aelianum* and *tripertita*', *Labeo* 19 (1973), pp. 26 ff.
[4] Unless they are still older!
[5] Cf., e.g., Watson, *Private Law*, pp. 126 f.
[6] For the argument that the *actio tutelae* is the oldest *bonae fidei* action see Watson, *Persons*, pp. 140 ff.
[7] Cf. *infra*, pp. 89 ff.
[8] The text is quoted *infra*, p. 25.
[9] As for instance does Nörr: 'Ciceros *Topica* und die römische Rechtsquellenlehre', *Romanitas* 9 (1971), 419 ff. at p. 424; *Divisio und Partitio* (Berlin, 1972), p. 12. Likewise in Cicero, *de inven.* 2. 22. 65, we cannot translate 'ius ex quibus rebus constet, considerandum est' as '[the parties] must consider the sources from which law arises' but rather as 'must consider the matters which make up law'.

definition by enumeration and by analysis Cicero claims that 'in enumeration there are, as it were, members, as the head, shoulders, hands, sides, thighs, feet, etc., are members of the body'.[1] Indeed, Cicero's list of the 'parts' of the civil law itself shows that it is not really meaningful to talk on any one level of 'sources' of law in the late Republic. Thus, for instance, *senatusconsulta* had no law-creating force,[2] *edicta* technically did not change the law, and the opinions and writings of the jurists had no official standing. Yet the last two especially modified the law profoundly and were the chief factors in its modernization. One might in theory draw a distinction between *lex* as a formal authoritative creator of law and these others, but it would have no real meaning, and it is to the credit of the Romans of the Republic that there is no sign of any attempt at such a distinction. There is no theory of 'sources of law' in the Republic and in truth there could hardly be one. Indeed, the notion of 'source of law' is foreign to the Republican texts. *Leges*[3] were authoritative in theory and practice; *edicta* were all-powerful in practice but in theory could not change the law; *senatusconsulta* were not thought of as making private law but they had a profound influence on the conduct of magistrates; jurists and their writings had no official standing, hence in theory there could be no distinction between the opinions of one jurist and another, but the opinions of some individuals would be decisive because of their quality and the reputation of the author.[4]

It is thus not surprising that in his definition by enumeration Cicero lists 'parts' of the civil law which no modern jurist would regard as a formal source. Equally it is not a matter for astonishment that the *Rhetorica ad Herennium*, 2. 13. 19, gives a rather different list of the parts: '. . . De eo causa posita dicere poterimus, si, ex quibus partibus ius constet cognoverimus. Constat igitur ex his partibus: natura, lege, consuetudine, iudicato, aequo et bono, pacto. . . .'[5]

---

[1] 6. 30.   [2] Cf. *infra*, pp. 21 ff.
[3] For private law this means *plebiscita*.
[4] Jurisprudential scholars are, of course, skilled in distinguishing the various meanings of 'source of law'. But we need not, I think, go into these meanings here. Modern theory seems even to reject as unhelpful the notion of sources of law.
[5] See also Cicero, *de inven.* 2. 22. 65 ff.

Perhaps it is impossible to discover the precise sense in which the author of *ad Herennium* and Cicero[1] were using the idea of 'the parts of the law', but the practical purpose of the former at least is apparent. When a lawsuit turns on a point of law and the facts are not in issue, the items on the list provide the orator with the appropriate argument for asserting that the law is on his side.[2] That is to say, the orator can claim that his client's case is right in law because of nature, equity, precedent etc. The *partes*, accordingly, would seem to be the factors which an orator can argue have determined the existence of a particular principle, rule, or point of law.[3]

It seemed right, therefore, to consider the importance for the development of private law of all Cicero's 'parts of the civil law'. But the scope appropriate to the book seemed wider and to involve the questions: Where would a Roman find the law in the later Republic? i.e. what categories of thing would he regard as binding (or even highly persuasive)?; what arguments (e.g. from equity) were regarded as acceptable when there was a gap to be filled or when two interpretations appeared possible?; and what active influences (e.g. Greek rhetoric) were there on the development of the law? It thus appeared justifiable to write sections in the appropriate places on matters such as the role of the censors, innovations resulting from the magistrates' control of the courts, Greek influence, and the degree of organization of legal concepts and materials.

[1] It is right, I think, to believe that both authors are using the idea in the same way.
[2] This appears from *Rhet. ad Herenn.* 2. 10. 14; 2. 11. 16.
[3] Or perhaps as Kaser, discussing *top.* 5. 28, says: 'For the orator it is not a question here of how the *ius civile* comes to be, but of how one can recognize the law in accordance with which the Romans live': '*Mores maiorum* und Gewohnheitsrecht', *ZSS* 59 (1939), 52 ff. at p. 97.

1

THE ORGANS OF LEGISLATION
FOR PRIVATE LAW

IT seems to be generally agreed that during the later Republic legislation on private law matters was passed by the *comitia centuriata* and by the *concilium plebis*, especially—for some unknown reason—by the latter.[1] The Senate was a deliberative body, and its *decreta* on private law were not law-creating.[2]

The demarcation line between private law legislation by the *comitia centuriata* and by the *concilium plebis* is very obscure. In most cases we do not know which body was responsible for a particular statute. Kunkel observes that Roman statutes are called by the family name of their proposers and suggests that a double title, for instance the *lex Poetilia Papiria*, usually points to a comitial statute proposed (as was usual) by both consuls together, while a simple title, for instance the *lex Aquilia*, points to a *plebiscitum* proposed by a tribune. But the suggestion is not wholly helpful. To begin with, some *leges* which we know had a simple name were not *plebiscita*. Thus, the *lex Valeria* of 300 B.C. was proposed by the consul, Valerius.[3] Others which had two proposers may in some texts be given a double name, in others a simple name; for instance the *lex Iunia Vellaea*[4] of around A.D. 28 is sometimes referred to as the *lex Vellaea*.[5] Equally important, some of the names given to statutes are not found in the sources but are the creation of later scholars, hence they cannot

---

[1] Cf., e.g., Buckland, *Textbook*, p. 4; Wieacker, *Vom römischen Recht*, 2nd edit. (Stuttgart, 1961), p. 62; Taylor, *Roman Voting Assemblies* (Ann Arbor, 1966), p. 60; Watson, *Private Law*, pp. 5 ff.

[2] Cf. *infra*, pp. 21 ff.

[3] Livy 10. 9. That this is not a statute concerning private law is irrelevant to the point at issue.

[4] G. 2. 134; D. 26. 2. 10. 2; 28. 3. 13.

[5] D. 28. 2. 29. 5, 6, 7; 28. 5. 6. 1.

be relied upon. This is true even of the so-called *lex Poetilia Papiria*.[1]

In this chapter I wish to argue that the evidence available points to the conclusion that the *comitia centuriata* did not legislate on private law matters during the later Republic except in very exceptional circumstances. Near the beginning of our period there is an important clue which seems to be overlooked. In 186 B.C. a freedwoman prostitute, Hispala Faecenia, revealed to her lover, Publius Aebutius, the dangers of the Bacchanalian orgies.[2] He thereupon refused his mother's request that he be initiated and he was driven from home by his mother, stepfather, and four slaves. Next day he reported the matter to one of the consuls, Spurius Postumius, who by means of threats dragged the story of the Bacchic rites from Hispala Faecenia. The cult and its adherents were savagely put down, and the consul raised the question of a reward for these two informers. A *senatusconsultum* was passed that the urban quaestors should pay each of them 100,000 *asses* from the treasury; that the consul should propose to the tribunes of the plebs that they put before the people as soon as possible that Publius Aebutius be regarded as having completed his military service, that he should not serve in the army against his will, and that the censor should not assign him an *equus publicus* without his consent, and also that Hispala Faecenia be given the right to convey ownership, enter contracts, and marry outside her *gens* all without her tutor's consent, and that she be given *optio tutoris* as if her husband had granted her that right by will,[3] and so on. These proposals were put before the plebs and carried.[4] What concerns us most is the private law rights granted to the woman. Contrary to what seems to be the opinion of Mommsen[5] and Kübler[6] the grant was not made by a *senatusconsultum* but, as Rotondi noticed,[7] by a *plebiscitum*. Only the

---

[1] Cf. *infra*, pp. 9 ff.   For the whole story see Livy 39. 8–19.

[3] On all this see now Watson, '*Enuptio gentis*', *Daube Noster* (Edinburgh and London, 1974), pp. 331 ff.

[4] Livy 39. 19. 3–7.

[5] 'Die römischen Eigennamen der republikanischen und augusteischen Zeit', now in *Römische Forschungen*, i (Berlin, 1864), pp. 1 ff. at p. 9, n. 5; *Staatsrecht* iii. 21, n. 1. But he is more accurate in *Staatsrecht* iii. 1121, n. 5.

[6] *RE* 7, s.v. *gens* at 1186.   [7] *Leges*, p. 276.

reward of 100,000 *asses* was directly given by the *senatusconsultum*. What is possibly surprising is that the Senate did not ask the tribunes of the plebs to bring the matter of the grant of private law rights before the *concilium plebis*,[1] but requested the consul to take up with the tribunes of the plebs the putting of the grant before the *concilium plebis*. Of course, the consul, Spurius Postumius, was very much involved in the whole affair, which may help to explain the course adopted. What is obviously important, though, is that the decree of the Senate was not that the consul should put the matter of the grants before the *comitia centuriata* which Spurius Postumius himself could have summoned. The true significance of this approach of the Senate can only be revealed by an examination of all the Republican statutes subsequent to the XII Tables which bear on private law.

Of these, the sources show the following to be *plebiscita*:[2] *lex Canuleia* of 445 B.C.;[3] *lex Aquilia* of 287;[4] *lex Cincia* of 204;[5] *lex Furia* on wills, dating from before 169;[6] *lex Voconia* of 169;[7] and the *lex Falcidia* of 40.[8]

No sure evidence of the method of promulgation exists for the *lex Aebutia*, *lex Appuleia* on suretyship, *lex Atilia* on tutors, *lex Atinia* on usucapion, *lex Calpurnia* on the *legis actio*, *lex Licinnia* on the *actio communi dividundo*, *lex Laetoria* (or *Plaetoria*) of 193/192, *lex Cicereia*, *lex Furia* on suretyship, *lex Hostilia* on representation in the *actio furti*, *lex Iulia et Titia* (whether one statute or two), *lex Mamilia Roscia Peducaea Alliena Fabia*, *lex Maenia* (if it did concern private law), *lex Minicia* (whether or not it is Republican), *lex Plautia* on violence,[9] *lex Publilia* on surety-

---

[1] But the senate often avoids direct dealings with the tribunes.

[2] They are arranged in historical order in so far as it is known.

[3] Livy 4. 1–4; Cicero, *de re pub.* 2. 37. 63; Florus, *Epit.* 1. 17 (1. 25).

[4] D. 9. 2. 1. 1 (Ulpian, 18 *ad ed.*).

[5] From Cicero, *de senec.* 4. 10, the *lex Cincia* can be dated to 204 B.C., and we know from Livy 29. 20. 11 that in that year M. Cincius Alimentus was a tribune of the plebs.

[6] Argued (possibly too simply) from Cicero, *pro Balbo*, 8. 21; cf., e.g., Steinwenter, *RE* 12. 2355, s.v. *lex Furia*.

[7] Livy, *epit.* 41.

[8] Dio Cassius 48. 33. 5; Isidorus, *etym.* 5. 15. 2.

[9] In the main this cannot be considered a private law statute. But it is listed because it forbade the usucapion of things seized by violence: G. 2. 45.

ship, *lex Scribonia* on the usucapion of servitudes, *lex Silia* on the *legis actio*.[1]

Sulla's legislation around 81 B.C. while dictator is a special case (which we will discuss later); *lex Cornelia de confirmandis testamentis, lex Cornelia de falsis, lex Cornelia de iniuriis, lex Cornelia de adulteriis, lex Cornelia de sponsu*.[2] The same will be true of Julius Caesar's *lex Iulia de vi*, possibly of around 46 B.C., if it existed and if it had any relevance for private law.

This leaves us with only one statute, the famous law on *nexum* from the late fourth century B.C., the so-called *lex Poetilia Papiria*. This, on the basis of Livy 8. 28, is generally believed to have been passed by some *comitia* in 326[3] at the instigation of C. Poetilius Libo and L. Papirius Cursor, the consuls of that year. The testimony of Livy in 8. 28. 8 is indeed unambiguous. The story is that the *lex* was passed as a result of the abuse of an unfortunately handsome debtor, C. Publilius, by the creditor, L. Papirius. But Livy's is not the only account. According to Varro, *de lingua latina*, 7. 105, the alteration in the law of *nexum* was made by C. Poetilius Libo Visolus when he was dictator.[4] C. Poetilius C. f. C. n. Libo Visolus, the son of the consul mentioned by Livy, appears in the Fasti as dictator in 313 B.C., and Livy also names C. Poetilius as dictator in 313.[5] Dionysius of Halicarnassus, 16. 5 (9) tells us that the unhappy debtor was Publius, the son of one of the military tribunes surrendered to the Samnites after the Caudine Forks disaster. The tribunes of the plebs,[6] Dionysius says, brought a capital indictment against the creditor. A law was passed on *nexum*, but Dionysius does not specifically reveal who

[1] On all these see the appropriate entry in Rotondi, *Leges*.

[2] Not all of these are conclusively proved to be the work of Sulla. The point is not of vital importance at this stage.

[3] Cf., e.g., Rotondi, *Leges*, pp. 230 f.; Girard, *Manuel élémentaire de droit romain*, 8th edit. by Senn (Paris, 1929), pp. 514 f., 515, n. 1; Berger, *RE* supp. 7. 405 ff.; Kaser, *RPR* i. 154, n. 36: *contra*, Rudorff, *Römische Rechtsgeschichte*, i (Leipzig, 1857), p. 47.

[4] Rotondi dismisses the Varro text as corrupt: loc. cit. But though the dictator's name is corrupt in the manuscripts and appears as 'C. popillio vocare sillo', the text is not corrupt where it makes the person responsible for the *lex* a dictator.

[5] 9. 28. 2. But in 9. 28. 6 he mentions that according to one tradition Poetilius was dictator *clavi figendi causa*.

[6] This is the only possible meaning of Dionysius' δημάρχοι.

the instigators were. Since the Caudine Forks disaster was in
321 B.C., Dionysius' account is very much contrary to that of Livy
with regard to the dating, and hence to the attribution of responsibility to the consuls Poetilius and Papirius. Valerius Maximus,
6. 1. 9, says the debtor was T. Veturius, the son of that Veturius
who in his consulate was surrendered to the Samnites because of
the dishonourable treaty. The creditor he gives as P. Plotius.
Veturius complained to the consuls, and the Senate ordered Plotius
to be imprisoned. Nothing is said of legislation, nor of who was
responsible for any. Again, because of the reference to the Caudine
Forks disaster, Valerius Maximus' account is at odds with Livy's
dating and with Poetilius' and Papirius' being responsible for the
legislation as consuls.

Modern juristic belief in the accuracy of Livy's version seems
to derive mainly from Mommsen,[1] though he himself was rather
less positive. Mommsen pointed out that there is no record of the
dictator Poetilius ever having been consul, yet in his view the
consulship was in practice a requirement for the dictatorship at
that time. Further, he pointed to the discrepancy of Livy and
Varro in dating the *lex* and suggested that this was obviously
connected with the relationship made out between the *lex* and the
Caudine disaster. Since we can see no reason, he claims, for prag-
matically linking that disaster with the *lex*, then, unless the connection is historically accurate, it must belong to the tradition
through which knowledge of the *lex Poetilia* was itself kept alive.
This, he thinks, is information which would not be in the *Annales*
from the start but be part of a legal tradition, thoroughly reliable in
itself, which was known to the later annalists. To this tradition
clung both the name of the *rogator*, C. Poetilius Visolus, and the
link with the Caudine disaster. But these two pieces of information
were inconsistent with one another, hence history had to be improved, and either a non-Caudine Visolus had to be produced or
the link with the Caudine Forks had to be abandoned. Most of the
later *Annales*, used by Dionysius, Varro, and Valerius Maximus,
took the former course and introduced the dictatorship of Poetilius

---

[1] 'Fabius und Diodor', now in *Römische Forschungen*, ii (Berlin, 1879),
pp. 221 ff. at pp. 242 ff.

Visolus. But the other and less objectionable approach was also taken, says Mommsen, since Livy places the statute in 326 B.C. But Livy, too, he thinks, took part in the first manipulation since he makes Poetilius Visolus dictator in 313.

Mommsen is, of course, completely justified in not solving the discrepancy by the simple expedient of counting heads—Livy on one side, Dionysius, Varro, Valerius Maximus on the other; and in not seeking the solution in the annalistic sources of these four writers. He is also surely right in claiming that the relevant tradition linked both the name of a Poetilius and the Caudine Forks disaster with the passing of the *lex* on *nexum*. But in other respects his arguments are not convincing. First, he claims that the discrepancy between Livy and Varro in dating the *lex* is obviously connected with the relationship made out between the *lex* and the Caudine disaster. But this point is not at all obvious. Varro, who mentioned Poetilius, *dictator*, says nothing of the Caudine disaster.[1] Nothing indicates that he accepted the tradition of Poetilius, *dictator*, as the *rogator* of the *lex* because of any idea that the *lex* was also connected with the Caudine disaster. Similarly, Dionysius and Valerius Maximus who link the *lex* with the Caudine Forks make no mention of any Poetilius. Thus, we may well feel that though the *lex* was traditionally linked with a Poetilius and the Caudine disaster the tradition was not unitary but double; and hence, that Dionysius' and Valerius Maximus' accounts are based on separate sources from that of Varro and so are some confirmation of Varro's dating, provided Poetilius *dictator* is historical. It is, in fact, Mommsen's refusal to accept the historicity of Poetilius, *dictator* in 313, which makes him favour the accuracy of Livy's account of the *lex* on *nexum*. This refusal is based entirely on his view that at that time the consulship was in practice a necessary prerequisite for the dictatorship and that no such Poetilius is listed as having been consul.

But as Münzer has pointed out,[2] Mommsen's argument is weakened by Mommsen himself. Mommsen showed elsewhere that until 323 B.C. more dictators were non-consuls than were consuls.[3]

---

[1] Neither, of course, does Livy in this connection.   [2] *RE* 21. 1166 f.
[3] *Staatsrecht* ii. 145 f. and the list given, p. 146, n. 1.

313, the date given for Poetilius' dictatorship, is only ten years after 323, and the tradition demanding that a dictator should have been consul need not have been too firmly established. Mommsen also seemed to accept that after 323 there were four non-consul dictators and he considered they had more or less an oppositional character. It cannot be regarded as established that C. Poetilius Libo Visolus was not dictator in 313.[1]

Thus, the whole question of the origins of the *lex Poetilia* is at least open. But the balance of probability, I suggest, is strongly in favour of Varro's being accurate and of the *lex*'s being the work of Poetilius, *dictator*. To begin with, his dating would harmonize both with Dionysius and Valerius Maximus, and nothing in these writers is actually contrary to what Varro says.[2] Secondly, Varro was a learned man, Livy was not, hence the former is more likely to be right except where his sources have been falsified, and, as has been shown, the argument that his sources here are corrupt is weak. Thirdly, if Livy has made a mistake such as I am suggesting then a plausible explanation of his error can be found. In the year 313 when Poetilius was dictator, L. Papirius Cursor was one of the consuls.[3] Livy met the names Poetilius and Papirius in the tradition of the *lex* on *nexum*, and assumed that the *lex* was passed in 326 when a Poetilius and the same Papirius were the consuls.

It would, of course, be going too far to claim that the statute on *nexum* was certainly the work of a dictator in 313 B.C. But it is enough for our purposes if it is accepted that there is no strong reason for holding that it was passed by a *comitia* at the request of the consuls.[4]

We then reach the position that there is no positive reason for attributing any statute concerned with private law in the Republic

[1] Cf. Münzer, loc. cit., who points out that this dictatorship need not be wiped from the record even if Poetilius' supposed exploits in battle are not historical. He further observes that Beloch also weakens his case against the historicity of this dictatorship by raising the possibility that Poetilius held in 326 B.C. the consulship which is normally attributed to his father.

[2] Though in one account the consuls are prominent, in the other the tribunes of the plebs, we are not told that they were responsible for the *lex* on *nexum*.

[3] Livy 9. 28. 2.

[4] If this is acceptable, then it will also appear that there is no reason to call the statute the *lex Poetilia Papiria*.

after the XII Tables to the *comitia centuriata* summoned by consuls or lesser magistrates.[1] Where there is positive evidence for the legislative body this always points even in the earliest days towards the *concilium plebis* when the Republic was not under extraordinary rule by *decemviri* or a *dictator*. An *argumentum e silentio* thus suggests that the *comitia centuriata* did not legislate in private law matters. The argument, however, is not just from silence. We now have an explanation of why in 186 B.C. the Senate, wishing to reward Hispala Faecenia, did not adopt the apparently obvious course of telling the consul who was involved to bring appropriate legislation before the *comitia centuriata*. The *comitia centuriata* just did not legislate on private law. Hence the *senatusconsultum* told the consul to ask the tribunes of the plebs to place legislation before the *concilium plebis* as soon as possible giving Hispala various private law rights.

This conclusion that in the Republic the *comitia centuriata* did not legislate on private law immediately raises two questions very sharply. How could Livy be mistaken and think that the statute on *nexum* was comitial, and how could Gaius distinguish between *lex* and *plebiscitum* and give both as sources of law?[2] Before we can give an answer we must glance at the Principate.

In the early Empire a change occurred in the methods of legislating. The most important factor was the Emperor, who in reality exercised control over the organs of legislation. In July 23 B.C. Augustus obtained *tribunicia potestas* for life[3] and, for a time, in virtue of this authority, he brought legislation affecting private law before the *concilium plebis*: the *lex Iulia de maritandis ordinibus*, *lex Iulia de adulteriis coercendis*, both of 18 B.C.[4] But later he preferred to have private law legislation proposed by the consuls: the *lex Fufia Caninia* on manumissions proposed by the consuls,

---

[1] For legislation by dictators see *infra*, pp. 16 ff.

[2] G. 1. 2, 3.

[3] For the settlement of 23 B.C. cf., e.g., Salmon, *A History of the Roman World 30 B.C. to A.D. 138*, 6th edit. (London, 1968), pp. 16 f.; Scullard, *From the Gracchi to Nero*, 3rd edit. (London, 1970), pp. 220 ff.

[4] For both these statutes this emerges from the *Res gestae divi Augusti* 6. 2 placed in conjunction with other texts, especially Suetonius, *Augustus*, 34; Seneca, *de benef.* 6. 32: cf., e.g., Brunt and Moore, *Res gestae divi Augusti* (London, 1967), pp. 46 f.; Rotondi, *Leges*, pp. 443 ff.

L. Caninius Gallus and C. Fufius Geminus, in 2 B.C.;[1] *lex Aelia Sentia* also on manumission proposed by the consuls, Sex. Aelius Catus and C. Sentius Saturninus, in A.D. 4;[2] *lex Papia Poppaea* on marriage proposed by the *consules suffecti*, M. Papius Mutilus and C. Poppaeus Sabinus, in A.D. 9.[3]

Tiberius seems to have continued the custom of having *leges* proposed by consuls. J. 1. 5. 3 refers to a *lex Iunia Norbana* (elsewhere called simply *lex Iunia*)[4] on manumissions and M. Iunius Silanus and L. Norbanus Balbus were consuls in A.D. 19;[5] D. 40. 1. 24pr. (Hermogenianus, 1 *iuris epit.*) concerns a *lex Iunia Petronia* on actions *de libertate* and P. Petronius was *consul suffectus* also in A.D. 19.[6] Many texts discuss a *lex Iunia Vellaea*[7] concerning institution and disinherison of *postumi* and L. Iunius Silanus and C. Vellaeus Tutor were *consules suffecti* apparently in A.D. 28.[8] Even if not all the attributions to particular consuls are wholly accurate, the attested double names of the statutes are good evidence of how they originated.

We know of two private law statutes from the reign of Claudius who, Tacitus says, took upon himself all the duties of laws and magistracies.[9] One, for which we are expressly told that he was personally responsible, forbade loans to *filii familiarum* 'in mortem parentum'.[10] The other was the famous *lex Claudia* which abolished the perpetual tutelage of women.[11] We are not directly told the method of promulgation of these two statutes but there is little doubt they are *plebiscita*. We know that Claudius was directly responsible for these measures,[12] *plebiscita* are expressly mentioned

---

[1] As appears clearly from the name, *lex Fufia Caninia* which is well attested in the sources: G. 1. 42, 46, 139; 2. 228, 239; P. S. 4. 14; *Epit. Ulp.* 1. 24; C. 7. 3. 1.

[2] As appears clearly from the name, *lex Aelia Sentia*, which is well attested in the sources: G. 1. 13, 27, 29, 31 etc.; *Epit. Ulp.* 1. 11; *Coll.* 16. 2. 5; D. 40. 9. 5; C. 7. 2. 5.

[3] Isidorus, *Etym.* 5. 15. 1.   [4] Cf. Rotondi, *Leges*, p. 463.

[5] Cf. Hohl, *RE* 10. 1098; Groag, *RE* 17. 931. But see Rotondi, loc. cit., for doubts on the attribution.

[6] Cf. Hanslik, *RE* 19. 1199.   [7] e.g. G. 2. 134; D. 26. 2. 10. 2; 28. 3. 13.

[8] Cf., e.g., Stein and Petersen, *Prosopographia Imperii Romani saecc. I, II, III*, pars IV, 2nd edit. (Berlin 1952–66), p. 350.

[9] *Ann.* 11. 5: 'cuncta legum et magistratuum munia in se trahens'.

[10] Tacitus, *Ann.* 11. 13.

[11] See, e.g., G. 1. 157, 171; *Epit. Ulp.* 11. 8.

[12] The name *lex Claudia* shows this for the *lex* on *tutela*.

for his reign,[1] and we can be sure that *plebiscita* were not then proposed by ordinary tribunes.[2] The Emperor Claudius, it will be recalled, was well known for his antiquarian interests and attitudes.[3]

There thus seems to be a pattern in legislating in the early Empire which, I submit, is important for our understanding of private law legislation in the later Republic. Augustus at first legislated by means of *plebiscita*, later through the *comitia*, Tiberius followed the latter procedure, Claudius used *plebiscita*. In the first place this pattern supports the contention that in the Republic *plebiscita* alone were used for private law legislation: Augustus at first followed the Republican procedure, the antiquarian scholar Claudius reverted to it. Secondly, the very fact that the pattern can be established so clearly is in itself some confirmation that we were right in discerning a pattern in the Republic. Thirdly, the ease with which transitions occur in the early Empire between using the *concilium plebis* and the *comitia centuriata* indicates that in theory either was equally competent to pass private law legislation, and which did was a matter of practice and established custom. It should be stressed that there is no sign of any law in the early Empire which modified the powers of these bodies. Hence for the Republic we should decide that the *comitia centuriata* did not legislate on private law matters but there was nothing in its constitution which forbade it to do so.

We are now in a position to explain why Gaius distinguished between *plebiscitum* and *lex* and gave both as a source of law. In the early Empire both means of legislating existed and were used. Nor is it so difficult to understand how Livy came to think that the *lex* on *nexum* was passed by a *comitia*. The *comitia* did, in fact, frequently legislate and, though in practice it did not deal with private law matters but with public law, this distinction was capable of being overlooked by Livy, who never shows much interest in law.[4]

---

[1] Tacitus, *Ann.* 11. 14.

[2] For the argument see Mommsen, *Staatsrecht* ii. 882 f. and 882, n. 5, 883, n. 1.

[3] Cf., e.g., Scullard, *From the Gracchi*, p. 299; Momigliano, *Claudius, the Emperor and his Achievement* (repr. Cambridge, 1961), pp. 1 ff. This is not to deny that in some senses he was also revolutionary.

[4] Livy, book 8, will have been written before Augustus began to use the *comitia* for private law legislation.

At this stage, now that the Republican pattern can be regarded as confirmed, it may be observed that those Republican statutes which concern private law and whose mode of promulgation is not clear[1] have—with one single exception—a simple, not double, name, and this is a slight (but only slight) indication that they too are *plebiscita*. The exception is the *lex Mamilia Roscia Peducaea Alliena Fabia*, which assuredly was not passed by the *comitia centuriata*.[2]

A further reason for the attitude of Livy, and possibly also of Gaius, may be found if we look at the exceptional case of the legislation of the XII Tables and, probably, also of Sulla.[3] The *decemviri* responsible for the XII Tables were appointed with extraordinary powers to make new laws,[4] but they voluntarily chose to submit their proposals to the *comitia centuriata*.[5]

Sulla was appointed dictator in 82 B.C., according to Appian,[6] 'for the enactment of such laws as he might deem best and for the regulation of the commonwealth'.[7] Hence we might expect from him both a considerable body of legislation (as there was) and also great freedom in its promulgation. Most of his statutes were concerned only with public law; some, which have already been listed,[8] also at least touched on private law.

There is no direct evidence of his method(s) of promulgating those statutes which affected private law. But we can be certain that he did not proceed through the *concilium plebis*. He himself was not a tribune of the plebs yet the statutes bear his name.[9]

---

[1] Listed *supra*, pp. 8 f.

[2] It was probably an agrarian law of 59, or more probably 55 B.C., instigated by Julius Caesar: cf., e.g., Rotondi, *Leges*, pp. 388 f.; Herrmann, 'La Date de la *lex Mamilia*', *RIDA* i (1948), 113 ff.; Torrent, *La Iurisdictio de los Magistrados Municipales* (Salamanca, 1970), p. 142.

[3] On the whole subject of extraordinary constitutive powers see Mommsen, *Staatsrecht* ii. 702 ff.

[4] Aulus Gellius, *N.A.* 14. 7. 5; 17. 21. 15; Cicero, *de re pub.* 2. 36. 61; *CIL* vi. 2011; Diodorus Siculus 12. 23; Livy 34. 6. 8; Suetonius, *Tiberius*, 2. 2: cf. Mommsen, *Staatsrecht* ii. 702, n. 2.

[5] Livy 3. 34; Dionysius of Halicarnassus 10. 57; Zonaras 7. 18.

[6] *Bell. civ.* 1. 99.

[7] In the *Fasti* he is described as dictator *rei publ(icae) constit(uendae) caussa*: cf. Degrassi, *Fasti Capitolini* (Turin, n.d.), pp. 74 f. As Mommsen pointed out, the indication of the purpose of the dictatorship was not part of the dictator's title: *Staatsrecht* ii. 703, n. 3.   [8] Cf. *supra*, p. 9.

[9] See, e.g., D. 28. 3. 15 (Iavolenus, 4 *epist.*); 48. 10. 1pr. (Marcian, 14 *inst.*); 47. 10. 5 (Ulpian, 56 *ad ed.*); G. 3. 124.

Moreover, he held the tribunate in deep detestation and deliberately weakened that office. Appian[1] said he reduced the tribunician power so much that it seemed to be destroyed, Velleius Paterculus[2] that he left the form but not the substance, and Livy[3] that he took away from the tribunes the right of legislating.[4]

There is evidence that some of his other statutes went before the *comitia centuriata*,[5] and this was probably at least his usual procedure. But in view of the *lex Valeria* which made him dictator he had absolute power, and did not need to submit his *leges* to any body in order to make them legally valid.[6] Mommsen argues very forcefully, in fact, that his *lex* on the sale of the goods of those who had been proscribed was not laid before any *comitia*.[7] Nothing definite, then, can be said about his private law statutes, though we might imagine that they went before the *comitia centuriata*. Possibly he followed the example of the *decemviri*. What must be emphasized is the wholly extraordinary powers given to the dictator which enabled him to legislate in whatever manner he chose.[8]

We should not, I think, be too ready to find any significant pattern in that the very exceptional legislation of both the *decemviri* and (presumably) Sulla was laid before the *comitia centuriata*. Once the *decemviri* had decided that they wanted the approval and ratification of the people the *comitia centuriata* was the obvious

[1] *Bell. civ.* i. 100.
[2] 2. 30.   [3] *Epit.* 89.
[4] Cf. also Cicero, *de leg.* 3. 9. 22; *in Verrem* II, i. 60. 155; *pro Cluentio* 40. 110; Caesar, *bell. civ.* i. 5; i. 7; Suetonius, *Divus Iulius*, 5; Dionysius of Halicarnassus 5. 77. 5; Sallust, *Hist.* i. 55; *lex Antonia de Termessibus, praescriptio.*
[5] Cicero, *de domo*, 30. 79, on exclusion of Italians from citizenship: 'Populus Romanus L. Sulla dictatore ferente comitiis centuriatis municipiis civitatem ademit.' Aulus Gellius, *N.A.* 2. 24. 11, 'L. Sulla dictator . . . legem ad populum tulit', discussing his sumptuary law (cf. Macrobius, *Sat.* 3. 17. 11) must have the *comitia centuriata* in mind. Mommsen, *Staatsrecht* ii. 726, claims that among the 'organische Gesetze' of Sulla there is none which did not probably go through the *comitia*.
[6] Cf. Mommsen, *Staatsrecht* ii. 724 ff.
[7] *Staatsrecht* ii. 725, n. 1. The argument is that in discussing it Cicero calls it *sive Valeria sive Cornelia* and it is only of an indirect law that the question could be raised whether it was valid in itself or because of the *lex* which authorized it. Cf. Cicero, *de leg. agrar.* 3. 2. 5. Mommsen, loc. cit., also thinks the dictator Julius Caesar's law on debt (*bell. civ.* 3. 1; Tacitus, *Ann.* 6. 16) was not brought before the *comitia*.
[8] Again one might refer to Mommsen, *Staatsrecht* ii. 702 ff.

assembly to turn to. *Plebiscita* did not then have the force of law.[1] Moreover, the *concilium plebis* did not represent all the citizens, and there was at that time great tension between the plebeians and the patricians.[2] As for Sulla, as was emphasized, it was his hatred of the office of tribune which made him turn, so far as we can tell, to the *comitia centuriata*.[3] The *lex Poetilia* which has already been discussed may well fit into this framework and be a dictator's *lex* which was laid before the *comitia centuriata*.[4]

We have in this chapter ranged far beyond the time boundaries set down for this study: backwards to the XII Tables, forwards to the reign of Claudius. The purpose of this was none the less clarification of legislation in the later Republic, hence problems which concern solely a different time, for instance the date when *plebiscita* became binding with the force of *leges*, have been ignored. None the less a certain unity in the mode of promulgating private law statutes throughout the Republic after the XII Tables has become apparent.

But though the *comitia centuriata* did not legislate on private

---

[1] In fact, modern scholars even doubt whether the tradition is accurate that *plebiscita* had the force of law after the *lex Horatia* of 449 B.C.: Livy 3. 55; Dionysius of Halicarnassus 11. 45. For the problem see Jolowicz and Nicholas, *Introduction*, pp. 24 f. and the authorities they cite.

[2] See Livy 3. 9 ff.

[3] And apart from the fact that each *lex* bears his name we have no evidence, except for this hatred, that he did not proceed through the *concilium plebis*.

[4] There is, of course, no positive evidence that this was the course adopted. The important thing for us is still that there is no real indication that the *comitia centuriata* when summoned by a consul or lesser magistrate was ever used in the Republic to pass legislation on private law topics. Even if, for the sake of argument, we accept that the *lex Poetilia* was such a statute, this would have relatively little effect upon our understanding of the mode of legislating on private law in the later Republic. It is widely believed that only in 287 B.C., as a result of the *lex Hortensia*, did *plebiscita* come to have the force of law and be binding on all citizens, patricians as well as plebeians: cf., e.g., Jolowicz and Nicholas, loc. cit. If this belief is correct (or even if the force of *plebiscita* had to be restated by statute from time to time), then proof that statutes on private law were passed by the *comitia centuriata* before 287 B.C. would be no evidence that they were also so passed after 287. The subject need not be pressed here. But we should remember the tradition that *plebiscita* had the force of *leges* after the *lex Horatia* was passed by the *comitia centuriata* in 449 B.C.: Livy 3. 55; Dionysius of Halicarnassus, 11. 45. The *lex Canuleia* of 445 B.C. which permitted intermarriage between patricians and plebeians was a *plebiscitum* (Livy 4. 1–4; Cicero, *de re pub.* 2. 37. 63; Florus, *Epit.* 1. 17 (1. 25)) and it obviously affected patricians as well as plebeians.

law matters (except in exceptional cases), the *comitia calata* did. This *comitia* had a very different composition from that of the *comitia centuriata*,[1] it was concerned with sacral business, and it was summoned under the presidency of the *pontifex maximus*.[2] In early times wills, in the form known as *testamenta calatis comitiis*, were made before it, but the practice probably did not survive into our period.[3] Though the proposition has been disputed, it is generally agreed that each *testamentum calatis comitiis* involved legislation by the *comitia*.[4] The adoption of a male *sui iuris*—termed *adrogatio*—also required the approval of this *comitia* from early times right through our period.[5] A *rogatio* was put to the people:[6] 'Velitis, iubeatis, uti L. Valerius L. Titio tam iure legeque filius siet, quam si ex eo patre matreque familias eius natus esset, utique ei vitae necisque in eum potestas siet, uti patri endo filio est. Haec ita, uti dixi, ita vos, Quirites, rogo.'[7] The form shows that this was true legislation and this is confirmed for the first century B.C. by a text of Cicero which also indicates, however, that, as legislation, *adrogatio* was treated rather lightly.[8]

Testamenta calatis comitiis and *adrogationes* were dealt with by the *comitia calata* because of their sacral implications. But it is also

[1] Since this present book is not a work on public law the composition and organization of the assemblies will not be discussed. See now on all such matters, Jolowicz and Nicholas, *Introduction*; Staveley, *Greek and Roman Voting and Elections* (London, 1972).

[2] For this *comitia* see in general, Botsford, *The Roman Assemblies* (New York, 1909), pp. 152 ff.

[3] Cf. Watson, *Private Law*, p. 100, n. 1.

[4] Cf., e.g., Kaser, *RPR* i. 66. For the arguments see also Botsford, *Assemblies*, pp. 157 ff.

[5] After a preliminary investigation by the *pontifices*.

[6] From Cicero, *de leg. agrar.* 2. 12. 31, it might appear that in his time the people in the *comitia* was represented by thirty lictors: cf. Buckland, *Textbook*, pp. 124 f. But Cicero says the lictors are there for the purpose of taking the auspices, and elsewhere in the speech, 2. 11. 27, he claims the *comitia curiata* had been retained only for the sake of the auspices. This latter statement is certainly too restrictive and it may be that only when the *comitia* met *auspiciorum causa* were the people represented by the lictors. The point is not material to the present discussion. (The *comitia curiata* was called *comitia calata* when it was summoned for sacral purposes.)

[7] Aulus Gellius, *N.A.* 5. 19. 9.

[8] *de domo* 16. 41: 'Si quod in ceteris legibus trinum nundinum esse oportet, id in adoptione satis est trium esse horarum, nihil reprehendo.' (Cicero is, in fact, complaining.) Cf. Watson, *Persons*, pp. 85 f.

proper to recognize the private law importance of both the will and the adoption. In the Empire the jurists certainly regarded both as concerning private law:[1] we have no evidence for the attitude of jurists in the Republic. But it should be emphasized that all this private law legislation of the *comitia calata* was passed at the request of individuals for the benefit of individuals and was not, nor was meant to be, of general application.

[1] Cf. G. 2. 101, 102, 103; *Epit. Ulp.* 20. 2: G. 1. 99, 100, 102.

2

THE LEGAL VALUE OF
SENATUSCONSULTA

IN the Empire Gaius wrote that a *senatusconsultum* had the force of
law although that had been questioned;[1] and Ulpian, 'It is not
uncertain that the senate can make law.'[2] The vigour of Ulpian's
statement—especially when it is taken in conjunction with the
text of Gaius—gives the impression that there was a time when it
was not certain that the Senate could make law, and it is not surprising that Pomponius explains how a *senatusconsultum* came to
be *ius*.[3]

In these circumstances it was only natural that modern scholars
should seek for the origins of the legislative powers of the Senate,
and in the event the general opinion came to be that during the
Republic *senatusconsulta* did not have legislative effect.[4] This has
in turn led to the more subtle question of the *effetto normativo* of
senatusconsulta.[5] Crifò puts it thus:

The essential problem, in fact, seems to us not that of seeing if the
Senate with a resolution can fix rules which are directly binding for all
citizens, but that of finding the effectiveness of the provisions; not
what it can do, but what it really does. In other words, it is a matter of

[1] G. 1. 4: 'Senatusconsultum est quod senatus iubet atque constituit; idque
legis vicem optinet, quamvis fuerit quaesitum.'

[2] D. 1. 3. 9 (Ulpian, 16 *ad ed.*): 'Non ambigitur senatum ius facere posse.'

[3] D. 1. 2. 2. 9 (Pomponius, *sing. enchirid.*): 'Deinde quia difficile plebs convenire coepit, populus certe multo difficilius in tanta turba hominum, necessitas
ipsa curam rei publicae ad senatum deduxit: ita coepit senatus se interponere
et quidquid constituisset observabatur, idque ius appellabatur senatus consultum.'

[4] Cf., above all, Loreti Lorini, 'Il potere legislativo del senato romano',
Studi Bonfante, iv (Milan, 1930), pp. 379 ff., the authors cited by her and by
Crifò in the article listed in the next footnote.

[5] Cf., e.g., Volterra, '*Senatus consulta*', *Novissimo digesto italiano* and, above
all, Crifò, 'Attività normativa del senato in età repubblicana', *BIDR*, 71 (1968),
31 ff.

identifying the facts which gave rise to the discussion and senatorial opinion, to take account of, successively, the existence or otherwise of a 'widespread conviction' according to which 'the principle fixed by *senatus consultum*'—not necessarily from the beginning of general application and of immediate realization—is 'a rule ("norma") of law which the magistrate will apply in the exercise of his jurisdiction'.[1]

A rather different formulation would please me more, but before we come to that a little should be said by way of background.

The Senate was originally the king's council and only patricians were members. At some early, but unknown, date plebeians were admitted. Apparently in the fourth century B.C. the power of choosing senators became the duty of the censors who were, however, limited by the right which ex-magistrates had, to be chosen unless they could be excluded for good reason. This right was accorded either by statute or by constitutional convention.

A survival of the original nature of the Senate was that all acts of the *comitia* needed the *auctoritas* of the patrician members of the Senate in order to be valid. Long before our period this had become a matter of form only. But of fundamental importance was the constitutional convention by which magistrates brought all matters of importance, including proposed legislation, to the Senate for discussion. Further, the Senate had control over the State's finances and over foreign affairs (although it could not declare war) and it had also power to dispense individuals from the operation of a law.[2] Dionysius of Halicarnassus puts into the mouth of Roman consuls of the early fifth century B.C.: 'We have had a law so long as we have inhabited this city by which the Senate is invested with sovereign power in everything except the appointing of magistrates, the enacting of laws, and the declaration or termination of wars; and the power of determining these three matters rests with the people, by their votes.'[3] The power of the Senate was, therefore, enormous.

It is against this background that we must judge the legal force of *senatusconsulta* in the later Republic. Obviously, given this posi-

---

[1] 'Attività', p. 35.

[2] On this last matter see Asconius, *in Cornelianam Ciceronis*, 51.

[3] 6. 66. 3; cf. 7. 56. 3; 9. 37. 2 (refers to 471 B.C.).

tion of power of the Senate, *senatusconsulta* would at all periods be regarded as legally important and relevant.[1] If *senatusconsulta* on matters of private law had been issued, directed towards all citizens, they would have been enforced to a greater or lesser extent by the magistrates in their courts. In times of social and political crisis magistrates might not have put the *senatusconsulta* into effect, but this would tell us as little about the legal value of the *senatusconsulta*, as would their general acceptance by magistrates in times of tranquillity.[2]

Because of these facts I would not formulate the fundamental question on the normative effect of *senatusconsulta* quite as Crifò does. To me the basic problem relates to attitudes, especially of the Senate itself, and the solution to the problem should be sought in the answers to a number of specific questions.

First, on matters of private law, do *senatusconsulta* contain commands addressed to all citizens, or only to magistrates? If the answer to the first alternative is positive, then the Senate thinks it has law-creating powers; if negative, then the Senate does not think it has such powers. *Senatusconsulta* which are addressed to non-Romans or which are concerned with foreign relations are, of course, not of significance for us in this context since foreign policy was in the hands of the Senate. Secondly, does the *senatus* ask magistrates to put its wishes before a legislative body? If it does, then again it does not think it has law-creating powers. Thirdly, are *senatusconsulta* incorporated into *edicta* or *leges* and in that form enforced by the courts? If so, the magistrates do not think the Senate has law-creating powers. Fourthly—and the answer to this depends primarily on the answers to the preceding questions—does the Senate act as if it has law-creating powers? Fifthly, do people think the Senate has legislative or quasi-legislative powers?

The fifth question should be answered at once. At the late end of the scale G. 1. 4, D. 1. 3. 9, and D. 1. 2. 2. 9[3] show that by the

---

[1] The vagueness of phrasing is deliberate and, indeed, necessary.

[2] The attitude of the plebs could be a very different matter, especially if they thought the Senate was trying to usurp legislative functions of the *concilium plebis*.

[3] Cf. *supra*, p. 21.

middle of the second century A.D. it was accepted that *senatus-consulta* did have the force of law.[1] At the other end of the scale Dionysius of Halicarnassus shows that it was believed in his time that in earlier days—at least in the fifth century B.C.—*senatus-consulta* did not have the force of law.[2] Crifò[3] argues, however, that the evidence of Dionysius does not exclude a normative power of the Senate but only that particular power which is equated with *leges publicae*. But this view takes little account of the moralizing and panegyric nature of Dionysius' work. In 6. 66. 3,[4] for instance, there would be no point in Dionysius' making the consuls say that the Senate was not vested with the power of making laws, if the Senate was regarded as having normative powers. The same is true of 7. 56. 3. Crifò relies mainly on 9. 37. 2:

ἦν γάρ τις ἐν τοῖς δημάρχοις θρασὺς καὶ λέγειν οὐκ ἀδύνατος ἀνήρ, Γναῖος Γενύκιος, παραθήγων τὰς ὀργὰς τῶν πενήτων. οὗτος ἐκκλησίας συνάγων ἑκάστοτε καὶ ἐκδημαγωγῶν τοὺς ἀπόρους προσηνάγκαζε τοὺς ὑπάτους τὰ ὑπὸ τῆς βουλῆς ψηφισθέντα περὶ τῆς κληρουχίας συντελεῖν. οἱ δ᾽ οὐχ ὑπήκουον οὐ τῇ ἑαυτῶν ἀρχῇ λέγοντες ἐπιτετάχθαι τὸ ἔργον ὑπὸ τῆς βουλῆς, ἀλλὰ τοῖς μετὰ Κάσσιον καὶ Οὐεργίνιον ὑπάτοις, πρὸς οὓς καὶ τὸ προβούλευμα ἐγράφη· καὶ ἅμα οὐδ᾽ εἶναι νόμους εἰς ἀεὶ κυρίους ἃ ψηφίζεται τὸ συνέδριον, ἀλλὰ πολιτεύματα καιρῶν ἐνιαύσιον ἔχοντα ἰσχύν.

This passage confirms that *senatusconsulta* were not the same as *leges publicae*, but really provides no evidence for a general norma-tive power of the Senate. It shows rather that decrees of the Senate—or at least the one in question—were addressed to magis-trates, not to the people at large. If we are to take as serious legal history the arguments of the consuls that the decree had been addressed not to them but to previous consuls and that *senatus-consulta* had validity for only one year then Dionysius in fact would be telling us more about the drafting of early *senatusconsulta* than about the permanence of their effect. By the early second century B.C. at the latest *senatusconsulta* were normally directed to a magis-trate designated by his title, not by name, 'who is now in office or who subsequently will be in office'.[5] It may well be that this careful

---

[1] The further question of whether they had the force of *ius civile* need not detain us.   [2] 6. 66. 3; 7. 56. 3; 9. 37. 2.
[3] 'Attività', p. 46.   [4] Cf. *supra*, p. 22.
[5] Cf. Livy 39. 19. 6, 'utique consules praetoresque qui nunc essent quive

formulation, expressing both present and future magistrates, was in direct response to real arguments of the type Dionysius puts into the mouth of the two consuls, namely that the *senatus-consultum* imposed no duty upon them because it simply said (for example) 'Let the consuls see to it . . .' and hence applied only to the holders of the office when the *senatusconsultum* was issued.

Between these texts showing the early and the later value of *senatusconsulta* stands, above all,[1] Cicero, *top.* 5. 28:

Atque etiam definitiones aliae sunt partitionum aliae divisionum; partitionum, cum res ea quae proposita est quasi in membra discerpitur, ut si quis ius civile dicat id esse quod in legibus, senatus consultis, rebus iudicatis, iuris peritorum auctoritate, edictis magistratuum, more, aequitate consistat.

This text is considered to be of fundamental importance by those scholars who believe *senatusconsulta* had the force of law or normative effect in the Republic. Volterra, for instance, claims that Cicero equates *senatusconsultum* with *lex publica populi Romani* as a source of *ius civile*, and that this text (with other later ones) puts the *senatusconsultum* on the same level as *lex* as a 'normative source'.[2] But Cicero also places in his list *aequitas, res iudicatae*, and *iuris peritorum auctoritas*.[3] Yet though the idea of *aequitas* might influence the development of the law it was never a formal source of law.[4] Though court decisions might be significant for showing what the law on a point was thought to be, the Romans, unlike the English, never developed a doctrine of precedent.[5] And although the authority of the jurists might in practice be of great importance

postea futuri essent' (186 B.C.); 41. 9. 11, 'ut dictator, consul, interrex, censor, praetor, qui nunc esset quive postea futurus esset' (177 B.C.). In the latter text 'quive postea futurus esset' is an addition, obviously reasonable, of Weissenborn: *Titi Livi ab urbe condita libri*, ix. 2 (Berlin, 1876), p. 19; accepted by, e.g., Sage and Schlesinger, *Livy* xii (Loeb Classical Library, London, 1938), p. 212. The justification for the mode of formulation does not lie in the nature of *senatusconsulta*, since the same formulation appears in statutes; e.g. the *lex Plaetoria de iurisdictione* (of uncertain date but probably later third century B.C.); 'praetor urbanus, qui nunc est quique posthac fiat'; cf. *lex Latina tabulae Bantinae*, lines 15 ff., 23; *lex Acilia repetundarum*, lines 16 f., 22.

[1] Nothing really helpful is to be found in Cicero, *part. orat.* 37. 130, or Horace, *Epist.* 1. 16. 41. Volterra takes the latter text as confirming his opinion of *top.* 5. 28.
[2] *Senatus consulta*, p. 10.   [3] For this list of Cicero see *supra*, pp. 3 ff.
[4] Cf. *infra*, pp. 173 ff.   [5] Cf. *infra*, pp. 171 f.

in systematizing the law through their writings and in developing the law by their interpretations, it could not, in the absence of the *ius respondendi*,[1] be a formal source of law in the Republic. Crifò[2] is more cautious and more subtle[3] but the problem remains. In view of the power and prestige of the Senate it was inevitable that *senatusconsulta* would be regarded as important and legally relevant.[4] But was Cicero in this text telling us anything more about *senatusconsulta* than this truism? Since he also lists *aequitas*, *res iudicatae*, and *iuris peritorum auctoritas*, the answer may easily be negative.[5]

Nor does the epigraphical material help the case of those who maintain the normative power of the Senate during the Republic. Lines 52 and 72 of the *tabula Heracleensis* of 45 B.C. are said by Volterra[6] and Crifò[7] to equate *senatusconsulta* with *leges*. This is true, but is not enough to show a law-creating power of the Senate in terms of the five specific questions which were posed earlier:[8]

[50] Quo minus aed(iles) et IIIIvir(ei) vieis in urbem purgandeis, IIvir(ei) vieis extra propiusve urbem Rom(am) passus ⟨M⟩ [51] purgandeis, queiquomque erunt, vias publicas purgandas curent eiusque rei potestatem habeant, [52] ita utei legibus pl(ebei)ve sc(itis) s(enatus)⟨ve⟩ c(onsultis) oportet oportebit, eum h.l. n(ihilum) r(ogatur).

The purpose of the clause is to show that it is not intended to take from the aediles and other magistrates mentioned any of the duties or powers in respect of street-cleaning imposed upon them by *leges*, *plebiscita*, or *senatusconsulta*. That means that any *senatusconsultum* actually envisaged was addressed to the magistrates, not to citizens at large. Thus, in terms of the first specific question, this clause does not show that the Senate thought it had law-creating powers. Line 72 concerns public areas and arcades under

---

[1] This, whatever it was, was introduced by Augustus.
[2] 'Attività', pp. 80 ff.
[3] Particularly in linking their legal effect with *ius consuetudine*.
[4] Cf. *supra*, p. 22.
[5] A more satisfactory approach to the text is that of Kaser, '*Mores maiorum* und Gewohnheitsrecht', *ZSS* 59 (1939), 52 ff. at p. 97. He suggests the orator was not concerned with the sources of the *ius civile*, but with how the law in accordance with which the Romans lived was to be recognized.
[6] '*Senatus consulta*', p. 10.   [7] 'Attività', p. 70.
[8] *Supra*, p. 23.

the control of the aediles and other magistrates and directs that no one is to have any structure erected there etc., 'nisi quibus uteique leg(ibus) pl(ebei)ve sc(itis) s(enatus)ve c(onsultis) concessum permissumve e⟨s⟩t'. It is not so evident on the face of the text that any relevant *senatusconsulta* was addressed to the aediles and other magistrates, but in view of the jurisdiction of these magistrates it is permissible to assume that that was the case. At the very least it cannot be said that the clause shows *senatusconsulta* addressed to non-magistrates or to citizens in general.[1]

A different document, the *fragmentum Atestinum*[2] probably of 49 B.C. is again concerned at line 10 with *senatusconsulta* directed towards magistrates.[3]

To return to the major question in hand.[4] There is no evidence that in the Republic people thought the Senate had legislative or quasi-legislative powers.

We can now look at the first of the specific questions posed, namely, do *senatusconsulta* concerned with private law contain commands addressed to all citizens, or only to magistrates? There is, of course, a number addressed directly to magistrates,[5] though this by itself would be of limited significance. Others which are not directly addressed to magistrates relate to foreign affairs[6] which was the province of the Senate, hence they are not helpful. Only in

---

[1] For other arguments on the two clauses, see Loreti Lorini, 'Potere legislativo', pp. 382 f.; *contra*, Crifò, 'Attività', pp. 70 ff. Loreti Lorini, loc. cit., rightly calls attention to line 103 which is concerned with privileges granted by statute, plebiscite, or treaty and does not mention *senatusconsulta*. Crifò's counter-arguments seem forced: 'Attività', pp. 71 f.

[2] Bruns, *Fontes*, no. 17.

[3] On the *fragmentum Atestinum* see Loreti Lorini, 'Potere legislativo', p. 382; Crifò, 'Attività', p. 73.

[4] The fifth question, *supra*, p. 23.

[5] *SC* of 460 B.C. in Livy 3. 21. 2; *SC de Bacchanalibus* of 186 in Livy 39. 19. 4; *SC de manumissionibus* of 177 B.C. in Livy 41. 9. 11; *SC de Thisbensibus* of 170 (Bruns, *Fontes*, no. 37); *SC de philosophis et rhetoribus* of 161 in Suetonius, *rhet.* 1 and Aulus Gellius, *N.A.* 15. 11. 1; *SC de hastis Martiis* in Aulus Gellius, *N.A.* 4. 6. 2.

[6] e.g. *SC* of 257 B.C. in Dionysius of Halicarnassus 6. 1. 2; *SC de Campanis* of 211 or 210 B.C. in Livy 26. 34 (and the *concilium plebis* had also given the Senate authority in the matter); *SC de Bacchanalibus* of 186 (Bruns, *Fontes*, no. 36); *SC de Tiburtibus* of 159 (Bruns, *Fontes*, no. 39); *SC de pago Montano* (Bruns, *Fontes*, no. 44) (presumably; certainty is not possible, given the fragmentary state of the *SC*). There are many others but not all need be listed: see Volterra, '*Senatus consulta*'.

two cases might it be argued that *senatusconsulta* were issued addressed to citizens at large and yet not concerned with foreign affairs.

The first is that which introduced the concept of *quasi usus fructus* and declared there could be a *usus fructus* of all things which could be in a person's patrimony[1] (hence including things which were consumed by use). There is no direct evidence for dating this *senatusconsultum*, but it is almost universally held that it dates from the early Empire. Crifò disagrees and attributes it to the time of Julius Caesar.[2] The arguments are inevitably indirect and there can be varying opinions of their general plausibility, but it seems to me that the force of Cicero, *top.* 3. 17 (to which Crifò devotes much space),[3] is conclusive against him.

> Ex contrario autem sic: Non debet ea mulier cui vir bonorum suorum usum fructum legavit cellis vinariis et oleariis plenis relictis, putare id ad se pertinere. Usus enim, non abusus, legatus est.

There is no need, I think, to examine what Cicero understands by an argument *ex contrario* or to debate the precise sense to be attributed to *pertinere*. The significant fact is, that in discussing a legacy of the usufruct of *bona sua*, Cicero says that wine and the oil do not come to the legatee. A contrast is thus implicit between the usufructuary's right to oil and wine and her right to some other things. In the context of usufruct, oil and wine are precisely the standard examples of things consumed by use,[4] that is of things which are not contained within the usufruct. But the legatee, as a result of the *senatusconsultum* in question, did receive entitlement to usufruct in them. Hence Cicero's contrast would be meaningless, if the *senatusconsultum* had been issued by 44 B.C., the year when the *topica* was written, but full of meaning if the *senatusconsultum* was later.[5]

---

[1] e.g. D. 7. 5. 1 (Ulpian, 18 *ad Sab.*).

[2] *Studi sul quasi-usufrutto in diritto romano* (Milan, forthcoming), pp. 17 ff. I am deeply grateful to Professor Crifò for showing me the proofs of his book before publication.

[3] From p. 121.   [4] Cf. D. 7. 5. 7 (Gaius, 7 *ad ed. prov.*).

[5] Cicero, *pro Caecina*, 4. 11 (delivered in 69 B.C.) shows that there could then be a *usus fructus omnium bonorum suorum*, but should not be used to argue that it included things which were destroyed by use.

The second case where it might be argued that during the Republic *senatusconsulta* unconnected with foreign affairs were addressed directly to citizens in general concerns those[1] which ordered the dissolution of *collegia*. But the evidence is ambiguous, to say the least. One text of Asconius, *in Pisonianam Ciceronis*, 6, has simply 'senatus consulto collegia sublata sunt quae adversus rem publicam videbantur esse ⟨constituta⟩.' Another text of the same author, *in Cornelianam Ciceronis*, 67, concerning the same decree reads, 'postea collegia et S.C. et pluribus legibus sunt sublata praeter pauca atque certa quae utilitas civitatis desiderasset.' Cicero, *ad Quintum fratrem*, 2. 3. 5, seems to give us the wording of a later similar *senatusconsultum* of 58 B.C.: 'senatus consultum factum est ut sodalitates decuriatique discederent lexque de iis ferretur, ut qui non discessissent ea poena quae est de vi tenerentur.' In this third text—which is by far the most explicit of the three—the major provisions of the *senatusconsultum* are to be put into a *lex*. This probably clarifies the relationship between the *senatusconsultum* and the *leges* in the second text of Asconius, and it seems reasonable to assume that some similar arrangement was at the base of Asconius' first text: the initiative came from the Senate, hence the *senatusconsultum* is mentioned but it was given legal effect by a *lex*.[2]

The second specific question was, does the Senate ask magistrates to put its wishes before a legislative body? The answer is a clear yes both for the second century and for the first century B.C. For the former we have the *senatusconsultum* of 186 B.C. reported by Livy 39. 19. 4, 5, that the consul should raise with the tribunes of the plebs the matter of the tribunes' putting before the *concilium plebis* as soon as possible the granting of certain rights to P. Aebutius and Hispala Faecenia including, to the woman, 'datio, deminutio, gentis enuptio, tutoris optio item esset, quasi ei vir testamento dedisset'.[3] For the latter we have the *senatusconsultum* of 58 B.C. recorded by Cicero, *ad Quintum fratrem*, 2. 3. 5.[4] The obvious

---

[1] Apparently there were at least two.
[2] The texts relating to the *ludi compitalicii* concern the same *senatusconsultum*; Cicero, *in Pisonem*, 4. 8; Asconius, *in Pisonianam Ciceronis*, 6.
[3] Cf. *supra*, pp. 7 f.
[4] Quoted above.

conclusion to be drawn from the affirmative answer to this question is that the Senate did not think it had law-creating powers.

The third question was, are *senatusconsulta* incorporated into *edicta* or *leges* and made enforceable in that way? Clearly, in view of the affirmative answer to the second question the answer to this must also be yes. In addition to the two cases there, we have the *senatusconsultum de sociis* of 177 B.C. mentioned by Livy 41. 9. 9: 'legem dein de sociis C. Claudius tulit ex senatus consulto et edixit, qui socii nominis Latini . . .' In the early Empire the *senatusconsultum Silanianum* of A.D. 10 was enforced by an edict.[1] The conclusion which I think should be drawn from this affirmative answer is that the magistrates did not treat *senatusconsulta* as having law-creating effect. It should be remembered that edicts were not issued to give effect to *leges*.

The fourth, and last, question to be answered was whether the Senate in the Republic acted as if it had law-creating powers. A negative answer follows automatically from the answers given to the other questions.

The conclusion, therefore, is that *senatusconsulta* should not be regarded as creating law in the Republic. This present book is concerned with the development of private law in the Roman Republic, but it will have been observed that we have wandered far afield in the present section. That was inevitable in view of the extremely small number of Republican *senatusconsulta* which touch on private law—a fact which is in itself significant in assessing the normative effect of decrees of the Senate.

---

[1] D. 29. 5. 3. 18 (Ulpian, 50 *ad ed.*).

3

THE DEVELOPMENT OF THE
PRAETOR'S EDICT[1]

In the *de legibus*, 1. 5. 17, Cicero tells us that people used to think the science of law was to be drawn from the XII Tables, but most now consider it to be from the praetor's Edict.[2] Unquestionably, in fact, the Edict had become a major factor in legal development in the late Republic, though the stages in its growth are by no means so clear.[3] Technically the magistrates, including the praetors, could not alter the law by *edictum*, but they had control of the courts (each within his own sphere), and in their Edict they set out the circumstances in which they would allow a remedy to be sought.[4]

Two primary difficulties face any attempt to reconstruct the course of development of the praetorian Edict. The first is the extreme rarity of positive or virtually positive dates for the introduction of individual edicts. In fact there are only four. The *edictum de hominibus armatis coactisve et vi bonorum raptorum* was introduced by M. Lucullus,[5] who was *praetor peregrinus*—not *praetor urbanus*—in 76 B.C.[6] The *edictum de dolo* was the work of

---

[1] This chapter is a slightly revised version of the author's article of the same name which appeared in *JRS* 60 (1970), 105 ff.

[2] 'Non ergo a praetoris edicto, ut plerique nunc, neque a duodecim tabulis, ut superiores, sed penitus ex intima philosophia hauriendam iuris disciplinam putas?'

[3] The course of development of the Edict has been rather neglected by scholars, but see the broad studies of Dernburg, 'Untersuchungen über das Alter der Satzungen des prätorischen Edikts', *Festgaben Heffter* (Berlin, 1873), pp. 91 ff.; and Kelly, 'The Growth Pattern of the Praetor's Edict', *Irish Jurist*, 1 (1966), 341 ff.

[4] Cf., e.g., Jolowicz and Nicholas, *Introduction*, pp. 98 f.

[5] Cicero, *pro Tullio*, 4. 8.

[6] Asconius 75. For the vexed problem of the relationship of the peregrine Edict or the peregrine praetor to the urban Edict see *infra*, pp. 63 ff. Even if Lucullus' edict was not in the urban Edict from the start, it certainly was by 69 B.C.: Cicero, *pro Tullio*, 3. 7.

Aquillius Gallus[1] who was a praetor in 66 B.C.[2] An edict on *metus* was issued almost certainly by the Octavius[3] who was consul in 76 B.C. and hence praetor not later than 79. It is noteworthy that all positive dating for these three edicts comes from Cicero. An edict to restrict the right of patrons was issued by a praetor Rutilius, who is in all probability P. Rutilius Rufus who was praetor in 118 B.C. or just before. The identification here would be far less sure if we were without the information about Rutilius which is given by Cicero.[4] These are the only dates which can be asserted with a strong degree of probability.[5] There have been many attempts to attach individual parts of the Edict to individual praetors because of the names involved. Thus, for instance, Kelly links the *interdictum Salvianum* with a Salvius who was *praetor urbanus* in or about 74 B.C.;[6] the *actio Publiciana* with the Q. Publicius who was praetor about 67; the *actio Serviana* with the jurist Servius Sulpicius Rufus who was praetor in 65; the *actio Calvisiana* with a Calvisius who was praetor in 46; the *iudicium Cascellianum* with Cascellius who was praetor in 44 or 43; and so on.[7] Sometimes the correlation will be valid. But the flimsiness of the basis of the argument becomes apparent when one notices that an action which is at least very similar to the *actio Serviana*

---

[1] Cicero, *de nat. deor.* 3. 30. 74; *de off.* 3. 14. 60.

[2] The wording of two passages of Cicero, who was *praetor de repetundis* also in 66 B.C., indicates strongly that it was as praetor that Aquilius Gallus was responsible for the edict: *de off.* 3. 14. 60, 'nondum enim C. Aquilius, collega et familiaris meus, protulerat de dolo malo formulas'; *de nat. deor.* 3. 30. 74, 'inde everriculum malitiarum omnium iudicium de dolo malo, quod C. Aquilius familiaris noster protulit'. But Aquilius Gallus' sphere of praetorian jurisdiction seems to have been the *quaestio de ambitu* (Cicero, *pro Cluentio*, 53. 147), and the *edictum de dolo* could not have been issued for that court. In whatsoever way Aquilius Gallus is responsible for the *edictum*, it must be dated in the urban Edict relatively close to 66. On the problem see *infra*, pp. 72 ff.

[3] Cicero, *ad Quintum fratrem*, 1. 1. 7. 21; cf. *in Verrem* II, 3. 65. 152. But Cicero has C. Octavius, and the consul of 76 was Cn. Octavius: cf. Broughton, *Magistrates* ii. 93. Another possibility is L. Octavius who was consul in 75, hence praetor by 78.

[4] Cf. *infra*, pp. 55 f.

[5] Cf. Dernburg, 'Untersuchungen', pp. 100 f.

[6] So Kelly, but Verres was urban praetor in 74.

[7] 'Growth Pattern', 346 f. It must be emphasized at this stage that in general Kelly's view of the development of the Edict and my own are similar, though I disagree with much that he says.

was known to Cato the Elder who died in 149 B.C.;[1] and that there is no evidence of the existence of the important *actio Publiciana* before the time of Neratius who was active in the closing decades of the first century A.D.[2] The underlying danger of too readily attaching edicts etc. to particular praetors must be stressed. So few actual dates are known—and they all come fundamentally from Cicero—that if a number of possible, but conjectural, dates is added, a picture of a development will emerge which owes its existence mainly to an *a priori* conception of the pattern.[3]

The second major difficulty is, if anything, even more serious. We have for the Republic direct evidence of the actual wording or a substantial part of the actual wording of extremely few edicts, interdicts, or *formulae*. And the majority of these have undergone alteration in the wording by the time of Hadrian's Edict.[4] An extreme example—but perhaps extreme only because our sources here are more informative—is the *interdictum de vi armata*. In 73 or 72 B.C. it began: 'Unde dolo malo tuo, M. Tulli, M. Claudius aut familia aut procurator eius detrusus est'.[5] In 69 B.C. it ran: 'Unde tu aut familia aut procurator tuus illum vi hominibus

---

[1] Cf. *infra*, pp. 53 ff. It might be worth observing that the jurisdiction of Servius Sulpicius Rufus as praetor was the *quaestio de peculatu*: Cicero, *pro Murena*, 17. 35; 20. 42.

[2] Cf. *infra*, p. 57.

[3] A danger perhaps not entirely avoided by Kelly, 'Growth Pattern'.

[4] The *edictum* giving *bonorum possessio secundum tabulas*, cf. Lenel, *Edictum*, p. 349; that giving *bonorum possessio* to *legitimi*, cf. Kaser, 'Zum Ediktsstil', *Festschrift Schulz II* (Weimar, 1951), pp. 21 ff. at pp. 25 f.; the *edictum* on *metus*, cf. Kaser, 'Ediktsstil', p. 32; the *interdictum de vi*, cf. Lenel, *Edictum*, p. 462; the *interdictum de vi armata*, cf. Lenel, *Edictum*, p. 467; the *interdictum qui fraudationis causa latitabit*, cf. Lenel, *Edictum*, p. 415; the *interdictum uti possidetis*, no direct evidence of wording for Republic but there is for earlier and later versions in the Empire, cf. Kaser, 'Ediktsstil', p. 30; probably the *interdictum ne quid in loco publico*, no direct evidence of wording but see Watson, *Property*, pp. 10 f.; perhaps the *edictum* on *commodatum*, cf. now Watson, *Obligations*, pp. 168 f.; weighty doubts are expressed by Kaser on a *formula* for *fiducia*, 'Ediktsstil', p. 29; Rutilius' *edictum* on *bonorum possessio liberti* was replaced by another, D. 38. 2. 1. 2 (Ulpian, 42 *ad ed.*); from Cicero, *pro Quinctio*, 27. 84 we know the wording of an edict 'qui ex edicto meo in possessionem venerint', but we have no precise indication of its wording in classical law, cf. Lenel, *Edictum*, p. 423; Kaser, 'Ediktsstil', p. 28.

[5] Cicero, *pro Tullio*, 12. 29; cf. Watson, *Property*, p. 88. That the *interdictum* in question is an early form of *de vi armata* emerges from Cicero, *pro Caecina*, 17. 49.

coactis armatisve deiecisti, eo restituas.'[1] In Julian's Edict it read: 'Unde tu illum vi hominibus coactis armatisve deiecisti aut familia tua deiecit, eo illum quaeque ille tunc ibi habuit restituas.'[2] So the wording of the parts of the Edict was commonly subject to change. In no case where the date of an edict is unknown can we say, even with a fair degree of probability, that we have substantial knowledge of its original wording. The consequence is that we cannot use the form of an edict or its phraseology to help in dating the introduction of the edict.[3] Thus, observations of the type first produced by Dernburg,[4] that the latest and most mature stage of development of the Edict links the promise of the action not to a state of facts but to the allegation of a state of facts (that is, for instance, to 'si quis . . . fecisse dicetur, iudicium dabo', not to 'si quis fecerit . . . iudicium dabo'), will not greatly help in dating the introduction of an edict, but at the most in dating the known and surviving form of the Edict.[5] Moreover, even if the edicts which contain an allegation of facts represent a mature state of development, the choice of formulation, as Daube[6] has shown, is basically dependent upon factors other than the date. In fact, to maintain his theory Dernburg has to postulate—without any evidence—that the general edict on *metus* is very old, though that of Octavius, of which we know, introduced the *actio quod metus causa*.[7]

In these circumstances, any attempt to trace the Edict's development must be based on more or less indirect arguments. Plausibility can be maintained only if a distinct pattern emerges. Conversely, the degree of plausibility should not be measured in terms of any one particular piece of evidence. A number of minor

[1] Cicero, *pro Caecina*, 14. 41–17. 48; 19. 55; 21. 60 f.; 30. 88; *ad fam.* 15. 16. 3; cf. Lenel, *Edictum*, p. 467; Watson, loc. cit.

[2] Cf. Lenel, loc. cit.

[3] Cf. Kaser, 'Ediktsstil', pp. 24 f., who reaches the same conclusions primarily for other reasons.

[4] 'Untersuchungen', pp. 103, 109 ff.; cf. Kaser, 'Ediktsstil', p. 33; Burillo, 'Las formulas de la *actio depositi*', *SDHI* 27 (1962), 233 ff. at p. 246. Dernburg thinks three historical levels of development of the Edict can be traced from different forms of edicts. He assigns no dates to these.

[5] This remains true despite the power of survival of ancient forms. On which see Daube, *Forms*.

[6] *Forms*, pp. 30 ff.   [7] 'Untersuchungen', p. 101.

evidentiary points all tending in the same direction can have as much force as one very strong item of positive evidence. But the accuracy of each point must be established or again we run the risk of establishing a pattern by *a priori* reasoning.

A pattern of development is, in fact, visible, and it is proposed to outline the pattern, list the facts which illuminate the pattern, and then where necessary examine separately the strength and accuracy of these facts.

As early as the end of the third century B.C. the praetor could issue edicts, but the development of the Edict proper had scarcely begun. What edicts there were touching private law were restricted to making alterations in the measure of damages (and probably in procedure). Changes in substantive private law were not yet made by the Edict. As late as 140 B.C. major changes in the substantive law, which later would have been introduced by the Edict, still could not be so made, but were instituted by the introduction of new actions with what were later regarded as civil law *formulae*, though they were due to the praetor. But even before this the praetor was substantially changing the law by means of a praetorian action *in factum*, though no edict was issued. By the second-to-last decade of the second century B.C., edicts were being promulgated which profoundly modified the *ius civile*, but it is quite probable that the force of these was limited to restricting the rights of a plaintiff in a civil law action. Apparently only around 100 B.C. was the Edict so developed that individual edicts giving totally new actions on substantive law could be issued. The main period of the Edict was the following decades, but the development was not complete by the end of the Republic. Interdicts—concerned with the peace-keeping duty of the praetor—could be issued before 160 B.C., decretal remedies before 70 B.C.; and both civil law and edictal actions could be refused by the praetor by this latter date. Thus runs the pattern.

The facts which illuminate the pattern are as follows:

(i) *Bonae fidei* actions existed as *iudicia* with *formulae* which were not *in factum conceptae*. The development of this small group of actions for *tutela*, the four consensual contracts, *commodatum*, and *depositum*, presents many problems, one of the

greatest of which is to explain how they arose as actions *de novo* without a statute or edict.[1] This cannot have been easy or straightforward, and the fact is of significance for the history of the Edict. Law tends to develop in the simplest manner. Yet generally, development by the Edict seems extremely straightforward. If it did not occur in this case—as it did not—it must have been impossible, and this can only have been because the introduction of the *bonae fidei iudicia* took place before the Edict could introduce new provisions of substantive law. The most important of the *bonae fidei iudicia* for us are the *actio mandati* and the *actio commodati*. The former was the last to become a *bonae fidei iudicium* without first passing through an edictal phase.[2] The latter was the first which certainly began with an edictal phase, the *formula in ius concepta* being much later. Hence the major change in the power of the praetor to issue edicts which actually modified the substantive law came between the dates of introduction of these two actions.

The *actio mandati* was in existence by 123 B.C., but it is unlikely to be much earlier. In all probability a date around 140 B.C. can be set as the extreme terminus. The edictal *actio commodati* was known to Quintus Mucius Scaevola, so it was probably in existence by 100 B.C. Therefore the fundamental change is somewhere in the region of 140–100 B.C. Other evidence will tend to support a date nearer the later part of this period.

(ii) The evidence of the Edict in Plautus is very limited. The playwright Plautus was interested in law and his plays are studded with legal jokes and legal scenes. But virtually nothing is said about the Praetor's Edict. The argument here, though *e silentio*, is none the less strong. It becomes even stronger when one takes into account the nature of the one praetorian provision of which we seem to have evidence. This is the *edictum generale* of *iniuria*,

---

[1] The extent of the difficulty is fully seen in the accounts in Kaser, *ZPR*, pp. 109 f.; and Jolowicz and Nicholas, *Introduction*, pp. 221 f. See also, e.g., Wieacker, 'Zum Ursprung der *bonae fidei iudicia*', *ZSS* 80 (1963), 1 ff.

[2] There was both a *bonae fidei formula* and a *formula in factum* (and an edict) for the *actio negotiorum gestorum*, but the early history of these is most obscure. The *bonae fidei formula*, however, was known to Cicero, *top.* 10. 42; 17. 66. Cf. now Watson, *Obligations*, pp. 193 ff., especially at pp. 201 ff.

which originally changed the measure of damages but not the substantive law. The conclusions to be drawn are that in the time of Plautus the Edict was in its infancy; and, perhaps, that the praetor could make changes in the civil law penalties but not in the substantive law.

(iii) There are no traces of the Edict in the texts relating to the jurists before Publius Rutilius Rufus and Quintus Mucius. We have in the sources a reasonable amount of information on the opinions and attitudes of the jurists of the second century B.C., and there is no sign of any praetorian edictal provision in any of the discussions before Rutilius.[1] The point is of importance in a negative sense. More than that, if the Edict had been extensively developed we would have expected some trace of it.

(iv) The earliest known praetorian action with a formulation *in factum* which changed the substantive law existed before 160 B.C., but it was not introduced by an edict. The action in question was either the *actio Serviana* or an action akin to it and it appears in Cato's *de agri cultura* which was written around 160 B.C. It should not be thought to be merely a quirk of fate that this, the earliest known *actio in factum* which changed the substantive law, should have been introduced by the praetor without an edict. Such actions are extremely rare: the only other probable examples which seem to have been introduced by the praetor on his own initiative are the *actio in factum adversus nautas, caupones, stabularios*,[2] and the *actio si mensor falsum modum dixerit*.[3] It would be very odd if it were nothing but chance that the earliest known praetorian innovation in substantive law belonged to this tiny group.

It thus seems that, before the praetor began issuing edicts which modified the substantive law, he was already introducing a new action which was not formulated *in ius* and which did greatly change the law.

(v) Between the time of Plautus and the praetorship of P. Rutilius Rufus in or shortly before 118 B.C., we have no evidence of the introduction of any new edict. A Rutilius who is probably this one introduced a clause in his Edict that he would not give to the

[1] Cf. *infra*, pp. 55 f.   [2] Cf. Lenel, *Edictum*, pp 205 f.
[3] Cf. Lenel, *Edictum*, p. 219.

patron more than an *actio operarum et societatis*. The purpose of
this was to restrict the burden which a master could impose on his
slave in return for the gift of liberty. Now in a very real sense this
does alter the substantive law, but it is at the most a restriction on
a plaintiff's rights at civil law, and can still be seen as primarily
procedural. What it does not do is create a new right of action or
a new legal concept. Perhaps it is not possible to estimate the full
significance of our knowledge of such an edict before any edict
introducing a new right of action. There are many edicts which do
nothing but modify existing civil law rights; and there is no corpus
of background—as there is in the plays of Plautus—against which
the fragment of our knowledge can be judged.

(vi) The *edictum* on *commodatum* was certainly known to Quintus
Mucius Scaevola[1] whose death was in 82 B.C.[2] So it probably was
in existence around 100 B.C. This makes it the earliest known
edict which created an action unknown previously in the civil law.
It is possible—though by no means certain—that Quintus Mucius
also knew the *edictum* on *depositum*,[3] but in the surviving evidence
concerning him there is no sign of any other edict.

(vii) In the following few decades the Edict was well developed.
The *edictum de convicio* was probably in existence by the second
decade of the first century B.C.[4] Edictal clauses giving *bonorum*

---

[1] D. 13. 6. 5. 3 (Ulpian, 28 *ad ed.*); against suggestions of interpolation see
Watson, *Obligations*, pp. 169 f.

[2] Cf. Kunkel, *Herkunft*, p. 18.

[3] D. 46. 3. 81. 1 (Pomponius, 6 *ad Quintum Mucium*) as far as *teneri* is in
indirect speech and so goes back to Mucius. But it is possible he was concerned
with the XII Tables' provision on *depositum*.

[4] *Rhet. ad Herenn.* 4. 25. 35. But the matter is not so simple as would appear
from Watson, *Obligations*, pp. 250 f. In *Rhet. ad Herenn.* 2. 13. 19 'C. Caelius
iudex absolvit iniuriarum' a defendant who insulted Lucilius on the stage, yet in
a similar case Publius Mucius (consul in 133 B.C.) as *iudex* found against the
defendant. For the story to have much point the *actio* in question must have been
the same in both cases, and it cannot have been under the *edictum ne quid
infamandi causa fiat* or the *edictum de convicio* (despite Pugliese, *Il processo civile
romano, II: Il processo formulare I* (Milan, 1963), p. 198, n. 109) or Caelius, one
would think, would also have awarded the decision to the plaintiff. But an action
under at least the *edictum de convicio* would have been more sensible if that edict
was in existence. Hence, first, that edict was not known when Publius Mucius
acted as *iudex*, and secondly, the *edictum generale* had been extended by the
jurists to cases where there was no physical assault. *Rhet. ad Herenn.* 4. 25. 35
then lists as one form of *iniuriae* those caused *convicio*. This need not mean, as
was argued in *Obligations*, that *convicium* was subsumed under the *edictum*

possessio on several accounts, 'qui fraudationis causa latitarit', 'cui heres non exstabit', 'qui exilii causa solum verterit', were available by 81 B.C.;[1] an edict on *metus* was in all probability issued by L. Octavius in 79 or just before;[2] the *edictum de hominibus armatis coactisve et vi bonorum raptorum* was issued by M. Lucullus in 76;[3] and the *edictum de dolo* was the work of Aquillius Gallus, almost certainly in 66 B.C.[4] An edict giving *bonorum possessio secundum tabulas* was already *tralaticium* in 74 B.C.,[5] and so was at least *unde legitimi* for *bonorum possessio contra tabulas*.[6] An *edictum de bonis libertorum* had been issued before that date[7] and the *edictum de pactis* existed in 54 B.C.[8] *Qui nisi pro certis personis ne postulent* existed by 44 B.C.[9] Servius Sulpicius Rufus died in 43 B.C.[10] and he knew of the *edictum ne quid infamandi causa*,[11] the *edictum de ventre*,[12] the *edictum de suggrundis*[13] (and hence of *de effusis vel deiectis*),[14] and of that which introduced the *actio institoria*.[15] Since that last action must be later than the *actio exercitoria*, which in turn is apparently later than the *receptum nautarum cauponum stabulariorum*, the two edicts for these actions must also have existed. Alfenus dealt with aspects of the *actio servi corrupti*[16] and the *actio de peculio et de in rem verso*;[17] so considering the dependence of that jurist on his teacher, Servius, it is most probable that the relevant edicts had already been discussed by Servius. Trebatius discussed

generale. The wording of the text is perfectly consistent with *convicium*'s being regarded as a form of *iniuria* under its own edict. It would not be strange if the work of the jurists was legitimized by issuing an edict giving an action for *convicium* (and if at a later stage of development *convicium* was again engulfed by the *edictum generale*). Actually the wording of the text would be appropriate even if the *edictum de convicio* had not yet been issued.

[1] Cicero, *pro Quinctio*, 19. 60.
[2] Cicero, *ad Quintum fratrem*, 1. 1. 7. 21; cf. *in Verrem* II, 3. 65. 152.
[3] Cicero, *pro Tullio*, 4. 8.
[4] Cicero, *de nat. deor.* 3. 30. 74; *de off.* 3. 14. 60.
[5] Cicero, *in Verrem* II, 1. 45. 117.   [6] Cicero, *in Verrem* II, 1. 44. 114.
[7] D. 38. 2. 1. 2 (Ulpian, 42 *ad ed.*); Cicero, *in Verrem* II, 1. 48. 125–6.
[8] Cicero, *ad Att.* 2. 9. 1.   [9] *Lex Iulia Municipalis*, lines 108 ff.
[10] Cf. Kunkel, *Herkunft*, p. 25.
[11] D. 47. 10. 15. 32 (Ulpian, 57 *ad ed.*); cf. Watson, *Obligations*, p. 252.
[12] D. 37. 9. 1. 24, 25 (Ulpian, 41 *ad ed.*).
[13] D. 9. 3. 5. 12 (Ulpian, 23 *ad ed.*).
[14] Cf., e.g., Daube, *Forms*, p. 26 and n. 3; Watson, *Obligations*, p. 267.
[15] D. 14. 3. 5. 1 (Ulpian, 28 *ad ed.*).
[16] D. 11. 3. 16 (Alfenus Varus, 2 *dig.*).   [17] D. 15. 3. 16 (Alfenus, 2 *dig.*).

aspects of the *edictum de sumptibus funerum*,[1] and apparently *si quis mortuum in locum alterius*,[2] and the clause *unde cognati* for *bonorum possessio contra tabulas*.[3] Ofilius commented on *ne quis eum qui in ius vocabitur vi eximat*,[4] on the clause *de eo per quem factum erit, quo minus quis vadimonium sistat*,[5] and on the edict *de minoribus viginti quinque annis*.[6] The edict on *damnum infectum*, at least of the peregrine praetor, existed by 49 B.C.[7]

It might be suggested that this evidence shows that the Edict was well developed in the first century B.C., and even in the first half of that century, but does not indicate that the great development took place in this time.[8] The more extensive sources for this period, as compared with those for the last half of the second century B.C., present us, it might be argued, with an unbalanced picture. There is point to the argument, but it should equally be observed that to a considerable extent the survival of Republican juristic discussion in later legal sources is dependent upon the continuing relevance of that discussion. The relative paucity of information in the Digest on jurists up to and including the time of Quintus Mucius must be due in part to the fact that the law shortly afterwards underwent such changes that their discussions were largely irrelevant.

(viii) A few edicts were issued in the Empire before Julian's redaction: one of minor importance—which did not become permanently enshrined in the Edict—by Cassius on *restitutio in integrum*; one on *bonorum possessio*; and probably some others.

---

[1] D. 11. 7. 14. 11 (Ulpian, 25 *ad ed.*).

[2] D. 10. 3. 6. 6; cf. Watson, *Property,* p. 6.

[3] D. 38. 10. 10. 15 and 18 (Paul, *sing. de gradibus*); cf. Watson, *Succession*, p. 184.

[4] D. 2. 7. 1. 2 (Ulpian, 5 *ad ed.*).

[5] D. 2. 10. 2 (Paul, 6 *ad ed.*).   [6] D. 4. 4. 16. 1 (Ulpian, 11 *ad ed.*).

[7] *Lex Rubria de Gallia Cisalpina* xx. On the complicated history of the early law on *damnum infectum* see Watson, *Property*, pp. 125 ff.; and *infra*, pp. 78 ff. Elsewhere I have suggested that the grants of *datio deminutio* to Hispala Faecenia in 186 B.C. (Livy 39. 19. 5) shows either that the *edicta Fabianum* and *Calvisianum* existed or that similar provisions did: *Persons*, pp. 234. But the point of the grant is probably simply to allow Hispala Faecenia, though *in tutela mulierum*, to alienate her property despite the tutor's opposition, and nothing more need be read into it.

[8] Cicero, *de inven.* 2. 22. 67 cannot be used as evidence that substantive changes had been effected by the Edict for more than a few decades.

There were also adjustments in wording, and a few actions and *exceptiones* were added or subtracted. But the great days of the Edict had passed with the Republic.

(ix) Interdicts developed early. Though there is no sign of them in Plautus,[1] we know that at least one existed in 161 B.C., the date of production of Terence's *Eunuchus*. Lines 319 f. have: 'ipsam hanc tu mihi vel vi vel clam vel precario fac tradas.' The combination *vi, clam, precario*, is frequent in interdicts but occurs nowhere else. The *interdictum Salvianum* is older than the *actio Serviana* which seems to have been available by 160 B.C.[2] Unless Cicero is being anachronistic *uti possidetis* existed in 129 B.C., the year in which his *de re publica* is set.[3] A Rutilius, who is almost certainly the consul of 105 B.C.[4] (and praetor of around 118), commented on the interdict *quae arbor ex aedibus tuis*,[5] and Quintus Mucius discussed *quod vi aut clam*.[6] The interdict *de vi armata*[7] existed in 73 or 72 B.C.[8] and so did that *de vi*.[9] *Quam hereditatem* was established by 74 B.C.[10] and *quorum bonorum* is at least as old as 44 B.C.[11] Servius knew the *interdictum de rivis*,[12] Alfenus a version of *ne quid in loco publico*.[13] Trebatius discussed *de fonte*,[14] *de cloacis*,[15] and *quem liberum*

---

[1] Against the idea of the *interdictum utrubi* in Plautus' *Stichus* 696 and 750, see now Watson, *Property*, pp. 86 f.

[2] In Hadrian's Edict the formula of the *actio Serviana* appears, surprisingly, in the section on interdicts where it is appended to the *interdictum Salvianum*. This must mean: (i) that the action is later than the *interdictum* which has attracted it to that position; (ii) that both the *interdictum* and the *actio* go back to a time when the Edict was in its infancy and arrangement of it was lax. On the general view the *interdictum* dates from the first half of the first century B.C.: cf., e.g., Kaser, *RPR* i. 472, n. 22; Kelly, 'Growth Pattern', p. 347.

[3] It is parodied in *de re pub*. 1. 13. 20. Jolowicz and Nicholas, *Introduction*, p. 263, claim that *uti possidetis* evidently served as the model for three arbitrations between Greek cities in the second half of the second century B.C.: Dittenberger, *Sylloge Inscriptionum Graecarum* ii, 4th edit. (Hildesheim, 1960), nos. 679, 683, 685 (with *Supplementum Epigraphicum Graecarum* 2. 511). But the situations involved in these arbitrations and the language employed seem too far removed from the *interdictum* for the claim to be persuasive.

[4] Cf. *infra*, pp. 55 f.   [5] D. 43. 27. 1. 2 (Ulpian, 71 *ad ed*.).

[6] D. 50. 17. 73. 2 (Quintus Mucius, *sing*. ὅρων); 43. 24. 1. 5 (Ulpian, 71 *ad ed*.).

[7] An early form of it.   [8] Cicero, *pro Tullio*, 12. 29.

[9] Cicero, *pro Tullio*, 19. 44 f.   [10] Cicero, *in Verrem* II, 1. 45. 116.

[11] Cicero, *ad fam*. 7. 21.

[12] D. 43. 21. 3pr., 1 (Ulpian, 70 *ad ed*.).

[13] D. 8. 5. 17. 2 (Alfenus, 2 *dig*.); cf. Watson, *Property*, pp. 10 f.

[14] D. 43. 20. 1. 8 (Ulpian, 70 *ad ed*.); cf. Watson, *Property*, p. 197.

[15] D. 43. 23. 2 (Venuleius, 1 *interd*.). So did Ofilius.

dolo malo retines.[1] Ofilius disagreed with another Republican
jurist on a point concerning *de aqua cottidiana et aestiva*,[2] and we
have an opinion of his on *quod in itinere publico*.[3] The two interdicts
de itinere actuque also existed in the Republic.[4]

Of praetorian edictal stipulations we have evidence for the
Republic only for *de damno infecto*, which existed in 58 B.C.,[5] and
legatorum servandorum causa, which was known to Ofilius.[6]

(x) Though not a matter of the Edict, it is significant for the
praetor's legal activity that as early as the time of Servius he was
granting decretal remedies,[7] and this was not altogether a rare
practice.

By 70 B.C., too, we know that the praetor might refuse an action
on a valid civil law claim which he regarded as inequitable,[8] and
he was refusing *bonorum possessio* under his own Edict by 74 or
by 72 at the latest.[9]

Most of these points which I think illuminate the pattern now
require separate examination to test their strength and accuracy.

(i) As yet, no convincing explanation of the mechanics of
introduction—without statute or edict—of the *iudicia* with *dare
facere oportet ex fide bona* has, I think, been produced. But there
have been many attempts. The nature and effect of *oportet ex
fide bona* are also much disputed.[10] In Gaius' time these actions may
have been regarded *par excellence* as the civil law *iudicia*, but it has
been argued that originally they were not civil law actions at all.[11]
Whether they were or were not does not here concern us. It is
enough to emphasize first that the difficulties of modern scholars

[1] D. 43. 29. 4. 1 (Venuleius, 4 *interd.*).
[2] D. 43. 20. 1. 17 (Ulpian, 70 *ad ed.*).
[3] D. 43. 8. 2. 39 (Ulpian, 68 *ad ed.*).
[4] D. 43. 19. 4pr. (Venuleius, 1 *interd.*).
[5] Cf. Watson, *Property*, p. 140.   [6] D. 36. 3. 1. 15 (Ulpian, 79 *ad ed.*).
[7] D. 9. 3. 5. 12 (Ulpian, 23 *ad ed.*) (Servius); 3. 5. 20 (21)pr. (Paul, 9 *ad ed.*)
(Servius); 19. 5. 23 (Alfenus, 3 *dig. a Paulo epit.*) (Alfenus); 6. 1. 5. 3 (Ulpian,
16 *ad ed.*) (?Alfenus—see now Watson, *Property*, p. 75); 39. 2. 9. 2 (Ulpian,
53 *ad ed.*) (Alfenus—see now Watson, *Property*, p. 148); 44. 1. 14 (Alfenus
Varus, 2 *dig.*) (Alfenus, *exceptio in factum*); 9. 2. 9. 3 (Ulpian, 18 *ad ed.*) (Ofilius).
[8] Valerius Maximus 7. 7. 5.
[9] Valerius Maximus 7. 7. 7; Cicero, *in Verrem* II, 1. 47. 123, 124; cf. also
Valerius Maximus 7. 7. 6: on all see Watson, *Succession*, pp. 75 ff.
[10] Cf., e.g., Wieacker, 'Ursprung', pp. 2 ff.
[11] See the account in Wieacker, 'Ursprung', p. 9.

in accounting for their existence can have been exceeded only by the difficulties experienced by the ancients in creating them. And secondly that though the praetor must have been responsible for the mechanics of the actions,[1] he did not establish them by edicts and they were not formulated *in factum*.

The order of development of each of the actions and the date of introduction are also much disputed. But it is very widely accepted that the *bonae fidei actiones* of *tutelae, empti, venditi, locati, conducti, pro socio,* and *mandati*—for which institutions there was no edict—were in existence in the second half of the second century B.C. The majority, in fact, are probably considerably older.[2] In any event it is very likely that the *actio mandati* was the last to develop, and it existed in 123 B.C., as we know from *Rhet. ad Herennium* 2. 13. 19: '. . . M. Drusus pr. urbanus, quod cum herede mandati ageretur, iudicium reddidit, Sex. Iulius non reddidit. . . .' Sextus Iulius Caesar was *praetor urbanus* in 123 B.C.[3] But *mandatum* as a contract can scarcely be much older. It can have developed only in what was already a mature legal system and few scholars, if any, would suggest a date before 140 B.C.

Commodatum, on the other hand, gave rise to a *bonae fidei iudicium* in the Empire only.[4] Before that the action was *in factum concepta* and was established by an edict.[5] *Commodatum* was known to Quintus Mucius Scaevola who died in 82 B.C.:

D. 13. 6. 5. 3 (Ulpian, 28 *ad ed.*). Commodatum autem plerumque solam utilitatem continet eius cui commodatur, et ideo verior est Quinti Mucii sententia existimantis et culpam praestandam et diligentiam et, si forte res aestimata data sit, omne periculum praestandum ab eo, qui aestimationem se praestaturum recepit.[6]

---

[1] Whether *praetor urbanus* or *praetor peregrinus* can be here ignored. But see *infra*, pp. 90 ff.

[2] So is the unique *actio rei uxoriae*, which, I think, dates from around 200 B.C. If, as is generally believed (cf. Kaser, 'Die Rechtsgrundlage der *actio rei uxoriae*', *RIDA* 2 (1949), 511 ff. at pp. 542 ff., and the references he gives), the *actio* is praetorian, it fits into the pattern described here since there was no edict. If its civil law character (in Hadrian's Edict) derives from the censors' control over family morals (cf., e.g., Monier, *Manuel élémentaire de droit romain* 1, 6th edit. (Paris, 1949), pp. 291 ff.), it is irrelevant to us.

[3] Cf. Broughton, *Magistrates* i. 513.

[4] Cf., e.g., Watson, *Obligations*, pp. 167 and 160.

[5] Cf. Lenel, *Edictum*, p. 252.

[6] On the text see now Watson, *Obligations*, pp. 169 ff.

So it is likely that the *edictum* on *commodatum* was issued by, say, 100 B.C. The significance of this information cannot be over-emphasized. In the first place, so far as our knowledge goes, this is the earliest edict which introduced a new action. Secondly, since eventually an *actio in ius concepta* developed to take its place side by side with the *actio in factum*, one cannot argue that the edict was needed because the power to introduce actions with an *oportet ex fide bona* clause had been lost. Rather, the kind of development which occurred here must be attributed to a growth of power in the Edict, a power which did not exist when *mandatum* became actionable.

It might be suggested that the Edict already had the power to change the substantive law when *mandatum* arose, and that that contract had a *bonae fidei iudicium* because of the power of attraction of the older *bonae fidei iudicia*. The force of the argument cannot be denied, but it affects the problem only marginally. One would then have to say that the power of counter-attraction of the Edict was not strong enough to cause the issue of an edict on *mandatum*, but a few years later it was enough for an edict to be issued for *commodatum*. So, on this view, the praetor in, say, 140 B.C. was still only beginning to develop his power to issue edicts changing the substance of the law.[1]

The rather different objection might be raised that the advent of a new way of making legal changes does not necessarily mean the disappearance of old and successful ones, and therefore that edicts changing substantive law could have been issued for some considerable time before the introduction of the *actio mandati*. But it must not be forgotten that issuing a new *bonae fidei iudicium* had never been a common method of law reform—the last case having probably occurred more than half a century previously—and the practice would not have been in the forefront of a praetor's mind if he had been accustomed to making changes by edict. Moreover, an edict clearly putting the innovation before the public would have had its advantages, and a satisfactory *actio mandati in factum* could easily have been framed.

---

[1] It is possible that the *edictum* on *depositum* was as early, but the early history of *depositum* is too complicated for any help to be obtained from the possibility.

(ii) From earliest times, it seems, Roman magistrates had the right *edicere*.[1] In all probability, the *praetor urbanus* and the *praetor peregrinus* had this right from the date of creation of their offices. This, of course, is in itself no guide to the date of introduction of an annual Edict nor to the date of the first individual edicts altering the substantive private law.

The earliest known praetorian edict is from the year 213 B.C.:[2]

Livy 25. 1. 12: Is [i.e., M. Aemilius, *praetor urbanus*] et in contione senatus consultum recitavit et edixit ut quicumque libros vaticinos precationesve aut artem sacrificandi conscriptam haberet eos libros omnes litterasque ad se ante calendas Apriles deferret neu quis in publico sacrove loco novo aut externo ritu sacrificaret.

It is doubtful how significant the episode is for the general development of the Edict. In the first place, the edict was issued when the senate expressly gave the task of freeing the people from these superstitions to the *praetor urbanus*.[3] In the second place, the edict was not concerned with private law but was in the nature of a police measure. And in the third place, the edict was apparently issued by itself and was not part of a general, annual Edict.

The information in Plautus ont he provisions of the praetor's Edict is minute. It is likely, though not certain, that the *edictum generale* on *iniuria* is referred to in *Asinaria* 371, where the slave, Leonida, says: 'pugno malam si tibi percussero'. Lenel observes that this has the ring of a comic citation of the formula[4] for *iniuria* which began: 'Quod . . . Ao Ao pugno mala percussa est . . .' The argument, however, can only be from the similarity of words, since

[1] See, e.g., the *SC de Bacchanalibus* (Bruns, *Fontes*, no. 36: 186 B.C.). In Livy the right is ascribed to kings (e.g. 1. 29. 6; 1. 52. 6), consuls (2. 11. 5; 2. 24. 6, etc.), dictators (2. 30. 6; 3. 27. 5, etc.), the *decemviri* (3. 38. 13, etc.), the *tribuni militum* (6. 10. 5). See further the *TLL*, s.v. *edicere* 1, B; Mommsen, *Staatsrecht* i. 202 f.

[2] Cf. Weissenborn–Müller, *Titi Livi ab urbe condita libri* iii, 2nd edit. (Leipzig, 1896), p. 57; Broughton, *Magistrates* i. 263. But Dernburg gives the date as 215 B.C., and names the praetor as M. Atilius: 'Untersuchungen', p. 95 and n. 2.

[3] Livy 25. 1. 11: 'Ubi potentius iam esse id malum apparuit quam ut minores per magistratus sedaretur, M. Aemilio praetori [urbano] negotium ab senatu datum est ut eis religionibus populum liberaret.'

[4] *Edictum*, p. 398, n. 7, followed by, e.g., Watson, *Obligations*, p. 248; Simon, 'Begriff und Tatbestand der *iniuria* im altrömischen Recht', *ZSS* 82 (1965), 132 ff. at p. 181.

nothing else in the Plautine context indicates a legal joke, and this similarity may perhaps not result from imitating the wording of the *formula*.[1] Nothing like absolute certainty is possible. Some support for an early date for the *edictum generale* may be found in Aulus Gellius, *N.A.* 20. 1. 13. He tells us that the jurist Labeo in his work on the XII Tables recorded the story of L. Veratius who amused himself by striking passers-by in the face while a slave followed him with a purse full of *asses* and counted out twenty-five to each victim, according to the law of the XII Tables. It was precisely the fall in the value of money which led to the replacement of the fixed sums of the XII Tables by the flexible assessment of the *edictum generale*, and it is unlikely that the fixed penalty would long survive the behaviour of a Veratius. Indeed, the praetor's edict is said in the story to be the consequence of Veratius' conduct. Now the word used for purse or money-bag in Labeo's story is *crumena*, and *crumena* (or *crumina*) with this its fundamental meaning is rare outside Plautus.[2] In fact, the grammarians Festus[3] and Nonius[4] indicate that in their time the word was obsolete for all practical purposes. And Gellius in his account uses the verb *depalmare* which occurs nowhere else. Might one not suspect that this, too, is an archaism? So the story of L. Veratius— and hence the introduction of the *edictum generale*—is old. The account is circumstantial, with its otherwise unknown L. Veratius,

---

[1] Cf. Girard, *ZSS* 14 (1893), 24 '. . . et il y a en effet une concordance de termes très frappante. Elle cesse d'être bien étonnante si l'on réfléchit que long-temps avant l'édit il y a eu des poings qui sont tombés sur des visages et qui y sont même tombés contrairement à la loi des XII tables, et que la formule concrète d'action soumise comme modèle aux plaideurs a dû précisément être choisie parmi les variétés d'injures les plus usuelles.'

[2] Cf. *TLL* iv. 124. With this meaning it occurs fifteen times in the extant plays of Plautus: *As.* 590, 653, 657, 661; *Epid.* 360, 632; *Per.* 265, 317, 685; *Ps.* 170; *Ru.* 1318; *Tru.* 652, 654, 655, 956 (plus once as a corruption of the text: *Per.* 687). Apart from the two grammarians and the text of Gellius, it appears elsewhere with this meaning before the fourth century A.D. only in Apuleius, whose exoticisms, as is well known, include archaisms: *Met.* 2. 13; *Ap.* 42. Horace uses it once ('deficiente crumina') with the transferred sense of money, *Epist.* 1. 4. 11; and in this he is followed once ('deficiente crumina') by Juvenal, 11. 38.

[3] S.v. *Crumina, sacculi genus*. Plautus, 'Di bene vertant, tene cruminam, inerunt triginta minae.'

[4] 78 s.v. *Bulga, et folliculus omnis, quam et cruminam veteres appellarunt et est sacculus ad bracchium pendens.*

and is likely to have some foundation in reality.[1] But so long as each *as* weighed approximately 10 ounces, one slave with a bagful of *asses* would not have sufficed to give Veratius the pleasure of striking quite a few people, as the story suggests he did. Moreover, the story demands that Veratius be exhibitionist, a self-confident, suave young man.[2] As such he would not walk through the streets followed by an overburdened slave who had such an important role to play in his insolence. One might feel, therefore, that a date at least after the halving of the weight of the *as* has greater plausibility. The date of this reduction—and of the subsequent ones—is disputed. But Hersh shows that Sydenham's suggested 208 B.C.[3] is too late, and proposes a date around 227.[4] And Mattingly gives 217 as the date of the reduction of the 10-ounce *as* to 6 ounces, and suggests 209 as the year of reduction to 3 ounces.[5] The recent work of Crawford indicates that coins of semi-libral standard (or just below), but no others, were in circulation in 216, and that coins of sextantal standard were introduced in 211 or just before.[6] The *Asinaria* is one of Plautus' early plays and should be dated before 200 B.C.[7] Thus, a date for the *edictum generale* in the last quarter of the third century B.C. seems indicated.[8] If this is accurate, then in all probability the *edictum generale* is the work of the urban

---

[1] Contra, Dernburg, 'Untersuchungen', p. 106, n. 4. An argument of Dernburg's (p. 101) for the existence of the *actio iniuriarum aestimatoria* in 170 B.C. is based on a now abandoned reconstruction of the *SC de Thisbensibus*: cf. Dittenberger, *Sylloge inscriptionum Graecarum*, 4th edit. (reprinted Hildesheim, 1960), ii. 205; Bruns, *Fontes*, pp. 169 f.; Riccobono, *FIRA* i. 246. Most recently, Birks also rejects the historicity of the episode ('The Early History of *Iniuria*', *TvR* 37 (1969), 163 ff. at pp. 174 ff.), but he dates the edict to the third century B.C. (p. 195). Von Lübtow leaves the question open: 'Zum römischen Injurienrecht', *Labeo* 15 (1969), 131 ff. at p. 134.

[2] Not a bitter middle-aged man of moderate means. He obviously did not fear being struck in return, so he must have come from an upper-class background: cf. Kelly, *Roman Litigation* (Oxford, 1966).

[3] *The Coinage of the Roman Republic*, revised with indexes by Haines, edited by Forrer and Hersh (London, 1952), p. xxii.

[4] In Sydenham, *Coinage*, p. 220.

[5] 'The First Age of Roman Coinage', *JRS* 35 (1945), 65 ff. at p. 73.

[6] 'War and Finance', *JRS* 54 (1964), 29 ff.; *Roman Republican Coin Hoards* (London, 1969), pp. 4 f.

[7] Cf., e.g., Duckworth, *The Nature of Roman Comedy* (Princeton, 1952), p. 55.

[8] For further texts in Plautus which may concern *iniuria*, though they throw no light on our problem, see Simon, 'Begriff', pp. 181 ff.

praetor, since between 215 and 198 B.C. (with the sole exception of 210) a peregrine praetor was either not appointed or was employed outside Rome.[1]

Kelly produces an argument for a much later date for the *actio iniuriarum aestimatoria*.[2] He observes that the *Lex Fannia*, of as late as 160 B.C.,[3] 'set 10 *as* as the maximum expenditure for a normal day's dinner: it seems scarcely likely that the 25 *as* penalty (in other words 2½ good dinners) was so derisory by the mid-second century as to require supersession'. But the position is not quite so straightforward. The *lex Fannia* seems[4] to have permitted 100 *asses* as maximum expenditure on food on the days of the *ludi Romani, ludi plebei, Saturnalia*, and certain other days; 30 *asses* on ten other days in each month; and 10 *asses* on every other day. When one takes the nature of sumptuary laws into account, 30 *asses* will represent a good dinner[5] and 10 *asses* a frugal day's eating. Moreover, Roman accounting was so weak at this time[6] that it is likely that the cost of preparing the meal (labour and wood for cooking) would not be taken into account and the 30 *asses* would represent the cost of raw materials only. So 25 *asses* was not such a great sum. And the fact remains that it was worth much less than the 25 *asses* of the XII Tables, mainly because of the reduction in weight of the *as* but also because copper was not so scarce.

The *edictum generale* was confined to cases of physical assault and did not in any way change the substantive law.[7] This latter

---

[1] Cf. Mommsen, *Staatsrecht* ii. 210, n. 5.   [2] 'Growth Pattern', p. 347.

[3] 161 is perhaps better: cf. Rotondi, *Leges*, pp. 287 f.

[4] The provisions of the *lex* are not absolutely clear. The main source is Aulus Gellius, *N.A.* 2. 24. 2–7, but see also *N.A.* 20. 1. 23; Macrobius, *Sat.* 3. 17. 3; Pliny the Elder, *N.H.* 10. 50. 139; Athenaeus, *Deipnos.* 247 C.

[5] Breakfast was a frugal meal, cf. Marquardt, *Das Privatleben der Römer*, i, 2nd edit. (reprinted Darmstadt, 1964), p. 265. And so usually was lunch, cf. Warde Fowler, *Social Life at Rome in the Age of Cicero* (repr. London, 1965), pp. 273 f.; also Marquardt, p. 267.

[6] Cf. de Ste Croix, 'Greek and Roman Accounting', *Studies in the History of Accounting* (London, 1950), pp. 33 ff., especially at pp. 37 ff.

[7] Cf., e.g., Watson, *Obligations*, pp. 248 ff. In general the sole dispute is whether all kinds of physical assault were covered, or only the less serious. Birks, who takes a different view from other scholars of the early history of *iniuria*, agrees that the praetor was not creating a new form of action: 'Early History', p. 196.

point, indeed, emerges even from the unusual wording of the edict:
the praetor does not promise an action, but gives instructions on
how to proceed in one.[1] The widening of the scope of the edict
to include cases where no blow had been struck was the work of
jurists.[2] So on this score there is no evidence that the Edict was
yet used to introduce reforms of substantive private law. But the
survival of this edict indicates that already the praetor was issuing
an Edict, the more satisfactory of whose provisions would be
repeated in the Edicts of subsequent praetors.

Something more must be said about the nature of the action
given under the *edictum generale*. This—to judge from later
sources—was *in factum* and it is unlikely that this characteristic
of the action was due to subsequent development.[3] Thus it seems
that as early as Plautus, when the damages under the civil law were
changed by an edict, the action itself would become an *actio in
factum*.[4]

A parody of a praetorian edict appears in the prologue to
Plautus' *Poenulus*, lines 16–45:

> bonum factum esse edicta ut servetis mea.
> scortum exoletum ne quis in proscaenio
> sedeat, neu lictor verbum aut virgae muttiant . . .

and so on. At one time it was held that the prologue was post-
Plautine, but the basis for that opinion is now thought to be wrong.[5]

---

[1] Cf. *Coll.* 2. 5. 1 (Paul, *sing. de iniuriis*); D. 47. 10. 7pr. (Ulpian, 57 *ad ed.*);
Lenel, *Edictum*, pp. 397 f.
[2] By the later part of the second century B.C.: P. Mucius in *Rhet. ad Herenn.*
2. 13. 19; cf. Watson, *Obligations*, pp. 250 f. Pugliese (*Processo formulare*, p. 198,
n. 109) suggests that the text was concerned with *convicium*, but my argument
against *ne quid infamandi causa fiat* is also valid against the idea of *convicium*: cf.
supra, p. 38, n. 4.   [3] Cf. Lenel, *Edictum*, p. 399.
[4] It is possible that a further instance of praetorian intervention is to be found
in Plautus, *Poenulus*, 711–85. The pimp, Lycus, who is described as a *fur
manifestus*, is under threat of *addictio*. It is most reasonable to treat this *addictio*
as being due to the XII Tables' provision for manifest theft, but it is conceivable
that, if the praetor had already introduced the fourfold penalty for manifest
theft where the thief was a free man, the *addictio* would be due to Lycus' inability
to pay the condemnation: cf. his reaction to the accusation of *furtum nec manifestum* in lines 1343–54. In this event, the praetor would again have intervened
to change a penalty (but not by an edict), though not the substantive law. It must
be emphasized, however, that nothing positively indicates that here the threat of
addictio is not the direct consequence of *furtum manifestum*.
[5] Cf., e.g., Duckworth, *Roman Comedy*, pp. 80 f.

The date of the play is by no means certain,[1] and it is not known when and on what occasion the play was first produced. None the less, Plautus is representing the production as being under the auspices of the praetor, not of the curule aediles, as is shown by the reference to *lictor* in line 18. The praetors—as magistrates with *imperium*—but not the aediles, were accompanied by lictors. But the passage takes us little further forward. All the provisions named are, as one would expect, directly concerned with the smooth running of the performance. They are evidence that, just as the curule aediles early issued regulations for the streets and markets for which they were responsible,[2] so the praetor issued an edict of several clauses governing behaviour at festivals for which he was responsible.[3] But no wider conclusions for the development of the Edict can be drawn from the passage.

This paucity of information in Plautus on the praetor's Edict is all the more striking when one recalls the large number of legal jokes, legal scenes, and comic uses of legal terminology which occurs in his plays. Thus, to choose some instances, he jokes about *furtum manifestum*,[4] *fiducia*,[5] the *exceptio legis Laetoriae*,[6] *in diem addictio* (a standard term in sale),[7] makes puns on the forms of real security,[8] has an elaborate legal scene to enable a rogue to sell a free woman as a slave without becoming liable to reimburse the buyer,[9] and another to make a brothel-keeper a *fur manifestus*,[10] and tells us something about the role of *arra* in sale,[11] the forms of words used for divorce,[12] capacity to marry,[13] and *manumissio vindicta*.[14, 15]

---

[1] Cf., e.g., Duckworth, *Roman Comedy*, p. 55.

[2] There is considerable early evidence in Plautus and elsewhere for the development of the Edict of the curule aediles: a parody of aedilician edictal clauses appears in Plautus, *Capt.* 803 ff. Cato discussed the edict on the sale of slaves: D. 21. 1. 10. 1 (Ulpian, 1 *ad ed. aed. cur.*). Aulus Gellius, *N.A.* 4. 2. 1 gives the wording of an early form of that edict. But the argument from the aedilician Edict to the praetorian Edict is not straightforward. See *infra*, pp. 82 ff.

[3] So would the aediles for their games and festivals.   [4] *Aul.* 465 ff.

[5] *Most.* 37; cf., e.g., *Trin.* 116 ff.; Watson, *Obligations*, p. 173.

[6] *Rud.* 1376 ff.   [7] *Capt.* 179 ff.; Watson, *Obligations*, p. 98.

[8] *Epid.* 697 ff.   [9] *Per.* 524 ff., 665, 714 f.   [10] *Poen.* 711 ff.

[11] e.g. *Most.* 637, 643 ff., 915 ff.; *Rud.* 554 ff., 859 ff.; cf. Watson, *Obligations*, pp. 47 ff.

[12] *Am.* 928; *Trin.* 266; *Cas.* 210.   [13] *Cas.* 67 ff.   [14] *Mil.* 961.

[15] None of this is to be taken to imply that Plautus always accurately represents the legal institutions which he mentions.

Nothing can be deduced from Varro's words 'quod tum et praetorium ius ad

(iii) The jurists of the second century B.C. before P. Rutilius Rufus and Quintus Mucius of whose opinions on private law matters something of importance has survived are Sextus Aelius Paetus Catus, M. Porcius Cato,[1] M. Iunius Brutus, M'. Manilius, and P. Mucius Scaevola.

We know a little of Sextus Aelius' views on liability for late delivery in sale,[2] on the extent of a legacy of *penus*,[3] on old restrictions on mourning,[4] on the heir's action in *furtum*.[5] From Cato we have information on the adoption of slaves,[6] the complications of stipulations with penalty clauses,[7] what counted as *morbosus* under the aedilician Edict,[8] the *actio ex empto* against a seller who fraudulently concealed a legal defect,[9] and perhaps on the *actio rei uxoriae* and the institution of an heir.[10] Traces remain of Brutus' discussion of usufruct,[11] the *actio legis Aquiliae*,[12] *usucapio*,[13] *postliminium*,[14] *in diem addictio* in sale,[15] *furtum*,[16] the *lex Atinia*,[17] and the same problem of the heir's action on *furtum*. The same disputes on usufruct, *usucapio*, the *lex Atinia*, and the heir's action on *furtum* involved Manilius, who also wrote extensively on the stipulations to be taken on a sale,[18] and described *nexum*.[19] Views of Publius Mucius survive on the *actio rei uxoriae*,[20] *ambitus*,[21] inheritance and

legem et censorium iudicium ad aequum existimabatur' (*de ling. lat.* 6. 71), though *tum* refers to the time of an unrecognized *fabula palliata*, a line of which he has just quoted: cf. Ribbeck, *Scaenicae Romanorum Poesis Fragmenta* ii (Leipzig, 1897), p. 114. 'Praetorium ius ad legem' must mean praetorian enforcement of the clause of the XII Tables on *sponsio*.

[1] Whether this is the Cato who was consul in 195 B.C. or his son who died when *praetor designatus* in 152 B.C. is uncertain, but is not of vital importance at the moment.

[2] D. 19. 1. 38. 1 (Celsus, 8 *dig.*).   [3] D. 33. 9. 3. 9 (Ulpian, 22 *ad Sab.*).
[4] Cicero, *de leg.* 2. 23. 59.   [5] Cicero, *ad fam.* 7. 22.
[6] J. 1. 11. 12.   [7] D. 45. 1. 4. 1 (Paul, 12 *ad Sab.*).
[8] D. 21. 1. 10. 1 (Ulpian, 1 *ad ed. aed. cur.*).
[9] Cicero, *de off.* 3. 16. 66. This time we are certainly concerned with Cato the Censor.
[10] D. 24. 3. 44pr. (Paul, 5 *quaest.*). But the *Cato* of the text is probably a scribal error for *Capito*.
[11] D. 7. 1. 68 (Ulpian, 17 *ad Sab.*); Cicero, *de fin.* 1. 4. 12.
[12] D. 9. 2. 27. 22, 23 (Ulpian, 18 *ad ed.*).
[13] D. 41. 2. 3. 3 (Paul, 54 *ad ed.*).   [14] D. 49. 15. 4 (Modestinus, 3 *reg.*).
[15] D. 18. 2. 11. 1 (Ulpian, 28 *ad Sab.*); *h.t.* 13pr. (*idem*).
[16] Aulus Gellius, *N.A.* 6. 15. 1.   [17] Aulus Gellius, *N.A.* 17. 7. 3.
[18] Varro, *de re rust.* 2. 3. 5; 2. 4. 5; 2. 5. 11; 2. 7. 6.
[19] Varro, *de ling. lat.* 7. 105.
[20] D. 24. 3. 66pr. (Iavolenus, 6 *post. Labeonis*).   [21] Cicero, *top.* 4. 24.

legatum partitionis,[1] loss of citizenship,[2] and the problem of the heir's action on *furtum*.[3]

It cannot be claimed that our information on juristic attitudes in the second century B.C. is very extensive. On the other hand, it is not minute. What is totally lacking is evidence of the praetor's Edict. This would surely be surprising if the Edict was well developed in this time. It would be nos ufficient counter-argument to suggest that the Edict might have been well developed, but since, as we have seen, edictal provisions were subject to change, the views expressed by these jurists quickly became obsolete and would not be recorded. Certainly, obsolete views have a diminished survival rate, but it should be emphasized, first, that those opinions of the jurists which have survived were in many (and perhaps most) cases already overruled by the time they were recorded in the writing which we have; and secondly that many of the edictal alterations known to us[4] concern relatively minor matters, and that juristic opinions expressed in connection with the earlier form would not necessarily lose their interest when the wording of the edict was changed.

Sextus Aelius wrote a work on the XII Tables,[5] Cato a commentary in at least fifteen books on the civil law,[6] Brutus a commentary of either three or seven books on the civil law,[7] Manilius a collection of forms and three books probably of *responsa*,[8] and Publius Mucius ten books also probably of *responsa*. It might be thought that the emphasis on the civil law, at least in the writings of the first three jurists, explains the absence of information on the Edict. But it is not so simple. Accounts of the *ius civile* and collections of *responsa* cannot neglect the important modifications of the Edict. More than that, if these jurists concentrated on writing books on the *ius civile* to the exclusion of the Edict the most natural explanation is that edictal law hardly existed. It is undoubtedly

---

[1] Cicero, *de leg.* 2. 20. 50; 2. 21. 53.
[2] D. 50. 7. 18 (17) (Pomponius, 37 *ad Quintum Mucium*).
[3] For Rutilius, who is slightly older than Quintus Mucius, see *infra*, pp. 55 f.
[4] Cf. *supra*, p. 33, n 4.
[5] D. 1. 2. 2. 38 (Pomponius, *sing. enchiridii*).
[6] D. 45. 1. 4. 1 (Paul, 12 *ad Sab.*).
[7] Cicero, *de orat.* 2. 55. 224; D. 1. 2. 2. 39; cf. Lenel, *Pal.* i. 77, n. 2; Schulz, *Legal Science*, p. 92.   [8] D. 1. 2. 2. 39.

significant that the first commentary on the Edict was as late as
Servius' short work in two books, and that the first full treatment
was not until Ofilius.[1]

(iv) Cato, *de agri cultura*, 146. 2 . . . donicum solutum erit aut ita satis
datum erit, quae in fundo inlata erunt, pigneri sunto: nequid eorum de
fundo deportato: siquid deportaverit, domini esto.

149. 2 . . . donicum pecuniam ⟨solverit aut⟩ satisfecerit aut delegarit,
pecus et familia quae illic erit, pigneri sunto. si quid de iis rebus controversiae erit, Romae iudicium fiat.

150. 2 . . . conductor duos menses pastorem praebeat. donec dominum
satisfecerit aut solverit, pigneri esto.

The texts are certainly concerned with a legal, not just a moral
right: 'si quid de iis rebus controversiae erit, Romae iudicium
fiat.' What is involved is a real right, not a personal right, since the
purpose of the provisions is to bolster existing personal rights with
the same party. The contracts which are being supplemented are
contracts of sale, not of hire, hence the real remedy envisaged
cannot be the *interdictum Salvianum*. The conclusion to be drawn
from these facts is that the real right involved is the *actio Serviana*
(or *actio hypothecaria*) or a forerunner of this.[2] There is no evidence
of a forerunner to the *actio Serviana*, far less of a civil law forerunner,[3] so it seems that we have to do with a praetorian action
which innovated and gave a new real right. Since the *de agri
cultura* was written about 160 B.C.,[4] this action will be the earliest

---

[1] D. 1. 2. 2. 44.

[2] On all this see now Watson, *Obligations*, pp. 180 ff.

[3] Though Kaser, following out his theory of divided ownership, thinks that
originally the pledge creditor would have the *vindicatio*: see, e.g., *Eigentum und
Besitz im älteren römischen Recht*, 2nd edit. (Cologne, Graz, 1956), pp. 21 ff.;
'The Concept of Roman Ownership', *Tydskrif vir Hedendaagse Romeins-
Hollandse Reg* (1964), pp. 5 ff. at p. 8. Whatever the general attractiveness of
Kaser's concept of early ownership (and against it, see Watson, *Property*,
pp. 91 ff.), the fact that the *actio Serviana*, which is not based on an edict, is
formulated so totally in a praetorian fashion is very much against the idea of
a civil law forerunner. The *actio Serviana* in this respect contrasts very markedly
with the actions for servitudes and usufruct, which began 'si paret ius Ao Ao
esse . . .'; and servitudes especially are thought by Kaser to be illustrative of the
concept.

[4] To accept the traditional dating: Daube postulates a much earlier date,
Forms, pp. 96 f., but see Watson, 'The Imperatives of the Aedilician Edict',
TvR 39 (1971), 73 ff. at p. 76.

praetorian action known to us which introduced a change in the substantive law.[1]

The *formula* of the *actio Serviana*, as reconstructed from evidence for a later period by Lenel,[2] was as follows:

Si paret inter Am Am et L. Titium convenisse, ut ea res qua de agitur Ao Ao pignori esset propter pecuniam debitam, eamque rem tunc, cum conveniebat, in bonis Lucii Titii fuisse eamque pecuniam neque solutam neque eo nomine satisfactum esse neque per Am Am stare quo minus solvatur, nisi ea res arbitrio iudicis restituetur, quanti ea res erit, tantam pecuniam iudex Nm Nm Ao Ao condemna, si non paret, absolve.

The formulation was thus *in factum*, not *in ius*. Lenel points out that we have not the slightest trace of an edict for this action and that without doubt there was not one;[3] rather, the *formula* was given at the end of the clause on the *interdictum Salvianum*.

It would be extraordinary if it were nothing but chance that the earliest information we have concerning a praetorian action which changed the substance of the law relates to one which was introduced without an edict. Such actions—introduced at the praetor's initiative[4]—are extremely uncommon, the only other probable cases being the *actio in factum adversus nautas, caupones, stabularios* and the *actio si mensor falsum modum dixerit*. The implication is that, for one reason or another, when the praetor began to make significant modifications to the substance of private law he gave the action without issuing an edict. This is reminiscent of his behaviour in introducing the *bonae fidei iudicia*.[5]

---

[1] This is to ignore the very special case of the *bonae fidei iudicia*. If they are praetorian innovations and developed before or around 200 B.C. (cf. *infra*, pp. 89 ff.), then they fit very well into the development postulated here since they have no *edictum*. If they are *iuris civilis* they are irrelevant.

[2] *Edictum*, p. 493.

[3] loc. cit.

[4] The *actio si ager vectigalis petatur* has no edict, but this is probably because it was introduced at imperial instigation: cf. Lenel, *Edictum*, pp. 186 f. And similarly there is no evidence of an edict for the actions *ad senatusconsultum Velleianum*: Lenel, *Edictum*, p. 287.

[5] The *actio in factum adversus nautas, caupones, stabularios* is not significant here. It belongs to the group of *actiones in factum* clustered round the *lex Aquilia*—hence its position in the Edict—though it alone of these has an

Incidentally, Kaser explains the absence of an edict here by saying that the requirements for the *actio Serviana* were covered by the requirements for the *interdictum Salvianum* which also functioned as an edict for the *formula*.[1] But apart from any other difficulties this explanation works only if at this time the scope of the *interdictum Salvianum* was much wider than it later became— the *interdictum* lay only in the case of a lease of land—which is very unlikely, or if the *actio Serviana* had originally a narrower scope than it had in the time of Cato.

(v) D. 38. 2. 1 (Ulpian, 42 *ad ed.*). Hoc edictum a praetore propositum est honoris, quem liberti patronis habere debent, moderandi gratia. namque ut Servius scribit, antea soliti fuerunt a libertis durissimas res exigere, scilicet ad remunerandum tam grande beneficium, quod in libertos confertur, cum ex servitute ad civitatem Romanam perducuntur. 1. Et quidem primus praetor Rutilius edixit se amplius non daturum patrono quam operarum et societatis actionem, videlicet si hoc pepigisset, ut, nisi ei obsequium praestaret libertus, in societatem admitteretur patronus. 2. Posteriores praetores certae partis bonorum possessionem pollicebantur: videlicet enim imago societatis induxit eiusdem partis praestationem, ut, quod vivus solebat societatis nomine praestare, id post mortem praestaret.

It is usually,[2] though not always,[3] held that this *praetor Rutilius* is P. Rutilius Rufus, who was consul in 105 B.C. and praetor not later than 118 B.C. The identification cannot be regarded as certain, but it is at least very probable considering his general importance,

---

'edictal *formula*, presumably because it went beyond a straightforward extension of the *lex*: cf. Lenel, *Edictum*, p. 205. It is thus essentially a decretal action which has come to be provided with an edictal *formula*. Of the early history of the *actio si mensor falsum modum dixerit* little is known, though it is certainly Republican— D. 11. 6. 1pr. (Ulpian, 24 *ad ed.*)—and is presumably earlier than the *edictum de dolo*: cf. Rudorff, in Blume, Lachmann, and Rudorff, *Die Schriften der römischen Feldmesser* ii (Berlin, 1852), p. 320, n. 235.

[1] *RPR* i. 472 and n. 31.

[2] Cf., e.g., Bremer, *Iurisprudentiae Antehadrianae*, i. 43 ff.; Münzer, *RE* 1 A, 1269 ff.; Kaser, *RPR* i. 300.

[3] Thus Kelly also suggests as possibilities the praetors of 93 and 49: 'Growth Pattern', p. 347. But 49 B.C. is impossibly late, since D. 38. 2. 1. 2 tells us that it was later praetors who promised *certae partis bonorum possessio*, and this *bonorum possessio* was in existence when Verres was urban praetor in 74 B.C.: Cicero, *in Verrem* II, 1. 48. 125–6. On the other hand, P. Rutilius Calvus, praetor in 166 B.C., is perhaps a possibility.

his reputation as a jurist,[1] and his friendship with Publius Mucius and Quintus Mucius.[2]

Nothing more need be said about (vi) or (vii).

(viii) The Edict did not play a strong part in shaping the new law of the Empire.

Only two new edicts were certainly introduced in the great praetorian Edict during the Empire, apart from that of Julian, *de coniungendis cum emancipato liberis eius*;[3] Julian, of course, as redactor of Hadrian's Edict, is in a special position and one cannot argue from his behaviour to that of earlier praetors. Indeed, the fact that almost a century later this edict of his is described by Ulpian as *edictum novum* and by Marcellus as *nova clausula* indicates that even before his time the issuing of a new edict was, at the very least, a great rarity.[4] It is perhaps more than a coincidence that the other two edicts from the Empire known to us both come from the first half of the first century A.D.

One of them was issued by C. Cassius Longinus who was urban praetor around A.D. 27, and this promised *restitutio in integrum* if the magistrate could not *ius dicere* because of the proclamation of an extraordinary holiday. But this clause did not find a permanent place in the Edict.[5] The other edict declared: 'Uti me quaque lege senatus(ve) consulto bonorum possessionem dare oportebit, ita dabo.'[6] We know of no statute or *senatusconsultum* which gave someone the right to *bonorum possessio* earlier than the *lex Papia* of A.D. 9.[7] And when one considers how few statutes or *senatusconsulta* touched upon private law in the later Republic, it seems safe to assume that none was issued on this point. Hence,

---

[1] Cf. Cicero, *Brutus*, 30. 113–14; *de off.* 2. 13. 47. He is also likely to be the Rutilius whose opinions have survived on the extent of a legacy of *penus* (Aulus Gellius, *N.A.* 4. 1. 2; D. 33. 9. 3. 9 (Ulpian, 22 *ad Sab.*)), on the duration of *habitatio* (D. 7. 8. 10. 3 (Ulpian, 17 *ad Sab.*)), and on the interdict *quae arbor ex aedibus* (D. 43. 27. 1. 2 (Ulpian, 71 *ad ed.*)); and to be the inventor of the *formula Rutiliana* (Gaius 4. 35; *Vat. Fr.* 1 (Paul, 8 *ad Sab.*)), cf. Bremer, loc. cit.

[2] Cicero, *de off.* 2. 13. 47; Livy, *epit.* lxx; Diodorus Siculus 37. 5. 1.

[3] Cf. D. 37. 9. 1. 13 (Ulpian, 41 *ad ed.*); 37. 8. 3 (Marcellus, 9 *dig.*).

[4] Cf. Dernburg, 'Untersuchungen', p. 99.

[5] D. 4. 6. 26. 7 (Ulpian, 12 *ad ed.*): cf. Lenel, *Edictum*, pp. 120 ff.; Daube, 'Extraordinary Holidays', *Festschrift Leibholz* (Tübingen, 1966), pp. 311 ff. at pp. 315 ff.

[6] Cf. Lenel, *Edictum*, pp. 360 f.   [7] G. 3. 46, 49, 50.

this edict too dates from the Empire, and presumably from a time shortly after the passing of the *lex Papia*.

The *breve edictum* of the praetor Nepos, enforcing a *senatus-consultum* which is mentioned by Pliny the Younger,[1] may well not be directly relevant. Licinius Nepos, who is known to us only from four letters of Pliny,[2] was a praetor in A.D. 105,[3] but it seems that his sphere was the presidency of one or more criminal courts.[4] But one might argue that if this praetor could issue a new edict, then it is very likely that the urban praetor could still do so also.

At least some of the edicts which are not directly evidenced for the Republic will have been in existence then, so that there are rather few edicts remaining which could have originated in the Empire. Still, it must be emphasized that some of them could have done, and probably did. For instance, the very important *actio Publiciana*, which is usually thought to have been issued in 67 B.C., is not evidenced until the time of Neratius, who was active around the end of the first century A.D. and the beginning of the second. A Publicius Certus was praetor in A.D. 93.[5] Again, the Digest title D. 26. 7, *de administratione et periculo tutorum etc.*, is one of the longest in the Digest, but not one of the texts in it refers to the Republic and there is not the slightest indication elsewhere, either, that the edict *de administratione tutorum* existed before the Empire.[6] It should be stressed, too, that the absence of positive proof of more edicts' being issued in the Empire is not necessarily significant. We have so very few firm dates that the main argument for dating is normally from the lifespan of the first jurist to mention the edict. And we may easily underrate the time-lapse between the introduction of an edict and the earliest surviving mention of it.

It is clear that other changes, apart from the issuing of new edicts, also occurred before the time of Julian. Thus, Cassius cut out the *exceptio metus*, considering the *exceptio doli* sufficient.[7] Later

---

[1] *Epist.* 5. 9. 3.   [2] 4. 29; 5. 4; 5. 9; 5. 13.
[3] Cf. Sherwin-White, *The Letters of Pliny* (Oxford, 1966), p. 305.
[4] Cf. Sherwin-White, *Pliny*, p. 336.
[5] On all this see now Watson, *Property*, pp. 104 ff.; cf. Jolowicz and Nicholas, *Introduction*, p. 265.   [6] On all this see now Watson, *Persons*, pp. 131 ff.
[7] D. 44. 4. 4. 33 (Ulpian, 76 *ad ed.*).

praetors reinserted it.[1,2] Aulus Gellius tells of an edict no longer in the Edict.[3] Again, actions were given in the Edict under the *senatusconsultum Velleianum* of about A.D. 46[4] and the *senatusconsultum Trebellianum* of A.D. 56,[5] and the *senatusconsultum Macedonianum* of the time of Claudius or Vespasian[6] gave rise to an edictal *exceptio*.[7] And not all the alterations in the wording of edicts which have already been noticed[8] can reasonably be ascribed to praetors before the end of the Republic or to Julian. Julian himself, in his redaction of the Edict, was responsible for modifications.[9]

The main reason for the decline of the Edict as a source of new law is, it is agreed, the changed political climate of the Principate, though the theoretical powers of the praetors in this regard remained unaltered.

Nothing more need be said about (ix) or (x).

Finally on the development of the praetor's Edict a conjecture of Kelly should be noted. He suggests that the first edicts would be designed to assist the enforcement of the civil law, such as threatening some evil against someone who did not obey a summons, and that 'the history of the praetorian edict reveals itself as

---

[1] Cf. now Watson, *Obligations*, pp. 257 f. The alternative is to say that the *exceptio metus* is post-Cassius.

[2] On Cassius' activity see also D. 42. 8. 11 (Venuleius Saturninus, 6 *interdic.*). Lenel suggests that here Cassius was the jurist who formulated the action, not the praetor who proposed it, *Edictum*, p. 500, n. 2. Against suggestions of interpolation in the text see now Impallomeni, *Studi sui mezzi di revoca degli atti fraudolenti nel diritto romano classico* (Padua, 1958), pp. 112 ff.

D. 29. 2. 99 (Pomponius, 1 *senatus consult.*) does not seem relevant to the present discussion.

[3] *N.A.* 11. 17. 2: 'Qui flumina retanda publice redempta habent, si quis eorum ad me eductus fuerit, qui dicatur, quod eum ex lege locationis facere oportuerit, non fecisse.' On this, most recently, Viganò, 'Sull' *edictum de fluminibus retandis*', *Labeo* 15 (1969), 168 ff.

[4] Cf. Lenel, *Edictum*, pp. 287 f.: and it seems that the action *si ager vectigalis petatur* which is in the Edict—but has no edict—is also from the Empire: Lenel, *Edictum*, pp. 186 ff.

[5] Cf. Lenel, *Edictum*, pp. 183 f.

[6] For the view that it is likely the SC dates from Claudius, see Daube, 'Did Macedo kill his father?', *ZSS* 65 (1947), 308 ff.; *Roman Law: Linguistic, Social and Philosophical Aspects* (Edinburgh, 1969), p. 90, n. 4.

[7] D. 14. 6. 11 (Ulpian, 29 *ad ed.*).   [8] Cf. *supra*, p. 33, n. 4.

[9] This is really outside the scope of the present inquiry, but see, e.g., Jolowicz and Nicholas, *Introduction*, pp. 356 ff.

a progress from *adjective* to *substantive* law.'[1] In view of the sources this can be nothing but an informed conjecture—but it is extremely plausible.

Two other matters should be mentioned briefly.

A famous problem is the relationship in time of *lex* and *edictum*. *Leges* in private law were always uncommon, but what determined whether a reform be introduced by *lex* or *edictum*? The matter will not, in general, be discussed here, but it is argued by Kelly that there never was any conflict or concurrence between *lex* and *edictum* in substantive reform because the periods of their respective activity in this sphere simply did not coincide or overlap.[2] There are, he says, no known statutes in private law in the Republic after 125 B.C. and it is unlikely that there were any. After 125 B.C., he claims, the instrument of private law reform was the Edict.

But Kelly's view of the cessation of statutes changing private law does not seem accurate. Thus, the *lex Iulia et Titia* (either one or two statutes) which gave provincial magistrates the power to appoint tutors almost certainly dates from between 125 B.C. and the end of the Republic;[3] and so probably does the *Lex Minicia* which enacted that the offspring of a Roman and a peregrine, where there was no *conubium*, was a peregrine.[4] The *Lex Cornelia de sponsu*, which forbade anyone to act as guarantor for the same debtor to the same creditor in the same year for a sum greater than 20,000 sesterces, is probably the work of Sulla,[5] as is the *Lex Cornelia de captivis*, which ordered the execution of a will left by a citizen who died a captive.[6] The *Lex Scribonia* which excluded the usucapion of servitudes seems to date from 50 B.C.[7] The *Lex Falcidia*, which enacted that testamentary heirs were to take at least one-quarter of the *hereditas*, is a plebiscite of 40 B.C.[8]

It is, of course, true that a political motivation can be traced for at least some of these statutes,[9] but this is of little consequence in

---

[1] 'Growth Pattern', pp. 348 f.   [2] 'Growth Pattern', pp. 344 ff.
[3] Cf. the authors cited by Kaser, *RPR* i. 357, n. 47.
[4] But it may be that status should not be considered a matter of private law. For the difficulties in dating the *Lex Minicia* see Watson, *Persons*, p. 27, n. 4.
[5] Cf. Rotondi, *Leges*, pp. 362 f.   [6] Cf., e.g., Watson, *Persons*, p. 253.
[7] Cf., e.g., Watson, *Property*, pp. 22 f.   [8] Cf. Rotondi, *Leges*, p. 438.
[9] Especially the *lex Falcidia*: cf. now Watson, *Succession*, pp. 170 ff.

this connection; first, because the same also applies to particular edicts—a great deal of private law reform always has political overtones—and secondly, because Kelly's argument is that there were probably no statutes which changed private law in the last century of the Republic, and this should not exclude any enacted for political reasons.

As a corollary one must ask whether a difference in political or social outlook is to be discerned between *edicta* and *leges*. Could it be argued that the private law measures of the praetors—who as a class would be both wealthy and well connected—were more concerned with the problems of the rich and less sympathetic to the poor than were the laws which, as we have seen, were the work of the *concilium plebis*? The short answer must be negative. On the one hand, the deep and sympathetic concern of *plebiscita* with the problems of the wealthy is evident from such *leges* as the *lex Furia de testamentis* and the *lex Voconia*.[1] On the other, no *edictum* draws a legal distinction between rich and poor or between one class and another.[2]

Secondly, in a well-known passage Fritz Schulz claimed that the volume of Roman legal material based on state legislation— taking legislation in a wide sense to include *lex rogata* and *lex data*, *senatusconsultum* (from the time it attained the force of law), *constitutio principis* and the edict of the two praetors, of the aediles

---

[1] To restrict ourselves only to those *leges* which are known to be *plebiscita* from the sources. Otherwise we could equally mention as examples the *lex Appuleia*, the *lex Atinia*, and the *lex Licinnia*.

[2] This, of course, is not meant to deny that Roman law served a capitalist society. It is, though, perhaps worth observing that after the *lex Canuleia* of 445 B.C. there was no legal barrier between one class and another and no distinctions in private law between freeborn citizens of different classes. For private law at this time there were no *honestiores* and no *humiliores*, no bar against intermarriage, the law did not declare that delicts against *senatores* or *equites* would give rise to a higher scale of damages, the right of making contracts of all kinds was equally open to all, and so on. (A contrast could be drawn here with some ancient Near Eastern systems, late Roman law, and law in medieval Europe.) There were, however, some restrictions on marriage between *ingenui* and *libertini*, and the latter were subject to disabilities in public law. Women were from the earliest times in a much weaker legal position than men, and the *lex Voconia* of 169 B.C. discriminated against them still further by enacting that a person in the wealthiest class of citizens could not appoint a woman as heir. (Yet the position of women was improved by the virtual disappearance of marriage *cum manu*.)

and of provincial governors—'is revealed on examination as surprisingly small'.[1] And he concludes, 'The "law-inspired nation" is not statute-inspired.'[2] This view is, I think, contrary both to what the Romans themselves felt[3] and to the truth.[4]

As to what the Romans themselves felt, Cicero tells us that most people in his day thought the science of law was to be drawn from the praetor's Edict, earlier generations from the XII Tables.[5] Elsewhere Cicero could write of the innumerable statutes in civil law.[6] Both Pompey the Great[7] and Julius Caesar[8] felt the need to codify the *leges* existing at the end of the Republic. Suetonius describes the latter's intention as being to reduce the *ius civile* to manageable size and to publish in a few volumes whatever was best and necessary out of an enormous and scattered mass of *leges*. Livy, referring to his own time, speaks of 'the enormous heap of laws piled one on top of another'.[9] Likewise Tacitus could write of the infinite multitude and variety of statutes in the early Empire.[10]

The truth about the volume of legislation in Rome appears clearly from both this chapter and the first chapter of this book. During the late Republic there were a few *leges* affecting private law[11] and

---

[1] *Principles of Roman Law* (Oxford, 1936), pp. 6 ff.

[2] *Principles*, p. 7.

[3] Recognized to some extent by Schulz himself: *Principles*, p. 9.

[4] Interestingly, Schulz prefaces his chapter, 'Statutes and the Law' with a quotation from Livy 2. 3: 'legem rem surdam, inexorabilem esse': *Principles*, p. 6. But this, given its position and the contents of the chapter, conveys a false impression. The context of the quotation shows Livy rather in favour of statute. When the Tarquins were expelled and the Republic established, young men of high birth 'quorum in regno libido solutior fuerat' expressed their grave dissatisfaction: 'a king was a man on whom one could make demands when there was need for *ius* or *iniuria*; there was opportunity for favours and promotion; he could be angry and forgiving; he could make a distinction between friend and enemy; *legem rem surdam* etc.'

[5] *de leg.* 1. 5. 17; quoted *supra*, p. 31, n. 2.

[6] *pro Balbo*, 8. 21: 'tulit apud maiores nostros legem C. Furius de testamentis, tulit Q. Voconius de mulierum hereditatibus; innumerabiles aliae leges de civili iure sunt latae.'

[7] Isidorus, *Etym.* 5. 1. 5; cf. now Pólay, 'Der Kodifikationsplan des Pompeius', *Acta Antiqua Hungarica* 13 (1965), 85 ff.

[8] Isidorus, *Etym.* 5. 1. 5; Suetonius, *Divus Iulius*, 44. 2: cf. Pólay, 'Der Kodifizierungsplan des Julius Caesar', *IURA* 16 (1965), 27 ff.

[9] 3. 34. 6.

[10] *Ann.* 3. 25.

[11] The circumstances in which, according to Schulz, *Principles*, p. 10, the *lex* might play a part in shaping the civil law are really very wide.

a great many *edicta*, and indeed the latter were by far the most
important single factor in the growth and development of the law.[1]

---

[1] Schulz minimizes the significance of the Edict: *Principles*, p. 12: 'As regards
the edicts, it is true that those relating to judicature contain a considerable
number of rules—though taking it all in all even the Hadrianic edict is only
a "short booklet"—but they are strictly confined to the magistrate's own acts:
the magistrate issues rules for his *officium*. In so far the edict, though not actually
a system of procedure, is related to the *leges* regulating procedure. Above all,
however, until the edict was reformed by Hadrian it lacked the rigidity of a
statute, as it was a *lex annua* and each new magistrate was legally entitled to
change its entire content. Apart from judicature, the edicts dealt exclusively
with administrative law.' But this is sophistry. The 'short booklet' contains
about 200 separate provisions. It is so short because of the principles of drafting
and interpretation which were employed: cf. *infra*, pp. 131 ff. And in practice,
edicts do drastically change the substance of the law.

4

URBAN PRAETOR, PEREGRINE PRAETOR; CURULE AEDILES; CENSORS

THE PRAETORS

AT first there was only one praetorship, the second being created in 242 B.C. and being followed by others. The oldest office came to be known as that of the urban praetor, the second that of the peregrine praetor. In 227 two new praetorships were created for governing Sicily and Sardinia, in 198 another two for Spain. From 123/2 one of the praetors was appointed to deal with charges *de repetundis*. Sulla introduced two new praetorships and under his constitution there were, besides the urban and peregrine praetors, praetors in charge of particular standing courts, for the *quaestiones repetundarum, ambitus, peculatus, maiestatis, de sicariis et veneficiis*, and probably *falsi*.[1]

In this book we are not directly concerned with constitutional law but with the factors in the development of private law, and hence we are involved with the jurisdictional limits of the praetors only in so far as the question affects legal progress, in particular the development of the Edict. Each praetor of course had the *ius edicendi*, as had, indeed, all the higher magistrates, but inevitably we shall be mostly concerned with the roles of the urban and the peregrine praetor.

Nicholas[2] expresses with admirable clarity what is, I think, the almost universal opinion:

The Urban Praetor's Edict was not the only source of *ius honorarium*. The Peregrine Praetor also issued an Edict, and many of the features which we find in the Urban Praetor's Edict may well have originated

---

[1] For all this see Mommsen, *Staatsrecht* ii. 193 ff.
[2] *Introduction to Roman Law* (Oxford, 1962), p. 23.

in that of his colleague. For the Peregrine Praetor, since he did not work within the framework of the traditional law, must have built faster and more freely than the Urban Praetor.

This view is, I think, largely mistaken. In this chapter I shall argue that the urban praetor's Edict was both much the larger and the more important. It contained all the edicts, *formulae*, interdicts, and praetorian stipulations which applied only to Romans or to both Romans and peregrines and which were appropriate at Rome; and though it was primarily the responsibility of the urban praetor who inserted or cut out clauses as he saw fit, he was, in normal times, aided by the peregrine praetor and by the other praetors as well, who were given full credit for the innovations they proposed. By contrast the Edict of the peregrine praetor was very short and was restricted to clauses which could not apply to citizens. Clauses which appeared in the urban praetor's Edict and which were appropriate for peregrines were not repeated in the peregrine praetor's Edict.

None of this is intended to deny that each of these two praetors had a separate primary area of responsibility, a fact which appears clearly from their very names. Thus, the urban praetor is called *praetor urbanus* in the *senatusconsultum de Bacchanalibus* of 186 B.C.,[1] and in the so-called *lex Iulia municipalis* of 45;[2] *praetor qui inter cives ius dicet* in the *lex Papiria de sacramentis* of between 242 and 124 B.C.,[3] and in the *lex agraria* of 111;[4] and *qui ius populo plebique dabit summum* in the Marcian oracles of the third century B.C.[5] The peregrine praetor is called *praetor qui inter peregrinos ius dicit* in the *lex Acilia repetundarum* of 123–2,[6] and in the *lex Iulia municipalis* of 45;[7] *is qui Romae inter peregrinos ius dicet* in the *lex Rubria* of 49 (or 42) B.C.;[8] and in Greek ἐπὶ τῶν ξένων στρατηγός;[9] στρατηγοῦντος ἐπὶ δὲ τῶν ξένων;[10] and στρατηγός κατὰ πόλιν καὶ ἐπὶ τῶν ξένων.[11] Only in the Empire, though from the very beginning

---

[1] Lines 5, 8, 17, 21.   [2] Lines 8, 11.
[3] Festus, s.v. *Sacramentum*.   [4] Lines 73, 74.
[5] Livy 25. 12. 10; Macrobius, *Sat.* 1. 17. 28.   [6] Lines 12, 89.
[7] Lines 8, 12.   [8] I. 24, 34.
[9] Inscription from Dyme of later second century B.C.; *CIGr* 1543.
[10] Treaty with Thyrrheion of 94 B.C.: I. 580.
[11] *Senatusconsultum de Asclepiade* of 78 B.C. (Bruns, no. 41), line 2. In that year the urban praetor was also peregrine praetor.

of it, is the peregrine praetor named as *praetor qui inter cives et peregrinos ius dicet* or something similar.[1,2]

The first and most powerful argument[3] for the proposition that there was at Rome one main praetorian Edict, the responsibility of the urban praetor with the active co-operation of the peregrine praetor, is derived from the *edictum de hominibus armatis coactisve et vi bonorum raptorum*. For the promulgation of this edict we have the testimony of Cicero, *pro Tullio*, 4. 8–5. 12:

Cum omnes leges omniaque iudicia quae paulo graviora atque asperiora videntur esse ex improborum iniquitate et iniuria nata sunt, tum hoc iudicium paucis hisce annis propter hominum malam consuetudinem nimiamque licentiam constitutum est. Nam cum multae familiae dicerentur in agris longinquis et pascuis armatae esse caedisque facere, cumque ea consuetudo non solum ad res privatorum sed ad summam rem publicam pertinere videretur, M. Lucullus, qui summa aequitate et sapientia ius dixit, primus hoc iudicium composuit et id spectavit ut omnes ita familias suas continerent ut non modo armati damnum nemini darent verum etiam lacessiti iure se potius quam armis defenderent; 9. et cum sciret de damno legem esse Aquiliam, tamen hoc ita existimavit, apud maiores nostros cum et res et cupiditates minores essent et familiae non magnae magno metu continerentur ut perraro fieret ut homo occideretur, idque nefarium ac singulare facinus putaretur, nihil opus fuisse iudicio de vi coactis armatisque hominibus; quod enim usu non veniebat, de eo si quis legem aut iudicium constitueret, non tam prohibere videretur quam admonere. 10. His temporibus cum ex bello diuturno atque domestico res in eam consuetudinem venisset ut homines minore religione armis uterentur, necesse putavit esse et in universam familiam iudicium dare, quod a familia factum diceretur, et recuperatores dare, 11. ut quam primum res iudicaretur, et poenam graviorem constituere, ut metu comprimeretur audacia, et illam latebram tollere: 'DAMNUM INIURIA'. Quod in aliis causis debet valere et valet lege Aquilia, id ex huius modi damno quod vi per servos armatos datum esset . . . 12. ipsi statuerent quo tempore possent suo iure arma capere, manum cogere, homines occidere. Cum iudicium ita daret ut hoc solum

[1] *Lex Quinctia de aquaeductibus* of 9 B.C., line 18; *edictum de aquaeductu Venafrano*, probably of a few years earlier, line 65.
[2] On the foregoing paragraph see above all Mommsen, *Staatsrecht* ii. 193 ff.; Daube, 'The Peregrine Praetor', *JRS* 41 (1951), 66 ff.; Serrao, *La 'Iurisdictio' del pretore peregrino* (Milan, 1954), pp. 18 ff.; Arriat, *Le Préteur pérégrin* (Paris, 1955), pp. 14 ff.
[3] The arguments will not be given in historical sequence, since I have not been able to find convincing traces of a historical development.

in iudicium veniret, videreturne vi hominibus coactis armatisve damnum dolo malo familiae datum, neque illud adderet 'INIURIA', putavit se audaciam improborum sustulisse, cum spem defensionis nullam reliquisset.

The edict was issued a few years before Cicero was speaking by Marcus Lucullus who, we know, was peregrine praetor, not urban praetor, in 76 B.C.[1] Lucullus proposed this edict, Cicero tells us, because as a result of a *bellum diuturnum et domesticum* men resorted to violence with weapons, and it was necessary to give an action against a whole *familia* in respect of what was said to be done by the *familia*. This *bellum domesticum* which led to the unrest can only have been the Civil War between Sulla and the Marians,[2] and so the *edictum* must have been intended primarily for application in Italy. This, indeed, is implied by the tenor of Cicero's speech. But as a result of the Social War, the *lex Iulia* of 90 B.C., and the *lex Plautia Papiria* of 89, the free inhabitants of Italy had become full Roman citizens. Naturally there would also be some peregrines, especially merchants, but they would be relatively few in numbers and concentrated in the ports and other urban centres. The edict was intended principally for violence in the country, especially by someone's *familia*. Hence Lucullus' edict appears to have been meant for actions where both the wrongdoer and the victim were Romans. This is confirmed by the reference to the *lex Aquilia* which shows that the jurisdiction of both the *lex* and the *edictum* was the same, and tells us that the *edictum* was intended by Lucullus to improve on the *lex*.[3] But the *lex Aquilia* and the action on it were framed to apply only to citizens, and even in the time of Gaius a fiction was needed in the action if a peregrine was suing or was sued.[4,5] Thus, in 76 B.C. the peregrine praetor issued an edict which was primarily meant to apply to Roman citizens in Italy.

This seems impossible to explain on any theory of two equal praetorian Edicts, one of the urban praetor, one of the peregrine

---

[1] Asconius 75; cf. Broughton, *Magistrates* ii. 93.

[2] Cf. Schmidlin, *Das Rekuperatorenverfahren* (Fribourg, 1963), p. 45.

[3] 'Et cum sciret de damno legem esse Aquiliam, tamen hoc ita existimavit, etc.'

[4] G. 4. 37: cf. *infra*, pp. 70 f.

[5] On this see Serrao, *Iurisdictio*, pp. 74 ff.

praetor. Whether one says that the peregrine praetor had jurisdiction in cases involving only peregrines or in cases where at least one party was a peregrine, one still would not have expected him (on the normal hypothesis of the two Edicts) to have promulgated this particular edict. But the situation does become explicable if the urban Edict was issued by the urban praetor with the active co-operation of the peregrine praetor. In this particular instance the initiative for the clause in question did come from the peregrine praetor.

A second argument is drawn from what Cicero tells us about his own Edict issued when he was governing Cilicia as proconsul in 51–50 B.C.:

ad Att. 6. 1. 15. De Bibuli edicto: nihil novi praeter illam exceptionem de qua tu ad me scripseras 'nimis gravi praeiudicio in ordinem nostrum'. Ego tamen habeo ἰσοδυναμοῦσαν sed tectiorem ex Q. Muci P. f. edicto Asiatico, EXTRA QUAM SI ITA NEGOTIUM GESTUM EST UT EO STARI NON OPORTEAT EX FIDE BONA; multaque sum secutus Scaevolae, in iis illud in quo sibi libertatem censent Graeci datam, ut Graeci inter se disceptent suis legibus. Breve autem edictum est propter hanc meam διαίρεσιν, quod duobus generibus edicendum putavi; quorum unum est provinciale, in quo inest de rationibus civitatum, de aere alieno, de usura, de syngraphis, in eodem omnia de publicanis; alterum quod sine edicto satis commode transigi non potest, de hereditatum possessionibus, de bonis possidendis, magistris faciendis, ⟨bonis⟩ vendendis, quae ex edicto et postulari et fieri solent. Tertium de reliquo iure dicundo ἄγραφον reliqui; dixi me de eo genere mea decreta ad edicta urbana accommodaturum; itaque curo, et satis facio adhuc omnibus. Graeci vero exsultant quod peregrinis iudicibus utuntur. 'Nugatoribus quidem' inquies. Quid refert? ii se αὐτονομίαν adeptos putant. Nostri enim, credo, gravis habent Turpionem sutorium et Vettium mancipem.

Cicero thought he should have two *genera* of clauses in his Edict. The first *genus* was to be *provinciale*, clauses peculiar to regulating a province; and the second was to concern those matters which could not be satisfactorily dealt with except by edict.[1] A third he left unwritten but stated that his decrees would be fitted to the *edicta urbana*.[2] But why state that his decrees would be fitted to

[1] For the meaning of this see above all Buckland, 'L' *Edictum provinciale*', *RHD* 13 (1934), 81 ff. at pp. 82 ff.
[2] On these *genera* and the construction of Cicero's Edict see, e.g., Marshall,

the *edicta urbana,* not to the *edicta peregrina* or to the *edicta urbana et peregrina?* The peregrine praetor's Edict, if it had been full, would have been more suitable in general for the conditions of Cilicia.

Buckland says[1] that Cicero's expression *edicta urbana* could mean either the two Edicts of the praetors or the individual clauses, *edicta,* of the urban praetor. Serrao takes it as meaning the former,[2] as does Shackleton Bailey.[3] But it seems highly unlikely that the phrase *edicta urbana* could ever be used to mean the Edict of the urban praetor and the Edict of the peregrine praetor where the latter was as significant as the former. This artificial interpretation is forced on scholars who think there were two equally important praetorian Edicts at Rome, because they cannot otherwise see why the third *genus* of Cicero's Edict would be modelled on clauses of the urban praetor's Edict. The dilemma disappears if one holds that there was only one main praetorian Edict at Rome and Cicero is following its clauses. The adjective *urbanum* then—for the first time—becomes fully appropriate and is used to contrast with *provinciale.*[4]

A similar argument can be drawn from Verres' Sicilian Edict. At one point[5] Cicero says: 'Tu ipse ex Siciliensi edicto hoc sustulisti; voluisti, ex improviso si quae res nata esset, ex urbano edicto decernere.' A clause invented by Verres and placed in the Edict when he was urban praetor in 74 B.C. was not inserted in his Sicilian Edict. This is used by Cicero to strengthen his assault on the morality of the clause. But the rest of the passage quoted, from 'voluisti', cannot refer to that clause alone.[6] In framing an Edict

---

'The Structure of Cicero's Edict', *American Journal of Philology,* 85 (1964), 185 ff.; Shackleton Bailey, *Cicero's Letters to Atticus,* iii (Cambridge, 1968), p. 247.

[1] 'L'*Edictum*', pp. 84 ff.

[2] *Iurisdictio,* p. 116.   [3] *Letters* iii, p. 248.

[4] In this volume we are not concerned with Roman provincial law, but see now on Cicero's Edict, Pugliese, 'Riflessioni sull'editto di Cicerone in Cilicia', *Synteleia Arangio-Ruiz,* ii (Naples, 1964), pp. 972 ff. For the *edictum provinciale* see Martini, *Ricerche in tema di editto provinciale* (Milan, 1969), pp. 11 ff.

[5] *In Verrem* II, 1. 43. 112.

[6] Nor is it so taken: cf. Greenwood, *Cicero, The Verrine Orations* i (London, Cambridge, Mass., 1953), p. 242, n. (*a*). Presumably, too, Buckland is thinking of this passage when he says that Verres constructed his Sicilian Edict from the individual clauses of the urban Edict: 'L'*Edictum*', pp. 84 f.

a governor would not omit a particular clause and state his intention to give an action according to the urban edict if unforeseen circumstances arose. Cicero means that Verres did not insert this particular clause and some other clauses in his Sicilian Edict, but declared his intention, in circumstances not covered by this Edict, to follow the principles of the urban Edict. It is important to establish this point since the particular clause under discussion concerned succession and was appropriate only for citizens. This time Cicero speaks of *urbanum edictum* in the singular and he cannot be understood as referring to the Edict of the urban praetor *and* to the Edict of the peregrine praetor. Yet, again, if there had been two praetorian Edicts of equal importance at Rome, we would not have expected a provincial governor who was drafting his Edict where possible by reference back to what was done at Rome to exclude the Edict of the peregrine praetor. Nor can we imagine that Verres was the sort of man who, as urban praetor, was so involved with the technicalities of his Edict that later, as governor, he modelled his provincial Edict on the one he was familiar with. Indeed, Cicero is making the point that as governor Verres did not keep to his own earlier urban Edict.

A fourth argument is owed to the acute observation of Lombardi[1] that 'Cicero does not feel a precise contrast between the *praetor urbanus* and the *praetor peregrinus*, between the law applied by the one and the law applied by the other.' This was said in connection with *de legibus* 3. 3. 8, but the statement can be both generalized and strengthened. There is no sign anywhere in Cicero of a contrast, precise or imprecise, between the functions of the urban praetor and the peregrine praetor, and the law administered by them. Yet he makes us aware of the distinction between the urban Edict and the Edicts of provincial governors; of his own for Cilicia,[2] of Q. Mucius Scaevola's for Asia,[3] of Bibulus' for Syria,[4] and of Verres' for Sicily. [5,6]

---

[1] *Sul concetto di 'ius gentium'* (Rome, 1947), p. 90; cited with approval by Serrao, *Iurisdictio*, p. 112.   [2] *ad Att.* 6. 1. 15.   [3] Ibid.

[4] *ad Att.* 6. 1. 15; 6. 8. 5; *ad fam.* 2. 10. 2.   [5] *In Verrem* II, 1. 43. 112.

[6] It would be wrong to overstress this latter part of the argument. Cicero had his own reasons for being interested in the provincial Edicts which would also differ from the urban Edict more than any supposed Edict of the peregrine praetor would from any Edict of the urban praetor.

An argument of a very different type is drawn from G. 4. 37:

Item civitas Romana peregrino fingitur, si eo nomine agat aut cum eo agatur, quo nomine nostris legibus actio constituta est, si modo iustum sit eam actionem etiam ad peregrinum extendi, veluti si furti agat peregrinus aut cum eo agatur. ⟨nam si cum peregrino agatur,⟩ formula ita concipitur: IUDEX ESTO. SI PARET LUCIO ⟨TITIO A DIONE HERMAEI FILIO OPEVE⟩ CONSILIO DIONIS HERMAEI FILII FURTUM FACTUM ESSE PATERAE AUREAE, QUAM OB REM EUM, SI CIVIS ROMANUS ESSET, PRO FURE DAMNUM DECIDERE OPORTERET, et reliqua. item, si peregrinus furti agat, civitas ei Romana fingitur. similiter, si ex lege Aquilia peregrinus damni iniuriae agat aut cum eo agatur, ficta civitate Romana iudicium datur.

Gaius tells us that if a peregrine sues or is sued by an action established by statute then a fiction of citizenship is inserted in the *formula*. He illustrates this with reference to the *actio furti* and the *actio legis Aquiliae*. *Formulae* for such actions were certainly set out in the urban Edict.[1] It will be enough to look at one. The simplest is perhaps the first possible reconstruction offered by Lenel of the *actio legis Aquiliae*:[2]

Si paret Numerium Negidium illum servum iniuria occidisse, quam ob rem, quanti is servus in eo anno plurimi fuit, tantam pecuniam Numerium Negidium Aulo Agerio dare oportet, tantam pecuniam duplam iudex Numerium Negidium Aulo Agerio condemna, si non paret, absolve.

On the face of it there seems no reason why this *formula* could not have been used where either the plaintiff or the defendant was a peregrine. Certainly the *formula* contains the word *oportet*, 'It is proper', a reference to higher authority[3]—in this case to the *lex Aquilia*. But there is nothing inappropriate in *oportet*'s appearing in *formulae* applying to peregrines as well as to citizens—witness the actions for the consensual contracts. Again, there is no constitutional reason for Roman statutes' being applicable of necessity only to citizens. Hence we can say that if the peregrine praetor had

---

[1] Ulpian dealt with *furtum* in books 37 and 38 of his commentary *ad edictum*, Paul in book 39, Gaius in book 13 of his *ad edictum provinciale*; Ulpian with the *lex Aquilia* in book 18 *ad edictum*, Paul in book 22, Gaius in book 7 *ad edictum provinciale*.

[2] *Edictum*, p. 201. Neither this *formula* nor any relating to *furtum* can be reconstructed with certainty, but the point is not too material.

[3] Cf. Daube, *Forms*, pp. 8 ff.

issued a full Edict he could have inserted a clause of the above type. No fiction of citizenship would then have been needed, since the very fact of the *formula*'s being in that Edict would have shown that its application extended also to peregrines. There would, in fact, have been no reason for using the fiction, *si civis Romanus esset*. We are thus left with a choice. Either we say there was no full Edict of the peregrine praetor, or we admit that there was but it contained no *formulae* for *furtum* or *damnum iniuria datum*. The latter alternative is inconceivable, since one of the first protections a peregrine would want would be against theft and wrongful damage to property.[1]

But if there was only one main praetorian Edict at Rome and it gave *formulae* for actions based on statute, then the question would arise whether the particular statute, and with it the relevant actions, should apply to peregrines as well as to citizens. Not all statutes would be appropriate for peregrines. The fiction *si civis Romanus esset* would then be fitting in the *formula*, as showing that the praetors did feel that the particular statute in question should extend to disputes involving peregrines.

Sixthly, there is no sign apart from the ambiguous D. 4. 3. 9. 4a (Ulpian, 11 *ad ed.*)[2] that any of the jurists ever wrote a commentary on the Edict of the peregrine praetor. This is surely astounding in view of the importance attached to the peregrine Edict by modern scholars. Gaius wrote a commentary on the urban praetor's Edict, on the provincial Edict, and on the Edict of the curule aediles. The only Edict omitted, so far as we can judge, appears to be that of the peregrine praetor. At the request of Hadrian the jurist Julian revised and stabilized the praetor's Edict. The sources talk only of one Edict, not of two.[3] There is no indication of the fate of any Edict of the peregrine praetor. In none of the great commentaries on the Edict by the jurists after Julian's redaction is there any sign

---

[1] Pernice thinks these *formulae* were in the peregrine praetor's Edict: *Labeo* i (reprinted Aalen, 1963), p. 58.

[2] The text is discussed *infra*, pp. 76 ff.

[3] *Const. Tanta*, § 18; C. 4. 5. 10. 1; Eutropius, *Brev.* 8. 17; Aurelius Victor, *Caesares*, 19. 2; *Epitome legum*, praefatio (in Zachariae, *Jus Graeco-Romanum*, ii (Leipzig, 1856), p. 280, and Zepos, *Ius Graecoromanum*, iv (reprinted Aalen, 1962), p. 279).

that a particular clause or phrase being discussed was ever in a peregrine praetor's Edict—unless one can argue from D. 4. 3. 9. 4a —just as there is no evidence of such a provenance in any of the earlier commentaries. These facts are irreconcilable, it seems to me, with the view that there were two different praetorian Edicts at Rome of roughly equal development. If there was only one main praetorian Edict then, of course, not all its provisions could apply equally to citizen and peregrine, and in such a case, I suggested at the beginning of this chapter, the peregrine praetor would state separately on the album the course he intended to follow. There is, as it happens, evidence that this was done in one, and only in one, case, that of the *cautio damni infecti*. The significance of this evidence will be examined later.[1] At the moment it is enough to notice that it fits in with the argument brought forward here. The *cautio damni infecti* proposed by the urban praetor was not suitable for peregrines, and a separate provision was needed. And evidence of one separate provision where it was needed does not justify belief in a complete Edict of the peregrine praetor, or balance the almost total silence of the sources.

A final argument is drawn from the introduction of the *actio de dolo*, on which we have considerable information from Cicero.

de off. 3. 14. 60. Nondum enim C. Aquillius, collega et familiaris meus, protulerat de dolo malo formulas; in quibus ipsis, cum ex eo quaereretur quid esset dolus malus respondebat: cum esset aliud simulatum, aliud actum.

de nat. deor. 3. 30. 74. Inde everriculum malitiarum omnium iudicium de dolo malo, quod C. Aquillius familiaris noster protulit, quem dolum idem Aquillius tum teneri putat cum aliud sit simulatum aliud actum.

The texts tell us that Cicero's colleague (and friend) C. Aquillius brought forward the *iudicium de dolo* (alternatively expressed as *de dolo malo formulas*). Cicero was praetor in 66 B.C., and so was the famous jurist Gaius Aquillius Gallus, the inventor of the *stipulatio Aquiliana*. So, at first sight, the early history of the *edictum de dolo* seems straightforward. But, strangely, it appears that Aquil-

[1] *Infra*, pp. 78 ff.

lius Gallus was not the urban praetor, nor indeed the peregrine praetor. Rather he was the praetor in charge of the *quaestio de ambitu*.[1]

Approaches to the problem fall into two main groups. One is to deny that Aquillius Gallus was responsible, as praetor, for the *iudicium de dolo*. He was, according to this view, the jurist who suggested the *iudicium*, but it was a different praetor who inserted the *iudicium* in his Edict.[2] This opinion seems most implausible. In crediting him with the *formulae de dolo malo* in *de off.* 3. 14. 60 Cicero calls him *collega et familiaris meus*, and *collega* must refer to Aquillius as praetor. Again, in one text he is said *proferre de dolo malo formulas*, in the other *iudicium de dolo malo proferre*. Moreover, in both texts, but especially in the *de officiis*, Cicero is concerned with the actual introduction of the legal remedies, not with the discovery of the idea that *dolus* might be made actionable.[3]

The other approach is to consider that Aquillius Gallus was either urban praetor or peregrine praetor.[4] The evidence is, though, that he was praetor in the *quaestio de ambitu*.[5] In that year, 66 B.C., C. Antonius Hibrida probably was urban praetor,[6] but who was peregrine praetor is not known. There is, however, no argument for suggesting that Aquillius Gallus was peregrine praetor as well as being in charge of the *quaestio de ambitu*. Though on occasion the same man might be urban praetor and peregrine praetor there is, as Mommsen observes,[7] no real proof that either

---

[1] Cicero, *pro Cluentio*, 53. 147: 'Quid M. Plaetori et C. Flamini inter sicarios, quid C. Orchivi peculatus, quid mea de pecuniis repetundis, quid C. Aquili apud quem nunc de ambitu causa dicitur, quid reliquae quaestiones?'

[2] For the numerous distinguished scholars who have taken this view see von Lübtow, 'Die Ursprungsgeschichte der *exceptio doli* und der *actio de dolo malo*', *Eranion Maridakis*, i (Athens, 1963), pp. 183 ff. at p. 186.

[3] These facts outweigh by far, it seems to me, the opposing arguments, such as that Cicero in *de nat. deor.* calls Aquillius only *familiaris* and that Cicero speaks of *proferre iudicium*, not *proponere iudicium*. The real argument for this view is the *a priori* one that it seems impossible that the praetor in the *quaestio de ambitu* could introduce the *edictum de dolo*.

[4] See the scholars cited by von Lübtow, 'Ursprungsgeschichte', p. 186, n. 12.

[5] Cicero, *pro Cluentio*, 53. 147; quoted *supra*, n. 1.

[6] Cf. Broughton, *Magistrates* ii. 152.

[7] *Staatsrecht* ii. 215, n. 1.

of these praetors was ever also praetor over one of the *quaestiones*.[1,2]

Serrao suggests[3] that only after 66 B.C. was the *quaestio ambitus* organized as the exclusive jurisdiction of a single praetor, and that until then it was held by one of the two ordinary praetors. Since Hibrida was urban praetor, it follows from Serrao's argument that Aquillius Gallus was peregrine praetor. As the *quaestiones repetundarum* were entrusted to the peregrine praetor before the *lex de repetundis*, so, he suggests, was the *quaestio ambitus* at first. The argument fails to satisfy. Admittedly there is no convincing textual evidence that Sulla appointed a praetor to the *quaestio* for *ambitus*.[4] Yet there was a *quaestio perpetua* for *ambitus* before the end of the second century B.C.,[5] and hence it would be very surprising if this court did not have a praetor appointed to it by Sulla at the latest.[6] No relevant argument[7] can be drawn from the fact that for a time the *quaestio repetundarum* was bound up with the peregrine praetorship. That was before a praetor was allotted for dealing with *repetundae* in 123 B.C.

It should also be observed that it would not be plausible to claim that Aquillius' *iudicium de dolo* was in an *edictum* intended for

[1] Beseler seems to rely, wrongly, on Mommsen for the proposition that at the same time a man could be praetor for a *quaestio* and peregrine praetor: '*De iure civili Tullio duce ad naturam revocando*', *BIDR* 39 (1931), 295 ff. at p. 315, n. 1; cf. the more ambiguous von Lübtow, 'Ursprungsgeschichte', p. 186, n. 16.

[2] Even if the reference in D. 4. 3. 9. 4a to Labeo's book 30 *praetoris peregrini* is accurate, this would not be an argument for thinking the action discussed (*actio de dolo*) was a creation of the peregrine praetor. In such a work it might have been as appropriate to discuss the *actio* as in a commentary on the urban praetor's Edict. And the *actio de dolo* was discussed by both Ulpian and Paul in book 11 of their commentaries *ad edictum* and by Gaius in book 4 of his commentary *ad edictum provinciale*.

[3] *Iurisdictio*, p. 108.

[4] Cf. Rotondi, *Leges*, p. 361.

[5] Evidenced for 115 B.C.: Plutarch, *Marius*, 5. 3 ff.; Valerius Maximus 6. 9. 14; cf. Kunkel, *Untersuchungen zur Entwicklung des römischen Kriminalverfahrens in vorsullanischen Zeit* (Munich, 1962), p. 62.

[6] Serrao also finds significant 'C. Aquili apud quem n u n c de ambitu causa dicitur' in Cicero's *pro Cluentio*, 53. 147, and thinks it shows that Aquillius was not exclusively the person holding the *quaestio ambitus* and also that he was not in charge of any other *quaestio*. But Cicero seems to mean only that at the time when the *pro Cluentio* was delivered in 66 B.C. a case of *ambitus* was in process before Aquillius.

[7] *Pace*, e.g., von Lübtow, 'Ursprungsgeschichte', p. 186, n. 16.

his *quaestio de ambitu*. Both texts quoted from Cicero show him giving Aquillius credit for a *iudicium* on private law.[1]

On the face of the evidence it seems we have to accept that Aquillius Gallus, as praetor in the *quaestio de ambitu*, was responsible for the insertion of the *edictum de dolo* in the urban praetor's Edict. This seems explicable only if we admit that though the urban Edict was the responsibility of the urban praetor, he could in normal times expect the active co-operation of the other praetors (especially, one might think, of the peregrine praetor), and that their part in framing the Edict would be open and recognized. In favour of this opinion it should also be noticed that, apart from the ill-fated innovations of Verres, the only two clauses of the urban Edict whose originator and his praetorship are known to us are the work of a peregrine praetor and a praetor in the *quaestio de ambitu*.[2]

Up to this point we have been concerned primarily with the arguments showing the very subordinate position of the peregrine praetor's Edict. Three lesser aspects of the problem still require to be treated.

The first is the predominating position of the urban praetor's Edict, and of the urban praetor's role in framing it. The former emerges, as we have seen, from Cicero, *ad Att.* 6. 1. 15,[3] and *in Verrem* II, 1. 43. 112,[4] the latter from *in Verrem* II, 1. 46. 119.

Et cum edictum totum eorum arbitratu, quam diu fuit designatus, componeret qui ab isto ius ad utilitatem suam nundinarentur, tum vero in magistratu contra illud ipsum edictum suum sine ulla religione decernebat. Itaque L. Piso multos codices implevit earum rerum in quibus ita intercessit, quod iste aliter atque ut edixerat decrevisset; quod vos oblitos esse non arbitror, quae multitudo, qui ordo ad Pisonis sellam isto praetore solitus sit convenire; quem iste conlegam nisi habuisset, lapidibus coopertus esset in foro. Sed eo leviores istius iniuriae videbantur quod erat in aequitate prudentiaque Pisonis paratissimum

---

[1] Elsewhere I have suggested that the original scope of the *actio de dolo* was rather narrow: see now *Obligations*, p. 259.

[2] Of course, not enough instances are known for conclusions to be drawn with safety. But it would be a very odd coincidence if both instances known to us were complete exceptions, and if all the other clauses of the urban Edict were the sole work of the urban praetor.

[3] Cf. *supra*, pp. 67 ff.   [4] Cf. *supra*, pp. 68 f.

perfugium, quo sine labore, sine molestia, sine impensa, etiam sine patrono homines uterentur.

At the moment we are concerned with the first part of the text, which makes plain the great freedom Verres exercised in framing his Edict while he was urban praetor. It emerges that the peregrine praetor of that year was not consulted. We should not forget, though, that Verres' behaviour was almost certainly exceptional.

Second is the actual existence and importance of the peregrine praetor's Edict, which is shown by G. 1. 6, Boethius, *ad top. Ciceronis* 5. 28, probably by D. 4. 3. 9. 4a, and above all by the *lex Rubria*.

G. 1. 6. Ius autem edicendi habent magistratus populi Romani. sed amplissimum ius est in edictis duorum praetorum, urbani et peregrini, quorum in provinciis iurisdictionem praesides earum habent; item in edictis aedilium curulium, quorum iurisdictionem in provinciis populi Romani quaestores habent; nam in provincias Caesaris omnino quaestores non mittuntur, et ob id hoc edictum in his provinciis non proponitur.

The text need not be taken as implying that the Edict of the urban praetor and that of the peregrine praetor were equally large and equally important.[1] The text, like that of Boethius, gives no indication of the scope of the peregrine praetor's edictal clauses: 'Edicta magistratuum sunt, quae praetores urbani vel peregrini vel aediles curules iura dixere.'

A seemingly impossible problem is set us by D. 4. 3. 9. 4a (Ulpian, 11 *ad ed.*):

Haec de dolo actio noxalis erit: ideo Labeo quoque libro trigensimo praetoris peregrini scribit de dolo actionem servi nomine interdum de peculio, interdum noxalem dari. nam si ea res est, in quam dolus commissus est, ex qua de peculio daretur actio, et nunc in peculio dandam: sin vero ea sit, ex qua noxalis, hoc quoque noxale futurum.

Thus it appears that Labeo wrote a thirtieth book on the peregrine praetor. But there have been doubts. Mommsen suggested[2] the

---

[1] It might be argued if this text stood alone that the two praetors were responsible for one Edict, and that *in edictis duorum praetorum* was to be taken as meaning 'in the edictal clauses of the two praetors', just as later in the text *in edictis aedilium curulium* refers to only one Edict.

[2] *Digesta Iustiniani Augusti*, i (Berlin, 1870), p. 122; *Staatsrecht* ii, p. 221, n. 2; followed, e.g., most recently by Arriat, *Le Préteur pérégrin*, p. 73.

book's title was the result of a mistake arising from an abbreviation
—$p'\overline{ter}$ wrongly understood as $\overline{pr}$ $\overline{per}$—and the book was Labeo's
triginta posteriorum. He doubted the appellation *praetor peregrinus*
which otherwise is not found before Vespasian,[1] and it seems he
also considered odd the apparent omission of *ad edictum* in the
title. But the appellation *praetor peregrinus* could be Ulpianic, and
ad edictum is also—almost as surprisingly—not expressed in
another text from the same book of Ulpian, D. 50. 16. 19: 'Labeo
quidem libro primo praetoris urbani definit . . .' Mommsen thinks
ad edictum has dropped out of this text,[2] but its omission here
undoubtedly weakens the case for Mommsen's reconstruction of
D. 4. 3. 9. 4a.[3] Other jurists have equally felt it impossible that Labeo
wrote a commentary on the Edict of the peregrine praetor in at
least thirty books, and have suggested that all the references to
Labeo *ad edictum* in the Digest and in Aulus Gellius refer to the
same work, that Labeo wrote a commentary on the urban praetor's
Edict and that the differences between that Edict and the Edict of
the peregrine praetor were dealt with in an appendix.[4] Hence the
reference to Labeo's thirtieth book *praetoris peregrini* does not
imply a large-scale work on the Edict of that praetor. This view
is attractive, but it must be admitted that it is to some extent based
on *a priori* reasoning. For it, though, can be forcefully argued that
of the numerous fragments of Labeo's commentary on the Edict
which have survived in other sources—188 fragments are listed
by Lenel—only one, D. 50. 16. 19 already mentioned—is more
specific than *ad praetoris edictum*. The implication is that there was
only one commentary of Labeo *ad edictum*. Again, Gaius' two books
ad edictum aedilium curulium seem to have formed an appendix to
his commentary *ad edictum provinciale* and be books 31 and 32 of
that commentary.[5] In Paul's commentary *ad edictum*, books 1–78

---

[1] *Staatsrecht* ii. 197, n. 2. Arriat, *Le Préteur pérégrin*, p. 19, says that the title
praetor peregrinus already appears under Tiberius in Valerius Maximus 1. 3. 3.
But the passage in question is the work of Julius Paulus, an epitomizer of
unknown date.

[2] *Digesta Iustiniani Augusti* ii (Berlin, 1870), p. 935, n. 5.

[3] Krüger does not think so: *Geschichte der Quellen und Litteratur des römischen
Rechts*, 2nd edit. (Leipzig, 1912), p. 157, n. 26.

[4] e.g. Pernice, *Labeo*, i. 56 ff.; Schulz, *Legal Science*, p. 190.

[5] Cf. Lenel, *Pal.* i. 181, 235 ff.

are *ad edictum praetoris*, 79 and 80 *ad edictum aedilium curulium*;[1] in Ulpian's *ad edictum*, books 1–81 are *ad edictum praetoris*, 82 and 83 *ad edictum aedilium curulium*.[2] So there is nothing unlikely in the idea that a commentary on another *edictum* could be placed as an appendix to the commentary on the major Edict. Other scholars find less difficulty in accepting the title as genuine and in thinking that Labeo could write a commentary in at least thirty books on the Edict of the peregrine praetor.[3]

No certainty is possible, but I submit that the balance of probability seems to be that Labeo's book 30 *praetoris peregrini* was an appendix to his commentary *ad edictum* which was concerned with the urban praetor's Edict.

The strongest evidence of the existence of a separate Edict of the peregrine praetor is in the *lex Rubria*, xx:

Qua de re quisque, et a quo, in Gallia Cisalpeina, damnei infectei ex formula restipularei satisve accipere volet, et ab eo quei ibei i(ure) d(eicundo) ⟨*p(raerit)*⟩ postulaverit, idque non k(alumniae) k(aussa) se facere iuraverit: tum is, quo d. e. r. in ius aditum erit, eum, quei in ius eductus erit, d. e. r. ex formula repromittere et, sei satis darei debebit, satis dare iubeto decernito. Quei eorum ita non repromeisserit aut non satis dederit, sei quid interim damni datum factumve ex ea re aut ob e(am) r(em) eove nomine erit, quam ob rem, utei damnei infectei repromissio satisve datio fierei ⟨*iubeatur*⟩, postulatum erit: tum mag(i-stratus) prove mag(istratu) IIvir IIIIvir praefec(tus)ve, quoquomque d. e. r. in ius aditum erit, d. e. r. ita ius deicito iudicia dato iudicareque iubeto *c*ogito, proinde atque sei d. e. r., quom ita postulatum esset, damn[*e*]i infectei ex formula recte repromissum satisve datum esset. D. [*e. r.*] quod ita iudicium datum iudicareve iussum iudicatumve erit, ius ratumque esto, dum in ea verba, sei damnei infectei repromissum non erit, iudicium det itaque iudicare iubeat: 'I(udex) e(sto). S(ei), antequam id iudicium q. d. r. a(gitur) factum est, Q. Licinius damni infectei eo nomine q. d. r. a(gitur) eam stipulationem, quam is quei Romae inter peregreinos ius deicet in albo propositam habet, L. Seio repromeississet: tum quicquid eum Q. Licinium ex ea stipulatione L. Seio d(are) f(acere) oport*e*ret ex f(ide) b(ona) d(um)*t(axat)* HS e(ius)

---

[3] e.g. Lenel (objecting to Pernice's claim that it is 'impossible'), *Pal*. i. 501, n. 2; Bonfante (with signs of hesitation), *Storia di diritto romano* i, 4th edit. (Rome, 1934), p. 380. Jörs thinks our knowledge of the relationship of the two Edicts to one another is too small to maintain the impossibility of a thirtieth book on the peregrine Edict: *RE* I. 2550 f.

i(udex) Q. Licinium L. Seio, sei ex decreto IIvir(ei) IIIIvir(ei) prae-
fec(tei)ve Mutinensis, quod eius ⟨*is*⟩ IIvir IIIIvir praefec(tus)ve ex lege
Rubria, seive id pl(ebei)ve sc(itum) est, decreverit, Q. Licinius eo
nomine qua d. r. a(gitur) L. Seio damnei infectei repromittere noluit,
c(ondemnato); s(ei) n(on) p(aret), a(bsolvito)'; aut sei damnei infectei
satis datum non erit, in ea verba iudicium det: 'I(udex) e(sto). S(ei),
antequam id iudicium q. d. r. a(gitur) *f*actum est, Q. Licinius damnei
infectei eo nomine q. d. r. a(gitur) ea stipulatione, quam is quei
Romae inter peregrinos ius deicet in albo propositam habet, L. Seio
satis dedisset: tum q(uic)q(uid) eum Q. Licinium ex ea stipulatione
L. Seio d(are) f(acere) oporteret ex f(ide) b(ona) d(um)t(axat), e(ius)
i(udex) Q. Liciniu*m* L. Seio, sei ex decreto IIvir(ei) IIIIvir(ei) prae-
f(ectei)ve Mutinensis, quod eius is IIvir IIIIvir praefect(us)⟨*ve*⟩ ex lege
Rubria, seive id pl(ebei)ve sc(itum) est, decreverit, Q. Licinius eo
nomine q. d. r a(gitur) L. Seio damnei infectei satis dare noluit,
c(ondemnato); s(ei) n(on) p(aret), a(bsolvito)'; dum IIvir IIIIvir i(ure)
d(eicundo) praefec(tus)ve d. e. r. ius ita deicat curetve, utei ea nomina
et municipium colonia locus in eo iudicio, quod ex ieis quae proxsume
s(cripta) s(unt) accipie⟨⟨n⟩⟩tur, includ*a*ntur concipiantur, quae
includei concipei s(ine) d(olo) m(alo) oporteret debebitve, ne quid ei
quei d. e. r. aget petetve captionei ob e(am) r(em) aut eo nomine esse
possit: neive ea nomina, qua⟨*e*⟩ in earum qua formula ⟨⟨quae⟩⟩ s(upra)
s(cripta) s(unt), aut Mutina⟨*m*⟩ in eo iudicio includei concipei curet,
nisi⟨*i*⟩ iei, quos inter id iudicium accipietur leisve contestabitur, ieis
nominibus fuerint, quae in earum qua formula s(upra) s(cripta), *s(unt)*,
et nisei sei Mutinae ea res agetur; neive quis mag(istratus) prove
mag(istratu), neive quis pro quo imperio potestateve erit, intercedito
neive quid aliud facito, quo minus de ea re ita iudicium detur iudice-
turque.

The dating of the *lex Rubria* which deals with the conduct of
certain types of civil case in Cisalpine Gaul is not certain, but it is
generally believed that the most likely date is 49 B.C. when Julius
Caesar gave *civitas* to all Cisalpine towns, and that it is at least
before Augustus incorporated Cisalpine Gaul in Italy.[1] The chapter
quoted shows that for *damnum infectum* the *cautio* which is regarded as appropriate is that set out on the album of the peregrine
praetor. For us there are two problems. First, for our general

---

[1] Cf., e.g., *FIRA* i. 169 ff. and the references given there, and pp. 176 f.;
Chilver, *Cisalpine Gaul* (Oxford, 1941), pp. 9 f.; Schulz, *Legal Science*, p. 88;
Serrao, *Iurisdictio*, pp. 87 ff.; Johnson, Coleman-Norton, Bourne, *Ancient
Roman Statutes* (Austin, 1961), p. 86; Frederiksen, 'The *lex Rubria*: Recon-
siderations', *JRS* 54 (1964), 129 ff. at p. 129.

theory it must be shown that the provisions on *damnum infectum* set out in the Edict of the urban praetor were not appropriate for peregrines and hence separate provisions had to be propounded in the Edict of the peregrine praetor. Secondly, it must be explained why the provisions set out by the peregrine praetor were considered appropriate in this case for citizens. Elsewhere, concerned mainly with this second problem, I suggested that too many factors were unknown for even a clear balance of probabilities to emerge.[1] But I should now like to propose a further explanation which would deal with both problems at once. The urban praetor's edict on *damnum infectum* was not appropriate for peregrines because under it, by what is called *missio ex secundo decreto*, the person given possession of the dangerous property should be able to usucapt it,[2] yet, as is well established, *usucapio* was not available to peregrines. Hence there had to be a separate provision for *damnum infectum* in the Edict of the peregrine praetor. At the time of the *lex Rubria*, Cisalpine Gaul had not yet been incorporated into Italy and still had provincial status. But as the jurist Gaius tells us,[3] provincial land could not be usucapted. Hence the provisions set out in the urban praetor's Edict on *damnum infectum* were not appropriate for Cisalpine Gaul, not even for the Roman citizens there, and so it was most reasonable for the *lex Rubria* to say that the *stipulatio* to be given for *damnum infectum* was that set out in the *album* of the peregrine praetor.

Discussion of the *lex Rubria* brings us to the third lesser aspect of the problem which demanded attention, and it concerns the respective jurisdictions of the urban praetor and the peregrine praetor. The *lex Rubria* apparently allows the peregrine praetor jurisdiction over the Roman citizens of Cisalpine Gaul.[4] The *senatusconsultum de Bacchanalibus* of 186 B.C. declared that no Roman citizen or Latin or ally 'should wish to have associated'[5] with the Bacchae unless he had first approached the urban

---

[1] *Property*, pp. 134 ff. It is not proposed to go over the whole ground.
[2] Lenel, *Edictum*, p. 53, p. 372.
[3] G. 2. 46.
[4] But does not necessarily do so: cf. Watson, *Property*, pp. 135 f.
[5] For the significance of this formulation see above all Daube, *Forms*, pp. 37 ff.

praetor.[1] The *lex Acilia repetundarum* of 122 B.C. gave jurisdiction[2] to the peregrine praetor in cases of extortion, yet it appears that the action might be brought by a Roman[3] as well as by a non-Roman.[4] In the very early Empire the *edictum de aquaeductu Venafrano* of about 11 B.C. gave jurisdiction to the peregrine praetor over breaches of the edict.[5] Yet Venafrum was a colony established by Augustus in Campania and virtually all the free inhabitants would be Roman citizens. Similarly, by the *lex Quinctia* of 9 B.C. concerning aqueducts to Rome, the peregrine praetor was given jurisdiction.[6] In all these cases one praetor is given jurisdiction over a specific subject-matter, and the status of parties in the actions, whether citizens or not, is irrelevant. Under the so-called *lex Iulia municipalis* of 45 B.C. *professiones* are to be made to a consul; if he is not at Rome, then to the urban praetor; if *he* is not at Rome, then to the peregrine praetor.[7]

Of the above instances, only the *lex Rubria* concerns private law. No doubt they are all, to a greater or lesser extent, exceptional cases. It is difficult, perhaps even impossible, to argue anything from them for the limits of jurisdiction of the two major praetors in ordinary cases. But they do show that the boundaries of jurisdiction of these two praetors were not absolutely fixed by the status of the parties. The same is true of the right of *intercessio* available to one praetor against the judgment of another, which praetors did not hesitate to use.[8] This matter of the exact jurisdiction exercised by the two praetors is, however, not of great importance for the history of legal development once the scope of their respective Edicts is established. There would be no distinction in general in the social background or political outlook between those who came to hold the office of urban praetor and those who became peregrine praetor.

---

[1] Lines 7 ff.
[2] The extent of this need not be discussed here.
[3] Line 87; cf., e.g., Mommsen, *Römisches Strafrecht* (Berlin, 1899), p. 721, n. 4; Hardy, *Six Roman Laws* (Oxford, 1911), p. 10, n. 1.
[4] Line 1. [5] Line 65.
[6] When there was no *curator aquarum*: line 18.
[7] Lines 8 ff.
[8] See above all, Cicero, *in Verrem* II, 1. 46. 119 (quoted *supra*, pp. 75 f.); Caesar, *bell. civ.* 3. 20.

It remains to observe that the conclusion reached on the peregrine praetor's Edict, that it contained only the clauses which could
not apply to citizens (and not those which could apply to peregrines
and citizens alike), can be regarded either as support for, or supported by, Daube's views on the jurisdiction of the peregrine
praetor. Using a totally different approach and arguments, he
reached the conclusion that originally and throughout the Republic[1] the peregrine praetor had jurisdiction only in lawsuits
between peregrines, and not also in lawsuits between a citizen and
a peregrine.[2]

CURULE AEDILES

The aediles were magistrates with a lesser jurisdiction than that of
the praetors, but it included the care of the public streets and
market places and, in connection with this duty, the curule
aediles[3] issued an Edict which in Hadrian's redaction had basically
only three clauses concerned with private law. The first clause was
to compel sellers of slaves to declare their defects to buyers at the
time of the sale; if a slave was sold without such a declaration, or
was not in accordance with what was stated or promised, then the
aediles gave the buyer a choice of remedy. The second clause was
to compel sellers of beasts to declare their faults and to deliver
them as they were adorned for the sale; a breach also provided the
buyer with a choice of remedy. The third clause was to deter
persons from keeping fierce wild animals where people commonly
walked, and the damages awarded under the clause varied with the
injury caused. The right of magistrates entrusted with looking
after streets and markets to issue such edicts is obvious.

---

[1] At least until the late Republic.

[2] 'Peregrine Praetor'. The contrary arguments of Serrao, *Iurisdictio*, pp. 12 ff.,
are unconvincing. The principal argument (pp. 16 f.)—and at first sight it is
persuasive—is that on Daube's view there would be little work for the peregrine
praetor to do, and that by far the heaviest load would fall on the urban praetor.
However accurate this observation is (and the balance could be redressed by
laying particular extra burdens on the peregrine praetor), it is equally true that
when later praetors were allotted to particular *quaestiones perpetuae*, they
would (apparently) have far less to do than either the urban praetor or peregrine
praetor, and yet they too were of equal rank.

[3] Not also the plebeian aediles.

But the existence of such a small perpetual Edict immediately raises problems. Why did it not contain more clauses? It is easy to think of others which would seem to have been just as appropriate. Thus, there could have been a more general edict on sales in the market place, rather than clauses simply imposing very particular duties on one party only, the seller. Again, since the aediles issued an edict because of wild animals kept *qua vulgo iter fiet*, why did they not, as the praetors in fact did, issue edicts to restrain people from throwing or pouring something out on to a place *quo vulgo iter fiet vel in quo consistetur*,[1] or from placing something on an eave or projecting roof above a place *quo vulgo iter fiet inve quo consistetur*.[2] Or, since such clauses in fact do not appear in the aedilician Edict, how is one to account for those which are there? Given the very small extent of the Edict, the basic problem is, I suggest, to explain its very existence rather than the exclusions from it.

I would submit that private law in the aedilician Edict is in a sense accidental, that it was the result of a natural development, and was not intended by the aediles when they first issued edicts on sales and the keeping of wild beasts, and that, further, very particular reasons existed to persuade the aediles to intervene in these situations.

Aulus Gellius, *Noctes Atticae*, 4. 2. 1, gives us a version of the edict *de mancipiis vendundis* which is very different from that reported in the Digest.

In edicto aedilium curulium, qua parte de mancipiis vendundis cautum est, scriptum sic fuit: 'Titulus servorum singulorum scriptus sit curato ita, ut intellegi recte possit, quid morbi vitive cuique sit, quis fugitivus errove sit, noxave solutus non sit.'

Undoubtedly this is a form older than that in Hadrian's Edict.[3] First, there is Gellius' tense, 'scriptum sic fuit', which is all the more significant following upon his 'qua parte . . . cautum est'. Secondly, we are extremely well informed in the Digest of the

---

[1] Cf. the praetorian edict, *De his qui deiecerint vel effuderint*: Lenel, *EP*, p. 173.

[2] Cf. the praetorian edict, *Ne quis in suggrunda*: Lenel, *EP*, p. 174.

[3] Cf. Lenel, *EP*, p. 555, n. 1.

redaction of the edict *de mancipiis vendundis* in Hadrian's Edict,[1] and it is clear that the version in Gellius was not part of it. Since Hadrian's Edict must have the final version, and that of Gellius covers the same subject, the latter must be the earlier. Thirdly, as we shall see, the edict in Gellius is far less satisfactory than that in the Digest.

The Gellius edict orders sellers to see to it that the defects of each slave be so written on a notice that they can be properly understood. Nothing, so far as the text goes, indicates the nature of any remedy for the seller's disobedience. The private law actions of the later edict postulate a pre-existing civil law duty, and all that that edict was doing was giving a new remedy.[2] Hence we would expect that any private law action under the Gellius edict would also be providing an alternative remedy for a pre-existing civil law duty. But it is impossible that a civil law action could arise from the writing on the notice, hence it is reasonable to conclude that this early aedilician edict did not provide a private law action at all. Thus, any action under the edict in Gellius must have been more in the nature of a criminal remedy.[3]

This criminal remedy would have been very unsatisfactory in practice. Only some time after the sale, when the buyer became aware of the undisclosed defect, would the matter be taken up, and it would not then be easy to disprove a seller who maintained that the defect had indeed been disclosed on a notice. So a new edict was desirable. That recorded in the Digest is a great improvement. The seller has to declare orally the defects in the slave; if he does not, or the slave is sold contrary to what was stated, then he is liable to the buyer. In practice this would necessarily put upon the seller the burden of proving the existence and accuracy of the declaration,[4] and so the lapse of time between the sale and the discovery by the buyer of the defect would not be disadvantageous, in this respect, to the buyer.

[1] See Lenel's reconstruction and the texts cited by him, *EP*, pp. 554 ff.; Nicholas, '*Dicta Promissave*', *Studies in the Roman Law of Sale, dedicated to de Zulueta* (Oxford, 1959), pp. 91 ff.; Watson, *Obligations*, pp. 86 f.

[2] Cf. Watson, *Obligations*, p. 87 and the authorities cited, nn. 2, 3, 4.

[3] Like many others of their actions: cf. Mommsen, *Staatsrecht* ii. 492 ff.

[4] Whereas, normally, the burden of proving the existence of a stipulation would be on the person who claimed that a stipulation was made to him.

It was this need to improve the Gellius edict which led, I submit, to the introduction of the edict now reported in the Digest.[1] In the process the remedies ceased to be criminal and became private actions. None the less the history of the edict remains apparent even in this final form: it is its original criminal scope which determines its being directed against fraudulent (or arguably fraudulent) conduct of the seller,[2] and not its being concerned with sales generally.

The appropriateness of an edict *de iumentis vendundis* would follow very naturally from one *de mancipiis vendundis*.

Of the third clause, the *edictum de feris*, at least part is directly quoted by Ulpian in the Digest: 'Ne quis canem verrem vel minorem[3] aprum, lupum, ursum, pantheram, leonem, qua vulgo iter fiet, ita habuisse velit.'[4] Lenel[5] pointed out that the quotation ended there, and that the continuing words of Ulpian were not actually part of the edict:

. . . si adversus ea factum erit et homo liber ex ea re perierit, solidi ducenti,[6] si nocitum homini libero esse dicetur, quanti bonum aequum iudici videbitur, condemnatur, ceterarum rerum, quanti damnum datum factumve sit, dupli.

But Lenel considered these words closely followed the wording of the edict. Daube exhaustively studied the legislative form[7]— which appears in this edict—*ne quis fecisse velit*, and concluded that it contained a distinct threat, was particularly nasty, and that, in keeping with this, the punishment was indeterminate in most

---

[1] Or at least to some early form of it.

[2] Cf. D. 21. 1. 1. 2 (Ulpian, 1 *ad ed. aed. cur.*): 'Causa huius edicti proponendi est, ut occurratur fallaciis vendentium et emptoribus succurratur, quicumque decepti a venditoribus fuerint . . .'

[3] 'minorem' appears to be a scribal error, but the true reading does not concern us.

[4] D. 21. 1. 40. 1; *h.t.* 42 (Ulpian, 2 *ad ed. aed. cur.*).

[5] *EP*, p. 566.

[6] In Ulpian's time the sum of money would have been *sestertiorum ducentorum milium*: cf. Lenel, loc. cit.

[7] *Forms*, pp. 37 ff.; '*Ne quis fecisse velit*', *ZSS* 78 (1961), 390 f.; 'No Kissing, Or Else . . .', *The Classical Tradition; Studies in Honor of Harry Caplan* (Ithaca, N.Y., 1966), pp. 222 ff. Johnson, Coleman-Norton, and Bourne, *Ancient Roman Statutes* (Austin, 1961), p. 27, is unsatisfactory.

instances, and certainly in the earlier ones. The aedilician edict seems to be an exception, and it, he suggests, 'may have begun without a sanction, to be provided with one later', and also may not be very old.[1]

In view of the history of this form and the fact that Ulpian's direct quotation ends at *dare possit* it is reasonable to hold that the edict originally did not set out a sanction, and that the specific remedies were provided later.[2] The early edict then would have all the appearance of a police measure,[3] and I would suggest that it was originally conceived of as penal. More conjecturally I would submit that the private law remedies were not available when the edict was first issued but developed subsequently.

This edict, concerned with safety on the public streets, is very appropriate for the curule aediles. But there was a further particular reason for their action in this situation. The wild animals kept in the city would be there primarily to appear at public games, and, in general, the public games were under the control of the aediles.[4] The aediles therefore had a double responsibility in seeing to it that wild animals did no harm.

The precise dating of the clauses of the aedilician Edict seems to be virtually impossible. No text shows the edict *de feris* existing in the Republic. Cato—who may be Cato Censorinus who died in 149 or his son Cato Licinianus who died in 152—thought that a slave who had lost a finger or a toe was *morbosus*, but nothing in the text[5] indicates whether he was commenting on an edict in its earlier, non-private law version or on one which did give private law remedies. But the edict with private law actions did exist in the time of Servius.[6] Aulus Gellius' discussion of *morbus* and *vitium* does not help us to be more precise in dating, since he writes

---

[1] *Forms*, p. 44.

[2] On the evidence available to us it would be possible to argue that they never actually formed part of the edict.

[3] Regarded as the essential character of the form by Daube; *Forms*, p. 48.

[4] Cf. Mommsen, *Staatsrecht*, ii. 517 ff. Foreign animals were seen at the Roman games from about 200 B.C.: cf. Jennison, *Animals for Show and Pleasure in Ancient Rome* (Manchester, 1937), pp. 42 ff.

[5] D. 21. 1. 10. 1 (Ulpian, 1 *ad ed. aed. cur.*).

[6] Aulus Gellius, *N.A.* 4. 2. 12: cf. Cicero, *de off.* 3. 17. 71.

as if the only version which had existed was the old one, now obsolete.[1, 2]

CENSORS

Mention at least must be made of the censors, though they did not issue an edict important for legal development. They were elected in the *comitia centuriata* for the purpose of holding a census, and they continued in office only until this was done or for eighteen months at the longest. Only when a new census was to be made were censors re-elected, and the usual interval between censuses was five years.[3]

The drawing up of the census gave the censors very considerable powers to oversee Roman morality, since they could mark a man with *infamia*, remove him from his *tribus*, remove him from the Senate or ranks of *equites*, or increase the tax he had to pay. This they could do arbitrarily, though they had to give reasons for affixing the *nota censoria*, both censors had to be in agreement, and the man who was to be punished was usually given the opportunity to defend himself. The censors were able to use their powers fairly systematically to deal with wrongful conduct which was otherwise not punished; for instance, an *ingenuus* marrying a *liberta*, an over-hasty divorce, or too severe a punishment by a *pater familias*.[4]

More directly they did in effect change the law by allowing a slave, at his master's command, to inscribe himself as a free man on the census roll and so created a new form of manumission.[5]

---

[1] This appears most clearly from *N.A.* 4. 2. 2 (following upon his quotation of the old edict). 'Propterea quaesierunt iureconsulti veteres, quod "mancipium morbosum" quodve "vitiosum" recte diceretur . . .'

[2] On the jurisdiction of the aediles see, e.g., Kaser, 'Die Jurisdiktion der kurulischen Ädilen', *Mélanges Meylan*, i (Lausanne, 1963), pp. 173 ff.

[3] But there were at times much longer gaps. In earlier centuries four years seem to have been the common gap between censuses.

[4] Cf., e.g., Kaser, *RPR* i. 62 and the authorities he cites; Watson, *Persons*, pp. 32 ff.; Treggiari, *Roman Freedmen during the Late Republic* (Oxford, 1969), pp. 82 ff.

[5] On *manumissio censu* see now the authorities cited by Kaser, *RPR* i. 117, n. 17.

5

THE MAGISTRATES' CONTROL OF THE COURTS

THE annual Edicts of the magistrates, especially that of the urban praetor, were important for the development of private law because these magistrates were in charge of the courts and the bringing of actions. The same control of the courts also gave these magistrates other opportunities to advance the law. These opportunities can be subdivided basically into three groups. First the deliberate, conscious use of existing procedure at the *in iure* stage (i.e. in front of the magistrate) to produce an effect other than that originally envisaged for the procedure. Secondly, the development of new forms of action (without an edict) which in time would be stabilized and the *formulae* of which would come to be published in the Edict. Thirdly, the *ad hoc* granting of actions which were not envisaged by law or in the Edict, when this seemed desirable; and likewise the refusal of a remedy created by law or Edict when this was considered proper. Of these only the last can rightly be regarded as an invention of the later Republic. The other two are earlier but continued to be important.

Of the first, the conspicuous instances are *cessio in iure* and *manumissio vindicta*. *Cessio in iure* is an adaptation of the *legis actio sacramento in rem*, the old Roman action for ownership. But it was used for an amicable transfer of rights. The transferor and the transferee appeared before the praetor, the transferee claimed the thing was his, the transferor made no counter-claim and the praetor adjudged the thing to the transferee. *Cessio in iure* could be used for the transfer of ownership of all things including incorporeals, of *res mancipi* and *res nec mancipi* alike, for the creation of servitudes and usufruct, for adoption and for the cession of *tutela*. The genesis of *cessio in iure* imposes a logical

difficulty for the structure of the institution: in history and appearance it is a judicial procedure and should have effect only between the parties to that procedure; in intention (and function) it is a conveyance and hence effective against all the world. The logical difficulty is not made express in any of the surviving sources.[1]

Manumissio vindicta is an adaptation of the *vindicatio in libertatem* and hence closely related to *cessio in iure*. Anyone could bring a *vindicatio in libertatem* against someone who was wrongly holding a free man as a slave. In *manumissio vindicta* the owner who wished to free a slave appeared with the slave before a magistrate having *imperium*, and a friend of the master claimed the slave was free. The master put up no defence and the magistrate declared the slave a free man. Even in the time of Cicero, *manumissio vindicta* retained much of its character as a form of *vindicatio*.[2] This device, it may be noted, involves an illogicality in a subsidiary matter. The manumission does not appear to be the freeing of a slave but the recognition of the status of a citizen who was wrongly held as a slave; yet, because the truth is that *manumissio vindicta* is the freeing of a slave, it was accepted without question that the former master has all the rights of a *patronus*.[3]

The use of *cessio in iure* was restricted to Roman citizens, and in *manumissio vindicta* the slave's owner had to be a Roman and the slave became one. Hence the origin of these devices—and they may be very early—has to be sought in the activity of the urban praetor rather than of the peregrine praetor.

The second type of development resulting from the magistrates' control of the courts is that of new forms of action (created without an edict) which were eventually stabilized and whose *formulae* came to be published in the Edict. Of these the foremost group are the *bonae fidei iudicia*, the *actio tutelae*, and the actions arising from the four consensual contracts of *emptio venditio*, *locatio*

---

[1] On the difficulty see Wolff, 'The constitutive effect of *in iure cessio*', *Tulane Law Review* 33 (1959), 525 ff., and the authors he cites. On D. 40. 12. 23pr. (Paul, 50 *ad ed.*) see Watson, *Persons*, pp. 116 ff.

[2] Cf. Watson, *Persons*, pp. 190 ff.

[3] See now Watson, 'Illogicality and Roman Law', *Israel Law Review* 7 (1972), 14 ff. at pp. 16 f.

conductio, societas, and *mandatum,* and the *actio negotiorum gestorum*[1] with the condemnation in *quidquid . . . dare facere oportet ex fide bona.* But we should also include here probably the *actio rei uxoriae,* with its *quod eius melius aequius erit*; that *formula* for *fiducia* which contains *ut inter bonos bene agier oportet et sine fraudatione*; and the *actio Serviana* for real security with its *formula in factum.*

The origins of the *bonae fidei iudicia* have attracted by far the greatest attention. The actual mechanism by which they developed is indeed shrouded in the greatest mystery, and here I intend simply to accept the overwhelmingly prevalent opinion that they arose without the intervention of a *lex*—there is no sign of a *lex* in the early history of any of them—and were the creation of magistrates applying law in their courts.[2] The question of whether they were regarded at the outset, as they were in classical law, as actions *in ius conceptae* cannot, I think, be answered.[3]

The main problem is whether they were created by the urban praetor or, as has been believed by a long line of distinguished scholars,[4] by the peregrine praetor. Elsewhere and at different times I have maintained that there is not sufficient evidence for the view that *mandatum* was the work of the peregrine praetor and that it is much more likely that it was created by the urban praetor;[5] that the *formula* in the Edict for the *actio pro socio* was designed for partnerships between citizens and not for partnerships involving peregrines;[6] that the arguments commonly adduced for the proposition that *emptio venditio* was created by the peregrine praetor are invalid and that there is no particular reason for

---

[1] The development of both the *actio negotiorum gestorum in ius* and the *actio negotiorum gestorum in factum* is obscure, but the former is not likely to be as early as some of the other *bonae fidei iudicia.* The *bonae fidei* actions for *depositum* and *commodatum* date only from the Empire.

[2] Cf. on this Wieacker, 'Zum Ursprung der *bonae fidei iudicia*', *ZSS* 80 (1963), 1 ff.; Jolowicz and Nicholas, *Introduction,* pp. 220 ff.

[3] Indeed it is historically an unreal question.

[4] See the references given by Wieacker, 'Ursprung', pp. 9 ff., and in the works cited, *infra,* nn. 5–6 and p. 91, n. 1.

[5] *Contract of Mandate in Roman Law* (Oxford, 1961), pp. 18 ff.; cf. *Obligations,* p. 147.

[6] 'Consensual *societas* between Romans and the Introduction of *formulae*', *RIDA* 9 (1962), 431 ff.

giving the credit to him rather than to the urban praetor.[1] Similarly nothing specifically points to the peregrine praetor as the inventor of *locatio conductio* or of the *actio negotiorum gestorum* formulated *in ius*.

I have also argued that the *actio tutelae* was the earliest of the *bonae fidei iudicia*.[2] If that is correct—as I still firmly believe—then the point is of fundamental importance in the present context. The *actio tutelae* was the action brought by a *pupillus* (or former *pupillus*) against his *tutor*, and in the nature of things both the *pupillus* and the *tutor* would be Roman citizens. The *actio tutelae* was introduced for actions between citizens and was intended for use in the court of the urban praetor. This means that the earliest *bonae fidei iudicium* was created for the urban praetor's court.

The *formula* for *fiducia* which was framed *ut inter bonos bene agier oportet et sine fraudatione* probably also existed from about the beginning of our period.[3] Since the basis of *fiducia* was a *mancipatio* or *in iure cessio* this action, too, was restricted to *cives*. The *actio rei uxoriae*,[4] since it was for the recovery of a wife's dowry from the husband, would also be mostly used between *cives*, though perhaps it could also be employed when one of the parties was a Latin.[5] We cannot be so definite about the origins of the earliest known praetorian *actio in factum*, which also was introduced without an edict, namely the *actio Serviana* or a forerunner of this. All we can say is that around 160 B.C. when we first learn of its existence, Cato treats it as if it were freely available to citizens, and that at least later the *formula* was in the urban praetor's Edict.[6]

Thus this second type of development, too, seems to be mainly the result of needs felt in the urban praetor's court, and he must be given the credit for the earliest and most important new actions

---

[1] 'The Origins of Consensual Sale: a Hypothesis', *TvR* 32 (1964), 245 ff.

[2] *Persons*, pp. 140 ff.

[3] Cf. *Private Law*, p. 87. But whether it is earlier or later than the first *bonae fidei iudicia* cannot really be determined.

[4] This action is later than the divorce of Carvilius Ruga around 230 B.C.: Aulus Gellius, *N.A.* 4. 3. 1, 2; cf. Watson, 'The Divorce of Carvilius Ruga', *TvR* 33 (1965), 38 ff.

[5] Since there could be a valid marriage only between persons with *conubium*.

[6] For all this see *supra*, pp. 53 ff.

created without an edict but which became stabilized with *formulae* eventually published in the Edict. Though no strict proof is possible, this type of development began, I suggest, in the second half of the third century B.C.[1]

The third development relevant to this chapter is the *ad hoc* granting of actions or defences which were not envisaged by law or in the Edict, and the *ad hoc* refusal of remedies established by law or the Edict. This certainly is much later than the other two and is probably no older than the first century B.C. The earliest recorded instances of the decretal *actio in factum* go no further back than Servius, who was consul in 51 B.C. and died in 43.[2] Two cases relate to him,[3] three to his pupil, Alfenus,[4] and one to another pupil, Ofilius.[5] There is an instructive difference between the wording of the texts referring to Servius and those concerning the two younger jurists. In D. 9. 3. 5. 12 Servius says it is proper for an action *ad exemplum huius actionis* to be given, in D. 3. 5. 20 (21)pr. that it would be fair for the praetor to give an action. In D. 19. 5. 23 Alfenus says an *actio in factum* can be brought; in D. 6. 1. 5. 3 we are told simply that Alfenus gave an *actio utilis*; and likewise in D. 39. 2. 9. 2 it appears that Alfenus simply said the action would be given. In D. 9. 2. 9. 3 we are also told that Ofilius wrote that an *actio in factum* would be given. Thus the formulation reserved for Servius is rather more tentative. He thought it proper or fair that a decretal action be given. His pupils, on the other hand, could hold that a decretal action would be given. This is consistent with the view that for Servius decretal actions were a new phenomenon and the praetor's readiness to give them (in circumstances judged appropriate by the jurist) could not be regarded as certain, whereas slightly later, in the heyday of Alfenus and Ofilius, the granting of decretal actions could be relied upon as a mere matter of course.

---

[1] Cf., e.g., Watson, *Obligations*, pp. 40 f.   [2] Cf. Kunkel, *Herkunft*, p. 25.

[3] D. 9. 3. 5. 12 (Ulpian, 23 *ad ed.*) (cf. Watson, *Obligations*, p. 268); 3. 5. 20 (21)pr. (Paul, 9 *ad ed.*) (cf. Watson, *Obligations*, p. 206).

[4] D. 19. 5. 23 (Alfenus, 3 *dig. a Paulo epit.*) (cf. Watson, *Obligations*, p. 244); 39. 2. 9. 2 (Ulpian, 53 *ad ed.*) (cf. Watson, *Property*, p. 148); 6. 1. 5. 3 (Ulpian, 16 *ad ed.*) (but the text is probably interpolated to some extent; cf. Watson, *Property*, p. 75).

[5] D. 9. 2. 9. 3 (Ulpian, 18 *ad ed.*) (cf. Watson, *Obligations*, p. 244).

Another development is shown in D. 44. 1. 14 (Alfenus Varus, 2 *dig.*), where Alfenus decided it would be fair (*aequum*) to give an *exceptio in factum*.

Just as the praetor could grant *ad hoc* actions, so he could refuse established remedies. By 74, 73, or 72 B.C. we have evidence that he could refuse to grant *bonorum possessio* under the terms of his own Edict.[1] And there is proof that as early as 70 B.C. the praetor might refuse to allow an action on a claim which was valid at civil law.[2]

This power of the praetor was open to abuse, and abused it certainly was. Cicero claims that L. Piso, Verres' colleague in the praetorship in 74 B.C., filled many books with reports of cases in which he interceded because Verres had decided differently from his Edict.[3] Other praetors also gave *ad hoc* decisions for corrupt purposes.[4] In the time of Verres' urban praetorship it was not against the law for a praetor to decide contrary to his Edict. The worst thing Cicero said of Verres' conduct in this respect was: 'tum vero in magistratu contra illud ipsum edictum suum sine ulla religione decernebat.'[5] As a consequence, a tribune of the plebs, C. Cornelius, had a plebiscite passed in 67 B.C. that a praetor should give actions according to his *edicta perpetua*.[6] There has

---

[1] Valerius Maximus 7. 7. 7 (cf. Watson, *Succession*, pp. 75 f.); Cicero, *in Verrem* II, 1. 47. 123–4 (cf. Watson, *Succession*, pp. 77 ff.).

[2] Valerius Maximus 7. 7. 5 (cf. Watson, *Succession*, pp. 80 f.).

[3] *In Verrem* II, 1. 46. 119: 'Itaque L. Piso multos codices implevit earum rerum in quibus intercessit, quod iste aliter atque ut edixerat decrevisset.'

[4] Asconius, *in Cornelianam*, 52; Dio Cassius 36. 40: cf. Kelly, *Roman Litigation*, pp. 86 f.

[5] *In Verrem* II, 1. 46. 119.

[6] Asconius, *in Cornelianam*, 52: 'Aliam deinde legem Cornelius, etsi nemo repugnare ausus est, multis tamen invitis tulit, ut praetores ex edictis suis perpetuis ius dicerent; quae res studium aut gratiam ambitiosis praetoribus qui varie ius dicere assueverant sustulit.' Dio Cassius 36. 40: καὶ οὕτως ἐκεῖνόν τε διενομοθέτησε καὶ ἕτερον τοιόνδε.

Οἱ στρατηγοὶ πάντες τὰ δίκαια καθ' ἃ δικάσειν ἔμελλον, αὐτοὶ συγγράφοντες ἐξετίθεσαν· οὐ γάρ πω πάντα τὰ δικαιώματα τὰ περὶ τὰ συμβόλαια διετέτακτο. ἐπεὶ οὖν οὔτε ἐσάπαξ τοῦτ' ἐποίουν οὔτε τὰ γραφέντα ἐτήρουν, ἀλλὰ πολλάκις αὐτὰ μετέγραφον καὶ συχνὰ ἐν τούτῳ πρὸς χάριν ἢ καὶ κατ' ἔχθραν τινῶν, ὥσπερ εἰκός, ἐγίγνετο, ἐσηγήσατο κατ' ἀρχάς τε εὐθὺς αὐτοὺς τὰ δίκαια οἷς χρήσονται προλέγειν, καὶ μηδὲν ἀπ' αὐτῶν παρατρέπειν. τό τε σύμπαν οὕτως ἐπιμελὲς τοῖς Ῥωμαίοις κατὰ τὸν χρόνον ἐκεῖνον τὸ μηδὲν δωροδοκεῖσθαι ἐγένετο ὥστε πρὸς τῷ τοὺς ἐλεγχομένους κολάζειν καὶ τοὺς κατηγοροῦντας αὐτῶν ἐτίμων. τοῦ γοῦν Κόττου τοῦ Μάρκου τὸν μὲν ταμίαν Πούπλιον Ὄππιον ἐπί τε δώροις καὶ ἐπὶ ὑποψίᾳ ἐπιβουλῆς ἀποπέμψαντος, αὐτοῦ δὲ πολλὰ ἐκ τῆς Βιθυνίας χρηματισαμένου,

been considerable controversy about the scope and effect of this *plebiscitum*,[1] primarily because in practice it did not stop praetors giving *ad hoc* actions or refusing existing standard remedies. Certainty is not possible,[2] but in view of what we are told of the *plebiscitum* and its purpose, it seems right to conjecture that it was meant to stop praetors issuing subsidiary edicts after the publication of their *edictum perpetuum*, granting decretal remedies and refusing established remedies. On this view, of course, we must hold that the *plebiscitum* was not rigidly enforced. But this would not be surprising: Asconius tells us that many people were against the law though they did not speak out, and moreover the proper use of these powers by praetors could be extremely valuable. The purpose of the law would be served if it hindered the abuse of the power, or if it could be invoked against an unprincipled magistrate.[3]

Γάιον Κάρβωνα τὸν κατηγορήσαντα αὐτοῦ τιμαῖς ὑπατικαῖς καίπερ δεδημαρχηκότα μόνον, ἐσέμνυναν. καὶ οὗτος μὲν τῆς τε Βιθυνίας καὶ αὐτὸς ὕστερον ἄρξας, καὶ μετριώτερον οὐδὲν τοῦ Κόττου πλημμελήσας, ἀντικατηγορήθη ὑπὸ τοῦ υἱέος αὐτοῦ καὶ ἀνθεάλω· πολλῷ γάρ που ῥᾷον ἄλλοις ἐπιτιμῶσί τινες ἢ ἑαυτοῖς παραινοῦσι, καὶ προχειρότατά γε ἐφ' οἷς τιμωρίας ἀξίους τοὺς πέλας εἶναι νομίζουσιν αὐτοὶ ποιοῦσιν, ὥστε μηδεμίαν πίστιν ἐξ ὧν ἑτέροις ἐγκαλοῦσιν, ὅτι καὶ μισοῦσιν αὐτά, λαμβάνειν.

[1] Cf. Kaser, *RPR* i. 206 and the references he gives, n. 6.
[2] Cf. Schulz, *Principles of Roman Law* (Oxford, 1936), p. 230.
[3] Reference has been made to the praetor's right of *intercessio* in the decision of another praetor. The same right of *intercessio* was accorded to the consuls: Valerius Maximus 7. 7. 6; cf. Watson, *Succession*, p. 76.

6

THE PROBLEM OF REFORM AND
THE AUTOCRATS

SULLA, around 81 B.C. when he was *dictator*, was responsible for a considerable body of legislation affecting private law: *lex Cornelia de confirmandis testamentis, lex Cornelia de falsis, lex Cornelia de iniuriis, lex Cornelia de adulteriis, lex Cornelia de sponsu.*[1]

Both Pompeius Magnus and Julius Caesar are said to have planned codifications:

Suetonius, *Divus Iulius*, 44. 2. Ius civile ad certum modum redigere atque ex immensa diffusaque legum copia optima quaeque et necessaria in paucissimos conferre libros . . .

Isidorus, *etym*. 5. 1. 5. Leges autem redigere in libris primus consul Pompeius instituere voluit, sed non perseveravit obtrectatorum metu. deinde Caesar id facere sed ante interfectus erat.

These reports are too imprecise for us to deduce much about the nature of the plans, but it would clearly be unreasonable to hold that at least that of Caesar did not extend to private law.[2] Though the term *ius civile* is used even by jurists with more than one meaning, such as 'juristic interpretation', 'that part of law which applies only to citizens', or in contrast to *ius honorarium* or *ius naturale*, yet it is very much a term which is attached to private law. Both Suetonius[3] and Isidorus report that it was death which prevented

---

[1] For all these see, e.g., the relevant entries in Rotondi, *Leges*, pp. 356 ff. It is not proved that all these *leges* are Sullan, but that point does not concern us greatly.

[2] Contra, Sanio, *Über die von Julius Caesar beabsichtigte Gesetzsammlung und die juristischen Schriften des Aulus Ofilius* (Königsberg, 1845), p. 72. For views which have been advanced on the two planned codifications see Pólay, 'Der Kodifizierungsplan des Julius Caesar', *IURA* 16 (1965), 28 ff.; 'Der Kodifikationsplan des Pompeius', *Acta Antiqua*, 13 (1965), 85 ff.; and the references he gives.

[3] *Divus Iulius*, 44. 4, 'Talia agentem atque meditantem mors praevenit.'

Caesar fulfilling his plan, which therefore essentially dates from the end of his life when he was *dictator*. Isidorus tells us that Pompeius wished 'leges . . . redigere in libris' when he was *consul*, and it seems most likely that this refers to his third consulship in 56 B.C. when he was *consul sine collega*.[1]

Augustus in power embarked on a policy of private law reform. A first statute to coerce marriage was proposed probably in 28 B.C., but was withdrawn because of the opposition to it.[2] It was, however, followed by the *lex Iulia de maritandis ordinibus* of 18 B.C., the *lex Iulia de adulteriis coercendis* of the same year, the *lex Fufia Caninia de manumissionibus* of 2 B.C., the *lex Aelia Sentia* of A.D. 4, the *lex Papia Poppaea* of 9.[3] By rescript he enabled a soldier *filius familias* to make a will in respect of any *peculium* which he had acquired in military service;[4] and by edict he forbade a father to disinherit a soldier son.[5] He also had *fideicommissa* and codicils made enforceable.[6] And he introduced the *ius respondendi*.[7]

Thus, the four men who achieved exclusive power in the first century B.C. were all proponents of extensive law reform.[8] No doubt specific reasons can be given in each case: Sulla was eager for the restoration of tranquillity and anxious to improve the lot of his soldiers; the codification plans of Pompeius and Caesar, it has been said, are due to Hellenism;[9] Augustus' social and moral purposes have long been emphasized by the historians.[10] Yet the zeal of these four reveals something more fundamental, the absence in normal times of any assembly or office-holder capable

[1] For the argument see Pólay, 'Pompeius', pp. 88 ff.
[2] Propertius, *eleg.* 2. 7; Suetonius *Divus Augustus*, 34. 1: cf., e.g., Butler and Barber, *The Elegies of Propertius* (Oxford, 1933), p. 202; Last, *Cambridge Ancient History* x (Cambridge, 1934), p. 441; Williams, 'Poetry in the Moral Climate of Augustan Rome', *JRS* 52 (1962), 28 ff. at p. 28; Camps, *Propertius: Elegies Book II* (Cambridge, 1967), p. 97.
[3] For the sources for these *leges* see Rotondi, *Leges*, pp. 443 ff.
[4] *Epit. Ulp.* 20. 10; J. 2. 12pr.
[5] D. 28. 2. 6 (Paul, 3 *sent.*).
[6] J. 2. 23. 1; 2. 25pr.
[7] D. 1. 2. 2. 49 (Pomponius, *sing. enchirid.*).
[8] The point remains even if the proposed codification of Pompeius and Caesar was directed more to the revision of the form than the substance of law.
[9] e.g. Schulz, *Legal Science*, p. 62; Pólay, 'Julius Caesar', p. 47; 'Pompeius', pp. 88 f.
[10] Cf., e.g., Jones, *Augustus* (London, 1970), pp. 131 ff.

of undertaking large-scale, far-reaching reform of private law.[1] However much any individual praetor might want to reform the law, he could not dare to propose too many changes in his Edict in his one year of office. The *concilium plebis* could meet only when summoned by an officer of the plebs, and it could only deal with the matter which he put before it. The assembly could not discuss his proposal or suggest amendments, but could only accept or reject it. There would, of course, be a *contio* before the assembly met, at which the tribune could make, and allow, speeches on the proposal, but no one would dare disturb a *contio* held under the auspices of a tribune.[2] Thus proposals for legislation by the *concilium plebis* were in the hands of the individual tribune, and again no tribune could in normal times dream of proposing sweeping changes in private law. The same would apply to legislation by the *comitia centuriata*, which would be summoned by a 'patrician magistrate'. As we have seen,[3] the *comitia centuriata* was apparently not used at all for private law legislation in normal times, hence the extensive use made of it by Sulla, as sole ruler, for private law reform is doubly significant.

Thus, in the later Republic, there could be no extensive, planned law reform except when one man held complete power, and the innovations of any one year by a magistrate or assembly would be strictly limited. It seems reasonable to assume that most magistrates would have little interest in the reform of private law, but those who had were not able to indulge in grandiose schemes. Accordingly, although the first century B.C. at Rome was the period of the world's greatest legal development, changes would often not be systematic or made as quickly as could have been desired. One can, indeed, go further. In normal times the responsibility for a particular change in the law would very clearly rest on an individual politician, whether praetor or tribune,[4] whose future career could easily be jeopardized by a controversial proposal.

---

[1] Cicero had already urged Julius Caesar to moral law reform; 'constituenda iudicia revocanda fides, comprimendae libidines propaganda suboles': *pro Marcello*, 8. 23.

[2] Cf., e.g., Botsford, *The Roman Assemblies* (New York, 1909), p. 142.

[3] *Supra*, pp. 6 ff.

[4] Even if the tribune proposed the *lex* at the request of the Senate.

Hence some areas of the law would change more slowly and less satisfactorily than others. This can best be illustrated by a quick look at the main changes in private law resulting from Augustus' reforms.

The *lex Fufia Caninia* limited—for the first time—the number of slaves whom a master could manumit (by will). The *lex Aelia Sentia* imposed *inter alia* restrictions on the manumission of young slaves or by young owners. A chapter of the *lex Iulia de adulteriis* forbade a husband, without the consent of his wife, to dispose of land in Italy which had come to him as dowry.[1] The *lex Iulia et Papia Poppaea*[2] freed women for the first time (apart from Vestal Virgins) from *tutela mulierum*, on account of the *ius liberorum*.[3] The law extended even to freedwomen (who had four children). For the first time since the *lex Canuleia* of 445 B.C. marriage between certain classes was prohibited: senators and their descendants were forbidden to marry freedwomen.[4] For divorce, formalities—unknown in the later Republic at least, except where the marriage was by *confarreatio*—were introduced: seven witnesses were needed for a valid *repudium*.[5] For the first time, a husband who found his wife in adultery had to divorce her, and a criminal penalty was established against him if he failed to do so.[6] Augustus also first imposed disabilities on the unmarried (males above 25, females above 20) and on childless couples: the former could take nothing under a will, the latter only half.[7] Augustus' grant to a soldier *filius* of the right to bequeath his *peculium castrense* was the first breach in the exclusive property rights of the *pater familias*. His edict forbidding a *pater* to disinherit his soldier son was the

---

[1] P. S. 2. 21b. 2.

[2] In reality two statutes, but it is often difficult (and not important here) to distinguish the provisions of one from those of the other.

[3] e.g. G. 1. 145.

[4] Cf., e.g., Dio Cassius 54. 16; 56. 7; D. 23. 2. 23 (Celsus, 30 *dig.*) *h.t.* 44pr. (Paul, 1 *ad legem Iuliam et Papiam*): for the argument see Watson, *Persons*, pp. 32 ff. In the Republic marriage between an *ingenuus* and a *libertina* could lead to the former's disgrace.

[5] D. 24. 2. 9 (Paul, 2 *de adulteriis*); cf., e.g., Corbett, *The Roman Law of Marriage* (Oxford, 1930), pp. 228 ff. But it is widely held that the form requiring seven witnesses was designed to end *manus* without the wife's co-operation; cf. Kaser, *RPR* i. 327 and the authorities he cites, n. 32.

[6] e.g. D. 48. 5. 2. 2 (Ulpian, 8 *disput.*) *h.t.* 30 (29)pr. (Ulpian, 4 *de adulteriis*).

[7] *Epit. Ulp.* 16. 1; 16. 3; G. 2. 111; 2. 286a.

earliest provision to force a testator to leave a share to a particular person;[1] just as the recognition of the legal enforceability of *fideicommissa* and codicils was the first known step in making the classical will less formal.

These extensive innovations of Augustus, when considered together with Republican law, reveal something of great significance about the latter. During the period which concerns us, from about 200 B.C. to the end of the Republic, there was no innovation in the law between a *pater familias* and his dependants. Yet the inconveniences of a *filius'* having no property rights of his own are obvious.[2] There was no *lex* or *edictum* on any aspect of marriage or divorce, and no new action on these matters after the introduction of the *actio rei uxoriae*. This action came into being after 230 B.C. but probably not too long after, and, interestingly in the present context, its origins and the basis of the obligation under it are not at all clear.[3] But in the early first century B.C. there was an important change in the law of marriage when *manus* became virtually obsolete. The development, it cannot be emphasized too strongly, was not the work of *lex* or *edictum* but was due to a deliberate misinterpretation by the jurists of an irrelevant provision of the XII Tables.[4] Again, when we notice Augustus' edict forbidding the disinherison of a *filius miles* and the absence of any Republican *lex* or *edictum* requiring a testator to leave a share to any one individual, we should remember the *querella inofficiosi testamenti*. This was a dodge developed in the Republic by the jurists or the centumviral court, operating under the pretence that a testator who passed over near relatives was insane and therefore his will was invalid.[5] From all this we can conclude, I submit, that in the later Republic politicians—with an eye to their future—

---

[1] Of course, the *querella inofficiosi testamenti* was in existence during the Republic, but it was not introduced by edict or statute.

[2] Cf. Daube, *Roman Law, Linguistic, Social and Philosophical Aspects* (Edinburgh, 1969), pp. 75 ff., who rightly stresses that even Augustus' reform was not radical.

[3] Cf. now Watson, *Private Law*, p. 26.

[4] On this development see now Watson, 'Limits of Juristic Decision in the Later Roman Republic', *Aufstieg und Niedergang der römischen Welt'* I. ii (Berlin, New York, 1972), pp. 215 ff. at pp. 219 f.

[5] Cf. Watson, *Succession*, pp. 62 ff.

were unwilling during their year of office to tackle the reform of certain parts of private law where feelings might be sensitive. In these parts, innovations, if they came at all, had to result from juristic dodges.[1]

---

[1] And yet the jurists, as we shall see from the topics omitted from their systematic writings, were themselves often backward-looking: *infra*, pp. 151 ff., 162 ff.

7

THE FUNCTIONS OF THE JURISTS

FROM the chapters on what might be called the official factors in legal development it will have been clear that the most important of these was the Edict, especially of the urban praetor; and that the effectiveness of the Edict depended on the magistrates' control of the courts. The control of the courts also permitted the magistrates to make other far-reaching innovations. It was in their relationship with the magistrates and the courts that in their turn the jurists made their own most important contributions, which indeed give them the right to be recognized as the major force in the development of law. Though here the jurists remain very much in the background, there can be no doubt that it was they who were really responsible for new court remedies and for the Edict itself. The process is well described by Schulz.[1] As he says of one illustration:

> In the field of contract the most important development was the recognition of the legal validity of the consensual contracts. How this came about is no mystery: some jurist or jurists proposed to the praetor the formula of an *actio empti* or *venditi* which instructed the *iudex* to award to the plaintiff whatever as a matter of good faith (*ex fide bona* in contrast to *ex iure Quiritium*) was due to him from the defendant, and this formula was accepted by the praetor and acted on by the *iudex*, who himself was advised by jurisconsults.

Yet so far in the background are the jurists that we know only of one remedy,[2] the *iudicium Cascellianum* which was named after the jurist who—*qua* jurist—devised it.[3] And there is no other action

---

[1] *Legal Science*, pp. 49 ff.

[2] There are, of course, other possible instances: cf. Schulz, *Legal Science*, p. 51, n. 9.

[3] G. 4. 166a, 169; cf., e.g., Schulz, *Legal Science*, p. 51, n. 8. So far as our knowledge extends there is no other possible inventor than the jurist A. Cascellius, who was a member of the Senate by 73 B.C.: cf. Kunkel, *Herkunft*, pp. 25 ff.

which can be attributed to a specific jurist.[1] Though the evidence is again slight we do know that jurists might be appointed to a magistrate's *consilium*.[2]

When the *legis actiones* were relatively stereotyped and not easily subject to change there was little scope here for the jurists, but the introduction of *formulae*, somewhat before the beginning of our period, and the possibility of ever more innovations and changes, brought their skills to life. When, from around 100 B.C. to the end of the Republic, praetors were apparently eager to propound law reforms in their Edict, the jurists seized the opportunity. It is no coincidence that from this time on legal books assume a new character and importance.[3]

The secret of the Roman genius for private law is thus revealed. Development of the law was only to a very limited extent by political assemblies. The jurists, those individuals of high social rank who were passionately devoted to private law, had the real control of change. Though it may be observed that the praetorship was an elective office and that praetors might be subject to external pressures, the harm that any one praetor might cause to legal progress was limited. The office was for one year only, was not normally held a second time in the later Republic, and such was the fluidity of the Edict that any unsatisfactory clause could be modified or removed altogether by any subsequent praetor.[4]

What gave the jurists their high authority is for the later Republic no doubt a matter of history, whose roots should be sought in the College of Pontiffs, and the pontiffs' early control of private law. The authority of any individual jurist would derive from his recognized legal skill and also from the positions he had held in

Pomponius tells us that he was quaestor but did not want higher office, and refused the consulship from Augustus: D. 1. 2. 2. 45 (*sing. enchirid.*). Hence he could not have proposed the *iudicium* as praetor. Against the view that despite Pomponius, Cascellius did hold the praetorship, see Kunkel, *Herkunft*, p. 26, n. 55; Rodger, 'A note on A. Cascellius', *Classical Quarterly* 22 (1972), 135 ff.

[1] Provided it was as praetor and not *qua* jurist that Aquillius was responsible for the *edictum de dolo* and the remedies under it: cf. *supra*, pp. 72 ff.

[2] Cicero, *pro Flacco*, 32. 77; *de orat.* 1. 37. 168.

[3] Cf. *infra*, pp. 143 ff.

[4] For an indication of the frequency of changes in edictal clauses see *supra*, p. 33, and n. 4.

the state and the respect accorded to him in general. The worth
of any particular opinion would depend on the jurist's authority
and—when the legal point was disputed—on the quality of the
arguments adduced.

The Republican system was for lay judges. Naturally they
required assistance when the case involved legal technicalities, and
they too turned to the jurists. Cicero says:

For private law suits involving highly important matters depend, in
my opinion, on the wisdom of the jurists. For they are often present at
the trials and are invited to join the judge's advisers; and they provide
weapons for careful advocates who look for help in their skill. Thus, in
all these actions in which the words 'in accordance with good faith' are
added, or also 'as one ought to behave properly among good men', and
above all, in the *actio rei uxoriae* which has 'whatever on that account
is fairer and better', the jurists should be ready to advise. It is they who
have defined fraud, good faith, equity, what a partner owes a partner,
what a person looking after another's affairs owes that person, or the
reciprocal rights of principal and agent and of husband and wife.[1]

The passage of Cicero reveals that not only judges but also
orators asked the jurists for their legal opinion, *responsum*. So
indeed did other individuals. Sometimes, in fact, the person seeking
advice might ask more than one jurist in turn. Thus, Cicero had
spoken (or written) to the jurist Trebatius about a succession
problem which involved someone named Silius. Silius visited
Cicero again and Cicero told him Trebatius' opinion. Silius then
reported that Servius and Ofilius had given him a contrary answer:
he himself had not spoken to Trebatius, and he asked Cicero to
commend him and his case to that jurist.[2] From D. 28. 6. 39. 2
(Iavolenus, 1 *ex post. Labeonis*) it appears that Ofilius and Cascellius

[1] 'Privata enim iudicia maximarum quidem rerum in iuris consultorum mihi
videntur esse prudentia. Nam et adsunt multum et adhibentur in consilia et
patronis diligentibus ad eorum prudentiam confugientibus hastas ministrant.
In omnibus igitur eis iudiciis, in quibus EX FIDE BONA est additum, ubi
vero etiam UT INTER BONOS BENE AGIER OPORTET, in primisque in
arbitrio rei uxoriae, in quo est QUOD EIUS AEQUIUS MELIUS, parati eis
esse debent. Illi dolum malum, illi fidem bonam, illi aequum bonum, illi quid
socium socio, quid eum qui negotia aliena curasset ei cuius ea negotia fuissent,
quid eum qui mandasset, eumve cui mandatum esset, alterum alteri praestare
oporteret, quid virum uxori, quid uxorem viro tradiderunt': *top.* 17. 65, 66.
[2] Cicero, *ad fam.* 7. 21. This is not quite the way Schulz reports the matter:
Legal Science, p. 52.

both gave *responsa* to the same effect in a case of *substitutio*. In
D. 37. 7. 16. 1 (Alfenus, 2 *dig. a Paulo epit.*) we learn that someone
consulted Servius after getting a *responsum* from Cornelius
Maximus. The *responsa* were not the same.[1]

Throughout the whole of our period (and even earlier)[2] the most
eminent jurists were active in giving *responsa*.[3] Cicero records that
jurists like Sextus Aelius and Manius Manilius might be approached for advice when they were out walking and when they
were at home; that such was their reputation that their advice was
sought not only on points of law, but on every sort of matter, such
as marrying a daughter, buying an estate, or cultivating a field.[4]
Pomponius also reports that Sextus Aelius and his brother
Publius were very skilled in giving opinions.[5] Cicero makes us
aware that Cato—who might be Cato the Censor or his son
—and Brutus gave *responsa* to private individuals.[6] So also,
clearly, did P. Licinius Crassus who died in 130,[7] and Quintus
Mucius Scaevola the augur who was consul in 117.[8] P. Rutilius
Rufus sustained a great burden of *responsa*.[9] Speaking of Quintus
Mucius the consul of 95, Cicero declares that the house of a jurist
is the oracle of the whole society because so many citizens attend
there daily.[10] Pomponius recounts an anecdote that Servius (while
still an orator) did not understand a *responsum* given him by
Quintus Mucius.[11] Aquillius Gallus was noted for the speed with
which he gave *responsa*.[12] Servius Sulpicius Rufus was very active
in giving *responsa* and thought it necessary to give a reply to those

---

[1] See on this Schulz, loc. cit.
[2] Cf., e.g., Cicero, *de orat.* 2. 33. 134; D. 1. 2. 2. 38 (Pomponius, *sing. enchirid.*).
[3] *de orat.* 3. 33. 133.
[4] *de orat.* 3. 33. 133. On Sextus Aelius see also *de re pub.* 1. 18. 30.
[5] D. 1. 2. 2. 38.
[6] *de orat.* 2. 33. 142: 'Video enim in Catonis et Bruti libris nominatim fere
referri quid alicui de iure viro aut mulieri responderit.' In D. 24. 3. 44pr. (Paul,
5 *quaest.*) *Cato* should perhaps read *Capito*: cf., e.g., Lenel, *Pal.* i. 1198; Bremer,
Iurisprudentiae Antehadrianae quae supersunt i (Leipzig, 1896), p. 20.
[7] Cicero, *Brutus*, 26. 98; *de orat.* 1. 56. 239.
[8] Cicero, *pro Balbo*, 20. 45.   [9] Cicero, *Brutus*, 30. 113.
[10] *de orat.* 1. 45. 200. For a *responsum* of Quintus Mucius on sacred law see
Macrobius, *sat.* 1. 16. 11.
[11] D. 1. 2. 2. 43.
[12] Cicero, *Brutus*, 42. 154. On the giving of *responsa* by this jurist see also
Cicero, *pro Balbo*, 20. 45; *de off.* 3. 14. 60; *top.* 7. 32.

who consulted him even when they were opponents of his friends.[1]
Many of his *responsa* published by his pupil Alfenus Varus have
survived.[2] So have many of Aulus Ofilius'[3] and Trebatius Testa's.[4]

A further important function of the jurists in the later Republic
was *cavere*,[5] the drafting (and advising on drafting) of wills, forms
of contract, and other transactions.[6] Thus M'. Manilius appears to
have published a collection of clauses appropriate to sale,[7] and
Varro expressly recommends his formulation for warranties of
health and against eviction when she-goats are purchased.[8] Publius
Mucius invented a drafting dodge to enable a testator to leave a
large share of his property to an individual without that individual's
becoming liable to perform the *sacra*. He also showed how the
legatee could avoid this liability where the testator had not wished
to take the necessary precaution.[9] Quintus Mucius Scaevola devised the famous *cautio Muciana* to allow a widow who was left
a legacy by her husband on condition she did not remarry to
benefit from the bequest.[10] Aquillius Gallus was responsible both
for the form of the *stipulatio Aquiliana* which novated debts of
any kind so that they could then be discharged by *acceptilatio*,[11] and
for the form of institution of *postumi nepotes* who were to succeed
only if their father predeceased the testator.[12] A very fine instance
of cautelary jurisprudence is to be found in D. 28. 6. 39pr.
(Iavolenus, 1 *ex post. Labeonis*) where Labeo, Ofilius, Cascellius,
and Trebatius give their opinion on how a will should be drafted
so as to benefit the testator's two grandchildren, of whom one was

---

[1] Cicero, *pro Murena*, 4. 9; 9. 19; 9. 22; 13. 28.

[2] See the texts in Lenel, *Pal.* i. 38 ff.

[3] See the texts in Lenel, *Pal.* i. 799 f.   [4] See the texts in Lenel, *Pal.* ii. 343 ff.

[5] Cicero, *de orat.* 1. 48. 212. In *pro Murena*, 9. 19, Cicero praising Servius
(rather ironically) describes the lot of the jurists: 'Servius hic nobiscum hanc
urbanam militiam respondendi, scribendi, cavendi plenam sollicitudinis ac
stomachi secutus est, ius civile didicit, multum vigilavit, laboravit, praesto
multis fuit . . .' See most recently on the meaning of the word *cavere*, Cancelli,
'Per una revisione del *cavere* dei giureconsulti republicani', *Studi Volterra* v
(Milan, 1972), pp. 611 ff.

[6] In a sense one can regard the jurists' participation in framing *formulae* and
edicta as *cavere*.

[7] Cicero, *de orat.* 1. 58. 246.   [8] *de re rust.* 2. 3. 5.

[9] Cicero, *de leg.* 2. 20. 50; 2. 21. 53: cf. Watson, *Succession*, pp. 6 f.

[10] Cf. Watson, *Succession*, p. 115.

[11] D. 46. 4. 18. 1. This was still used in the time of Justinian.

[12] D. 28. 2. 29pr. (Scaevola 6 *quaest.*). This was still standard centuries later.

in potestate, the other not. The text shows that even at the end of the Republic leading jurists were still very interested in problems of drafting.[1]

In the time of Plautus it was still usual for educated men to appear in court for friends and relatives,[2] and frequently these *patroni* would be jurists. But in the course of the second century B.C. the art of oratory developed in Rome[3] and the *oratores*, specially trained in rhetoric, gradually drove the amateurs, including the jurists, from the floor of the court. None the less, Cicero still lists acting in court among the qualities of *iurisconsulti*.

Cato the Censor whose merits as a jurist are well known, is listed as one of the first Roman orators by Cicero, who claims to have read more than 150 of his orations and praises his simple but sophisticated style.[4] Among the other great jurists of that century who conducted actions Cicero mentions Publius Scaevola, Manius Manilius,[5] and Publius Rutilius.[6] The last, he says, appeared in many private actions but had no reputation as a great orator; his speeches are unadorned, with many splendid passages on points of law.

The great Quintus Mucius Scaevola argued at least one case in court, the famous *causa Curiana* of between 93 and 91 B.C.[7]

[1] Daube has called attention to one consequence of this interest: 'Slightly Different', *IURA* 12 (1961), 81 ff. A text structure is found in which the first part of the answer deals with a hypothetical term very similar to that under consideration but just different enough to require a different answer; and the second part gives the proper answer. The structure died out around the end of the Republic when the great jurists ceased to concern themselves with *cavere*.

[2] Cf. Plautus, *Cas.* 563 ff.; *Epid.* 462; *Tri.* 651; Terence, *Eun.* 335 ff. Scipio Africanus when he was eighteen (i.e. around 167 B.C.) told Polybius he was regarded as a quiet, lazy man without the energy of a Roman because he did not choose to speak in the law courts: Polybius 31. 23. 11; cf. 31. 29. 10.
The practice is much older, and Dionysius of Halicarnassus claims that Romulus assigned to *patroni* the duty of bringing law suits for their *clientes* and assisting them in court; 2. 9 f.

[3] Cicero is at pains to stress the lateness (and difficulty) of the art of oratory: in Greece, *Brutus*, 7. 26 ff.; at Rome, 14. 53. On early Roman rhetoric see now Kennedy, *The Art of Rhetoric in the Roman World* (Princeton, 1972), pp. 3 ff.

[4] *Brutus*, 17. 65 ff.; cf. Marrou, *A History of Education in Antiquity*, 3rd edit. translated by Ward (London, 1956), p. 244. For Cato as an orator see now Kennedy, *Rhetoric*, pp. 38 ff.

[5] *Brutus*, 28. 108.   [6] *Brutus*, 29. 110; 30. 113 ff.

[7] Cicero, *Brutus*, 52. 194 ff.; *de orat.* 1. 39. 180; 2. 32. 141; *de inven.* 2. 42. 122; *pro Caecina*, 18. 53. On this see now Watson, *Succession*, pp. 94 ff., and the authorities cited.

Cicero describes him as 'the best orator among the jurists',[1] and there is a hint that he also argued other suits.[2] Servius Sulpicius was a trained orator,[3] but he preferred law to oratory[4] and was reluctant to argue a case in court. We possess no evidence that Aquillius Gallus, Cascellius, Ofilius, Trebatius, or Alfenus ever acted as orators.[5]

The gulf between the jurists and the orators is well stressed by Schulz:

As a rule the jurisconsults were not masters of the higher flights of rhetoric and had no desire to become such, the truth being that they were not at ease in the unscrupulous atmosphere of Hellenistic forensic rhetoric. Faithful to the pontifical tradition they were not mere partisans, ready to forward a client's cause by any and every available means, including falsehood, calumny, and emotional appeals, but guardians and promoters of the law. To this tradition they were resolved to be true, and fortunate it was for Roman legal science that they stood fast and refused to suffer the noisome weed of rhetoric, which choked so much else that was fine and precious, to invade their profession. The history of Greek law demonstrates that Hellenistic forensic rhetoric was incapable of producing a legal science. As of the philosopher, so of the Roman jurisconsult, it may be said that he despised words and sought truth with a single mind: *res spectatur, non verba penduntur*.[6]

And at another place:

Rhetoric is a theory of advocacy, not of law; it arms its pupils against every eventuality, and thus equally to defend or to attack literal interpretation. It may be that rhetoricians were mostly opposed to literalness, but that was due not to rhetoric but to Hellenistic individualism. If it suited his client, a rhetorician was equally ready to plead for the letter of the law. What other purpose was served by the above-mentioned school exercises? Hence an orator makes no scruple '*eadem de re alias aliud defendere*'. The result was that the Roman jurists found nothing worth learning in rhetoric. They were not interested in how best to argue for or against the letter, which is a rhetorical question, but in the legal question how far it might be right and proper to depart from the letter.[7]

---

[1] Cicero, *Brutus*, 39. 145.   [2] In Cicero, *Brutus*, 30. 115; 42. 155.
[3] Cicero, *Brutus*, 41. 151.   [4] Cicero, *Brutus*, 41. 151; 42. 155.
[5] On the whole topic of oratorical activity by the Republican jurists see above all, Schulz, *Legal Science*, pp. 53 ff.
[6] *Legal Science*, pp. 54 f.   [7] *Legal Science*, pp. 76 f.

There were no law schools in Republican Rome but the *iuris-consulti* made themselves responsible for training the young. Since Cicero describes his own legal education we know the procedure:

When I had assumed the *toga virilis* I was taken by my father to Scaevola[1] with the intention that, so far as I was able and he would permit, I would never leave the old man's side. And so I committed to memory many points skilfully expounded by him and also many of his brief and well-expressed opinions. I studied to become more learned through his legal skill. After his death I took myself to Scaevola, the pontiff,[2] whom I dare to declare the outstanding man of our state both in ability and justice.[3] In order to study the civil law I paid much attention to Quintus Scaevola, the son of Quintus, who although he did not devote himself to teaching anyone, none the less by the replies he gave to those asking his opinion taught those who were anxious to hear him.[4]

Thus it appears that the young man went to live with his master and would go with him everywhere: he would hear his consultations with magistrates, judges, orators, and people with personal legal problems. He would, no doubt, be told stories of famous jurists of his master's own young days.[5] Cicero heard, for instance, from Scaevola,[6] that only the first three books of Brutus' *de iure civili* were written by that jurist.[7] Obviously Quintus Mucius did not give any formal teaching, but possibly other jurists may have done so.[8] We can be reasonably sure, however, that legal books written by the master—like Quintus Mucius' *ius civile*—would be studied by the student. The training, therefore, would be mainly practical and basically unsystematic. From what we know otherwise about the jurists we can conjecture that very little was said about the philosophy of law, but in view of the interest in the

[1] Quintus Mucius Scaevola, the augur, consul of 117 B.C.
[2] Quintus Mucius Scaevola, consul of 95 B.C.   [3] *de amic.* 1. 1.
[4] *Brutus*, 89. 306.
[5] Cicero describes Quintus Mucius the augur as *ioculator senex*, 'a jokey old man': *ad Att.* 4. 16. 3.
[6] He is not further described, but Scaevola the augur seems the more reasonable guess.
[7] *de orat.* 2. 55. 224.
[8] Though teaching, in general, was rather despised.

XII Tables there may have been considerable discussion of Roman legal history.

This method of training depended entirely on personal contact, and even by itself would be enough to account for the fact that the leading jurists of the Republic were all very much from the upper classes.[1] We may be surprised, though, that such great legal development could be due to a few jurists chosen from such a small section of the population.

Cicero was not the sole pupil of Quintus Mucius. We know that his lifelong friend, Pomponius Atticus, was also with that jurist at the same time.[2] According to the later jurist, Pomponius (who had learnt the fact from Servius), Quintus Mucius had several *auditores*, including Aquillius Gallus, Lucilius Balbus, Sextus Papirius, and Gaius (Titus?) Iuventius.[3] Servius learned from several jurists, was taught by Lucilius Balbus, and was above all instructed by Aquillius Gallus.[4] In his turn Servius had many distinguished *auditores*: Pomponius lists Alfenus Varus, Aulus Ofilius, Titus Caesius, Aufidius Tucca, Aufidius Namusa, Flavius Priscus, Gaius Ateius, Pacuvius Antistius Labeo, Cinna, and Publicius (Publius?) Gellius.[5, 6]

In helping the magistrates develop the law, advising them, judges, orators, and individuals with legal problems, drafting,

---

[1] Cf. above all, Kunkel, *Herkunft*, especially pp. 41 ff. Whether individual jurists or a majority of the influential jurists were of senatorial or equestrian rank would not have much effect on the development of private law, since for private law the interests of these classes did not conflict. Sometimes the narrow political affiliation of a jurist might affect his opinion in a particular case (cf. Wieacker, 'Die römischen Juristen in der politischen Gesellschaft des zweiten vorchristlichen Jahrhunderts', *Sein und Werden im Recht: Festgabe für von Lübtow* (Berlin, 1970), pp. 183 ff.) but would not determine his general viewpoint. The sources do not disclose a bias in interpreting in favour of the wealthy and well-connected, except possibly for Valerius Maximus 7. 8. 4. There a brother was passed over in his brother's will and the insult to him—relevant for the *querella inofficiosi testamenti*—was apparently regarded as aggravated because the *heredes scripti* were *humiles*. But the jurists appear to have been unsympathetic towards slaves: cf. Watson, 'Morality, Slavery and the Jurists in the Later Roman Republic', *Tulane Law Review* 42 (1968), 289 ff.

[2] *de leg.* 1. 4. 13. [3] D. 1. 2. 2. 42.

[4] D. 1. 2. 2. 43.

[5] D. 1. 2. 2. 44. And see now Casavola, '*Auditores Servii*', *Atti del secondo congresso della società italiana di storia del diritto*, i (Florence, 1971), pp. 153 ff.

[6] Cicero also seems to have had pupils (in rhetoric): Quintilian, *inst. orat.* 12. 11. 6.

appearing in court and in training the next generation, the Roman jurists showed both how they interpreted the law themselves and how they felt the law should be interpreted. They wrote books which illustrated their ideas about law. Interpretation and juristic books are the subject of the next few chapters.

8

THE XII TABLES IN THE
LATER REPUBLIC

WRITING in the Empire, the jurist Pomponius declared that the *ius civile* began to flow from the XII Tables and that the *legis actiones* were devised in accordance with them.[1] In our own period Cicero could write that if anyone looked to the origins and fundamentals of the laws, the little book of the XII Tables surpassed the libraries of all the philosophers in both weight of authority and richness of usefulness.[2]

Around 200 B.C. the law of Rome was still soundly based on the old code of the mid-fifth century, though there had been major modifications. Intermarriage between plebeian and patrician had been permitted by the *lex Canuleia* of 445, *nexum* disappeared as a result of the *lex Poetilia* perhaps in 313,[3] damage to property was regulated by the *lex Aquilia* of 287. Rather twisted interpretation of some of the code's provisions had produced *fiducia*[4] and adoption of a person *alieni iuris*.[5] The consensual contracts of sale, hire, and partnership had independently come into existence[6] and there was a *bonae fidei* action for *tutela*.[7] A praetorian edict had substituted flexible damages for the fixed penalties under the XII Tables for *membrum ruptum*, *os fractum*, and *iniuria*, though the substantive

---

[1] D. 1. 2. 2. 6 (*sing. enchirid.*): '. . . ex his (i.e. XII Tables) fluere coepit ius civile, ex isdem legis actiones compositae sunt.' What Pomponius understands by *ius civile* is discussed *infra*, pp. 137 f.

[2] *De oratore*, 1. 44. 195: 'Fremant omnes licet, dicam quod sentio: bibliothecas me hercule omnium philosophorum unus mihi videtur XII tabularum libellus, si quis legum fontis et capita viderit, et auctoritatis pondere et utilitatis ubertate superare.'   [3] Cf. *supra*, pp. 9 ff.

[4] For the argument see Watson, *Obligations*, pp. 172 ff.; *Private Law*, pp. 84 ff.

[5] Cf. Daube, 'Texts and Interpretations in Roman and Jewish Law', *Jewish Journal of Sociology* 3 (1961), 3 ff. at pp. 5 ff.

[6] Cf. Watson, *Obligations*, pp. 40 f., 100 f., 126.

[7] Cf. Watson, *Persons*, pp. 140 ff.

law was unchanged.[1] The new flexible procedural system *per formulas* could be used as an alternative to the *legis actio* for at least one old civil law action, the *condictio*.[2]

By the end of the Republic the situation was very different and the importance of the XII Tables in the totality of private law was much reduced. Further new concepts like *possessio* and *mandatum* had emerged, procedure *per formulas* had become more and more standard and available in more and more actions. What had been the usual form of marriage, with the woman *in manu* of her husband, virtually disappeared, to be replaced by the previously uncommon marriage *sine manu*. But the real decline in the importance of the XII Tables was caused by the growth of the praetor's Edict. Remedies of great importance were introduced where none had existed before: for instance, *actiones adiecticiae qualitatis, actio de dolo, actio quod metus causa, actio commodati, actio negotiorum gestorum* (which covered more than one situation). The law of succession, both testate and intestate, was profoundly modified by a number of edicts.[3] Other edicts also altered the scope of existing institutions, like *iniuria* and *depositum,* or changed the measure of damages, like that on *arbores furtim caesae.* Only in relatively few cases such as *pauperies,* the *actio finium regundorum, aqua pluvia,* and *furtum,* was no edict proposed though the *actio* itself, descending ultimately from the XII Tables, was set out in the Edict. The Edict, of course, could not abolish clauses of the XII Tables, but the new remedies of the Edict would supplant them in practice, whether because parties found them more suitable, or because praetors exerted pressure on parties to use them.

Against this background we must look at the attitudes to the XII Tables in the later Republic.

The period opens with a famous book of the consul of 198, Sextus Aelius. Only one text mentions the work.

D. 1. 2. 2. 38 (Pomponius, *sing. enchir.*) . . . Sextum Aelium etiam Ennius laudavit et extat illius liber qui inscribitur 'tripertita', qui liber

---

[1] Cf. *supra*, pp. 45 ff.

[2] Cf. now Watson, 'Some Cases of Distortion by the Past in Classical Roman Law', *TvR* 31 (1963), 69 ff.; *Private Law*, p. 127, n. 3 (against the different approach of Kaser, *ZPR*, p. 54 and n. 1).

[3] Cf. Watson, *Succession,* pp. 71 ff., 182 ff.

veluti cunabula iuris continet: tripertita autem dicitur, quoniam lege
duodecim tabularum praeposita iungitur interpretatio, deinde subtexitur
legis actio. . . .

This book is either the first or second¹ Roman law work to go
beyond simple collections of legal formulations, and Pomponius
describes it as containing, as it were, the elements of the law.² Its
title it owes to its threefold nature: first it gives the clause of the
XII Tables, secondly the interpretation of this, and thirdly the
appropriate *legis actio*. That the first or second Roman legal
treatise is on the XII Tables, two and a half centuries after their
promulgation, is eloquent evidence of the central position they
then held in legal thought. More significant still, the name,
tripertita, together with Pomponius' description of the book's
contents³—it was still extant in his time—excludes any possible
idea that it was a commentary on statutes generally. If the *lex
Canuleia, lex Aquilia*, and so on, were discussed at all it would
only be because they altered the effects of the XII Tables. This
must strengthen our belief in the importance attached to the XII
Tables around 200 B.C.

Possibly surprisingly, no treatise on the XII Tables was written
by subsequent Republican jurists,⁴ though one was by Labeo⁵ and
another by Gaius.⁶ Naturally, provisions of the XII Tables were
often discussed⁷ but, strangely, in only six surviving texts do

¹ Depending upon whether it is correct to attribute (cf. D. 1. 2. 2. 36) to
Appius Claudius Caecus, consul of 307, a book *de usurpationibus*. For the most
recent full discussion of this mysterious work see Mayer-Maly, 'Roms älteste
Juristenschrift', *Mnemosynon Bizoukides* (Thessalonike, 1960), pp. 221 ff.

² Cf. Schulz, *Legal Science*, p. 35, n. 9.

³ Discussion of the precise arrangement of the book is not needed here: but
cf., e.g., Krüger, *Geschichte der Quellen und Litteratur des römischen Rechts*, 2nd
edit. (Leipzig, 1912), p. 59 and n. 17; Schulz, *Legal Science*, p. 35 and n. 10.

⁴ Unless Servius Sulpicius wrote one, as some scholars think: e.g. Bremer,
Iurisprudentiae Antehadrianae quae supersunt, i (Leipzig, 1896), p. 228; Kübler,
RE 4A, 857.

It is also at times suggested that L. Acilius, a contemporary of Cato the Elder
(Cicero, *de amicitia*, 2. 6), wrote a commentary on the XII Tables: e.g. Bremer,
Iurisprudentiae i. 18; Kunkel, *Herkunft*, p. 10. If he did, the point which is
being made is not affected, but the evidence adduced in favour of a commentary
is not conclusive.   ⁵ For the surviving fragments see Lenel, *Pal.* i. 501.

⁶ For the surviving fragments see Lenel, *Pal.* i. 242 ff.

⁷ The total of texts involved cannot be counted, since it is not always clear
whether a text is concerned with a rule of the XII Tables or an aspect of the
institution which arose later.

Republican jurists appear actually to mention the XII Tables. Four of the texts relate to Servius and none of these concerns interpretation proper. All four are the result of the long passage of time which made an explanation of some words and phrases necessary. Thus, Servius said that in the XII Tables *pedem struit* meant *fugit*;[1] *sarcito* meant *damnum solvito* or *praestato*.[2] He seems to have explained who the *Sanates* were, also in the context of the XII Tables;[3] and to have observed that the singular *vindicia* was used as well as the plural *vindiciae*.[4] Though these texts may concern the meaning of a word or phrase they are not concerned with interpretation: no attempt is made to give a wide or narrow scope to the provision or even to define the scope. The two of these texts which most nearly approach interpretation simply give a synonym from current usage, which in its turn will require interpretation. Of the others, D. 47. 7. 1 (Paul, 9 *ad Sab.*) shows Trebatius discussing the concurrence of the *actiones ex lege Aquilia et ex duodecim tabularum* in respect of *arbores furtim caesae*, and he appears to hold that in the second action the judge will deduct from the condemnation whatever was obtained in the first action.[5] There is in the text no discussion of the meaning of the XII Tables' provision and no interpretation of the substantive law contained in it. The remaining text, Aulus Gellius, *Noctes Atticae*, 3. 2. 12, reports a view of Quintus Mucius on *trinoctium* and *usurpatio*. Thus, only this one text has a Republican jurist expressly mentioning the XII Tables and concerned with interpretation.[6]

But if we turn our attention to the extreme limits of juristic interpretation in the Republic we find (unexpressed) provisions of the XII Tables very prominent in the cases. Thus, Publius Mucius Scaevola, consul in 133 B.C., held that the *ambitus* of a house was

---

[1] Festus, s.v. *Pedem struit.*   [2] Festus, *s.v. Sarcito.*
[3] Festus, s.v. *Sanates.* Though it is not clear from the very corrupt texts—see, e.g., Lenel's reconstruction, *Pal.* ii. 334—that Servius actually expressly mentioned the XII Tables.   [4] Festus, s.v. *Vindiciae.*
[5] This part of the text is generally held to be interpolated, though the point does not affect us.
[6] In D. 40. 7. 21pr. (Pomponius, 7 *ex Plautio*) Republican jurists are shown interpreting the XII Tables, but the mention of the code—so far as the text goes—is by Pomponius.

'so far as a roof projects for the purposes of protecting a common wall, from which roof the water flows on to the house of him who did the protecting'.[1] On such an interpretation the XII Tables' provision on *ambitus* would have to be ignored in practice. The *actio finium regundorum* was strangely interpreted as applying only in the country, not also in the city.[2] Most jurists held that the *actio aquae pluviae arcendae*, which gave an action for damage caused by rain water (*aqua pluvia*), would lie if a neighbour joined channels of springs or sent in spring water dirty.[3] And Trebatius gave the same action where the damage was caused by a hot spring arising on a neighbour's land.[4] *Usus*, and with it marriage *cum manu*, virtually disappeared when the XII Tables' provision forbidding *mancipatio* of a woman's *res mancipi* without the consent of her *tutor*[5] was treated as applying to it. In the clause which allowed a man to collect his *glans* which fell on to a neighbour's land, the word *glans*, acorn, was interpreted as meaning fruit generally.[6] And in one particular situation of mis-statement in

---

[1] Cicero, *top.* 4. 24.

[2] This emerges from Cicero, *top.* 4. 23; 10. 43; D. 10. 1. 4. 10 (Paul, 23 *ad ed.*). Rodger claims that the jurists had a certain linguistic backing for their argument since the word *fines* 'was used of the country as opposed to the town': *Owners and Neighbours in Roman Law* (Oxford, 1972), p. 149.   But there seems to be a misunderstanding. The opposition (which does exist) is between the city (*urbs* or *oppidum*) and the boundaries (*fines*) of its territory, and it is irrelevant in our context. Cicero, *top.* 10. 43 itself shows that the word *fines* could properly be used of property boundaries within a town: '. . . si in urbe de finibus controversia est'.

[3] D. 39. 3. 3pr. (Ulpian, 53 *ad ed.*). Rodger asks rhetorically, 'Why ever should the jurists have allowed an action to do with rain-water where dirty spring water was sent down?': 'Roman Rain-Water', *TvR* 38 (1970), 417 ff. at p. 420. The answer is, obviously, the jurists wanted the injured party to have a remedy, and he had none unless the scope of this action was interpreted widely. Rodger also suggests that linguistically *vel si spurcam quis immittat* is bad, but the subjunctive is always very common in conditional clauses written by jurists. There is a difference in mood between *conrivat* and *immittat*, but this need suggest nothing more than a minor scribal error.

[4] D. 39. 3. 3. 1. *Pace* Rodger, 'Rain-Water', pp. 428 ff., this is still the best way to understand *aquae fluentes callidae*. He takes the phrase as meaning rain-water artificially heated. But, apart from anything else, nothing in the text tells us that the water was rain-water. Here, too, the explanation of the Roman jurist's opinion is that he wished to extend the scope of the *actio aquae pluviae arcendae* because no other remedy was available. Rodger, is, I think, unwilling to recognize this very reasonable desire.

[5] Or prohibiting the *usucapio* of such *res mancipi*.

[6] D. 18. 1. 80. 2 (Labeo, 5 *post. a Iavoleno epit.*).

a *mancipatio*, Servius excluded the *actio auctoritatis* where the damages awarded would have been very high relative to the loss sustained.[1] In all these instances involving extreme interpretation of provisions of the XII Tables, the XII Tables are in fact not mentioned. It should be further observed that about half of the cases of extreme interpretation known to us in the later Republic relate to the XII Tables; and that none of the others concerns statutes.[2,3]

All this suggests that in the late Republic, from a date after Sextus Aelius' *tripertita*, the jurists began to regard the XII Tables with some embarrassment. The code was, of course, still relevant and important. But it was also very old-fashioned and restrictive. Hence the jurists, when dealing with the law contained in it, prefer not to mention the code. Hence, too, the interpretation of it could be very free, perhaps freer than the interpretation of other statutes.

Cicero, as the quotation from him at the beginning of this chapter shows, had a very high opinion of the worth of the XII Tables. But his own writings confirm the changing attitude to the code, and an ambiguity is apparent even in his work.

In the speeches Cicero refers expressly to the XII Tables in five passages, four of which should be grouped in two pairs. In both *de domo*, 17. 43 and *pro Sestio*, 30. 65, he is concerned with the statute which caused his exile and the forfeiture of his property, and he maintains that the *leges sacratae* and the XII Tables forbid the passing of an enactment concerning an individual. Of course,

---

[1] D. 21. 2. 69. 3 (Scaevola, 3 *quaest.*).

[2] Except perhaps D. 46. 3. 67 (Marcellus, 13 *dig.*). On the foregoing paragraph see Watson, 'Juristic Decision'. Even though the sources of our knowledge are not always juristic, we can be sure that the decisions are.

[3] For another instance (of a different kind) of extreme interpretation of the XII Tables we should perhaps refer to the situation in G. 1. 165, though the interpretation in question may have occurred before our period. The interpretation of the XII Tables' words 'si aqua pluvia nocet' as 'si nocere poterit' (D. 40. 7. 21pr. (Pomponius, 7 *ex Plautio*)) may, but need not, imply a radical alteration of the scope of the remedy. At the least it shows a willingness to treat the apparent meaning in a cavalier fashion: cf. Watson, *Property*, p. 155. Whether Servius' opinion recorded in D. 50. 16. 237 (Gaius, 6 *ad legem XII tab.*) that two negatives permit rather than forbid, was expressed with regard to the XII Tables cannot be ascertained. That opinion, too, might have involved deliberate misinterpretation.

such enactments both for and against individuals were extremely common,[1] and their validity was never in doubt. Cicero's rhetorical point, very thinly disguised, is really about the immorality—not the illegality—of the statute against him. Hence he summons in aid the ancient *leges sacratae* and the XII Tables. This linking is very significant for our present investigation; they are all cited for their moral authority,[2] not for their legal effectiveness.

The third passage is *pro Milone*, 3. 9, where Cicero is defending Milo after his followers have killed Clodius in a brawl on the Via Appia. Cicero argues that if the XII Tables permitted a thief by night to be killed in any circumstances, a thief by day if he defended himself with a weapon, then who can think punishment should follow any killing, no matter what the circumstances were? The killing of a thief is, of course, not what Milo is accused of, and Cicero brings in the XII Tables by analogy, once again for their general moral authority. The use made of them becomes even more apparent when we look at the other passage of the pair, *pro Tullio*, 20. 47–22. 51. This time Cicero is replying to an opposing orator who used the very same provisions of the XII Tables on the killing of thieves in exactly the same way as Cicero himself did in the *pro Milone*, and who also recited the enactment from the *leges sacratae* which ordered that a person who struck a tribune of the plebs should be killed with impunity. Slaves belonging to Cicero's client, M. Tullius, had been killed. In § 48 he maintains that the provisions quoted by his opponent have no relevance for the case under discussion. From § 49 to § 51 he argues skilfully, misleadingly, and disingenuously, against the rhetorical point being made by his opponent, and in § 51 produces a further provision of the XII Tables, 'Si telum manu fugit magis quam iecit', to show that that code did regard killing as a very serious matter. The passage from the *pro Tullio*, put in conjunction with *pro Milone*, 3. 9, suggests it was a commonplace for counsel for the defence—and not just Cicero—to bring forward the XII Tables' provisions on the killing of thieves. This, on the one hand, tends to strengthen the belief in

---

[1] As even a quick glance at Rotondi, *Leges*, would show.

[2] Cf. Cicero, *de leg.* 2. 7. 18 where the XII Tables and *leges sacratae* are again linked.

I

the moral authority of the XII Tables, yet, on the other, might indicate that less thought went into their use or legal meaning. Cicero's opponent, moreover, had called in aid rhetorically not only the XII Tables but also a *lex sacrata*, just as did Cicero himself in the first pair of texts. Again this brings out the moral authority of the code, and the respect due to it.

The fifth text is *Philippica*, II. 28. 69. Mark Antony after riotous excesses has, according to Cicero, reformed and has divorced his *uxor mima*:[1] 'illam suam suas res sibi habere iussit, ex duodecim tabulis clavis ademit, exegit.' Thus, Cicero tells us, all the formalities were rigorously observed, including those demanded by the XII Tables.[2] But he is being ironic and farcical. Antony and his female mime never were married! This time the XII Tables are mentioned to achieve a comic solemnity. No question of the meaning of the provision is involved and on any serious level the XII Tables are completely irrelevant.

There are, however, passages in Cicero's speeches where he is, for one reason or another, concerned with the interpretation of the XII Tables but then he never mentions the code. Three instances are particularly noteworthy. In *pro Caecina*, 19. 54, he says that statute commands prescription of land and the seller's liability to be for two years, but that the same legal principle is used in respect of houses which are not mentioned in the statute.[3] The statute, which is not named, is the XII Tables.[4] Here he is using the provision and its interpretation as an argument for wide interpretation of the *interdictum de vi armata*. *Pro Murena*, 12. 27, shows him arguing that many clear statutory provisions have been perverted and distorted by the ingenuity of jurists. His first example is that 'Our ancestors wished all women, because of their

---

[1] She is so described in *Phil.* II. 8. 20.

[2] For the XII Tables' provision on divorce see, e.g., Watson, 'The Divorce of Carvilius Ruga', *TvR* 33 (1965), 38 ff., especially at pp. 42 f. Söllner rightly calls attention to two fragments of Titinius (in Nonius 306. 29 and 232. 20) overlooked in that article: *Zur Vorgeschichte und Funktion der actio rei uxoriae* (Cologne, 1969), p. 67, n. 16. But despite what he says, the texts do not conflict with my arguments.

[3] 'Lex usum et auctoritatem fundi iubet esse biennium; at utimur eodem iure in aedibus, quae in lege non appellantur.'

[4] Cf. G. 2. 42, 54.

lack of judgement, to be in the power of tutors, but the jurists discovered kinds of tutors who are in the power of women.'[1] The
unnamed (now perverted) statute issued by the respected *maiores*
must be the XII Tables, which contained a provision on *tutela
mulierum*.[2] In *pro Flacco*, 34. 84, arguing that a certain woman had
not been *in manu* of her husband, he reveals how the XII Tables'
provision on the usucapion of a woman's *res mancipi* was mis-
interpreted by the jurists to apply to the *usus* of the woman herself.[3]
But nothing appears in the text about any statute, far less the XII
Tables.

We can only conclude from these passages[4] that it would not
have been helpful to Cicero's case to mention that the interpretation related to the XII Tables: that is why he refers instead to 'a
statute' or 'our ancestors' or to nothing at all. This would suggest
first that there was no clear argument from the interpretation of the
XII Tables to the interpretation of other statutes, etc.,[5] that interpretation of the XII Tables was regarded as different and in fact
rather free;[6] secondly that on points of practical law the worth of
the XII Tables was suspect.

From Cicero's speeches it seems to emerge, therefore, that in
the courts the moral authority of the XII Tables was high but
their legal relevance to the modern world was considered doubtful.
It was no longer fashionable to argue by analogy from the XII
Tables: Cicero's idea that law is thought of as coming from the
Edict, not the XII Tables,[7] is an accurate reflection of legal
opinion.

Before we look at what can be learned from Cicero's rhetorical
and philosophical writings[8] about his own attitude to the XII

---

[1] 'Mulieres omnis propter infirmitatem consili maiores in tutorum potestate
esse voluerunt; hi invenerunt genera tutorum quae potestate mulierum continerentur.'

[2] This appears from G. 1. 144, 145.

[3] Cf. above all, Watson, *Persons*, pp. 21 ff.

[4] And to a lesser extent from other passages in which the XII Tables might
have been mentioned but were not: e.g. *de har. resp.* 7. 14; *pro Caecina*, 7. 19.

[5] This point relates specifically to *pro Caecina*, 19. 54, and *pro Murena*, 12. 27.

[6] This emerges especially from *pro Flacco*, 34. 84.

[7] Cf. *supra*, p. 31.

[8] Nothing significant for contemporary attitudes to the XII Tables emerges
from his letters.

Tables we should turn to the very special information contained in *de legibus*, 2. 23. 59. 'Nostis, quae sequuntur; discebamus enim pueri duodecim ut carmen necessarium; quas iam nemo discit.' Thus, when Cicero (who was born in 106 B.C.) and Atticus (born in 110) were boys in school, the XII Tables had to be learned by heart,[1] but no one learned them when *de legibus* was written. (Cicero had started that dialogue by 52 B.C. but he was still working on it in 46 B.C.[2]) No testimony could be more eloquent on the decline of the prestige of the XII Tables. If they were overvalued when they had to be learnt compulsorily or were taught as part of Roman tradition, all the more thoroughly and swiftly would reaction against them set in when schoolmasters took a different attitude. Revealing in another way for the decline is a subsequent part of the same text where Cicero tells us that older interpreters of the XII Tables, Sextus Aelius and Lucius Acilius, admitted they did not really understand a particular provision.[3] Even when modernized in wording, the XII Tables could fail to be of use because they were no longer comprehensible. In the same dialogue Cicero illustrates the extent of the decline. Atticus is made to say that people used to think that the science of law, *iuris disciplina*, was to be drawn from the XII Tables, but now most people say it is from the praetor's Edict.[4]

Elsewhere in his philosophical and rhetorical writings Cicero gives us what must be regarded as his own opinion of the XII Tables. In so far as he was writing for a public we can also be sure that he, as a politician, did not expect his views to be regarded as old-fashioned nonsense.[5] He expresses himself in the most laudatory terms, as we have already seen from *de oratore*, 1. 44. 195.[6] In authority and usefulness with regard to the origins of law,

[1] Cf. *de leg.* 2. 4. 9.

[2] Cf., e.g., Philippson, *RE* 7A, 1117 ff.

[3] '"Mulieres genas ne radunto neve lessum funeris ergo habento." Hoc veteres interpretes Sex. Aelius, L. Acilius non satis se intellegere dixerunt, sed suspicari vestimenti aliquod genus funebris, L. Aelius lessum quasi lugubrem eiulationem, ut vox ipsa significat.' Lucius Acilius was probably a contemporary of Cato the Elder: Cicero, *de amicitia*, 2. 6.

[4] 1. 5. 17: discussed, *supra*, p. 61.

[5] But he expects some contradiction (from the jurists?), though 'Fremant omnes licet' is a rhetorical exaggeration; *de orat.* 1. 44. 195.

[6] Quoted, *supra*, p. 111, n. 2.

the XII Tables, he claims, are worth more than the writings of all the philosophers; elsewhere, particular provisions are praised as being in accordance with nature;[1] others as excellent.[2] An orator is flattered; his ability is such that he could make 'Uti lingua nuncupassit' seem not a clause of the XII Tables, but a teacher's verse.[3] The code's provision prohibiting usucapion of a five-foot strip along boundaries is amusingly used as authority for not allowing Zeno to acquire complete rights to the Academy, for having three arbiters instead of one for fixing such boundaries, and for seeking and following the boundaries established by Socrates.[4] Respect for the XII Tables is inherent in the humour.

In many other places, too, Cicero draws illustrations from the XII Tables and usually he refers to them by name.[5]

These writings suggest, I submit, that the educated non-juristic population regarded the XII Tables with general approval. This need not mean that they would wish them applied in the courts, but the provisions were respected, not only for their antiquity and their Roman-ness, but also for their usefulness, which was still apparent.

To sum up. It seems that in the late Republic attitudes to the XII Tables were complex and in a state of flux. Around 200 B.C. jurists regarded the code very highly even though they admitted that not all its provisions could be understood with certainty. By the late second century and in the first century B.C. the jurists were embarrassed by the antiquity of the code; they preferred not to mention it even when they discussed its provisions; and they tended to interpret it with more freedom than was possibly allowable for other statutes. Orators in court would grandiosely refer to the XII Tables for their moral authority but were conscious of the jurists' hesitations, and did not like to argue too

---

[1] *de leg.* 2. 24. 61: 'Haec habemus in duodecim sane secundum naturam, quae norma legis est.' Cf. *de leg.* 2. 23. 59–25. 62.

[2] 'Praeclarissimae': *de leg.* 3. 19. 44. See, too, *de re pub.* 4. 10. 12 (in Augustine, *de civ. Dei*, 2. 9) where a provision is praised and misunderstood; it must refer to witchcraft, not defamation: cf. Jolowicz and Nicholas, *Introduction*, p. 171.

[3] *de orat.* 1. 57. 245.   [4] *de leg.* 1. 21. 55.

[5] *de off.* 1. 12. 37; 3. 15. 61; *de leg.* 1. 22. 57; 2. 23. 58–25. 64; 3. 8. 19; *Tusc. disp.* 2. 23. 55; 3. 5. 11; 4. 2. 4. The XII Tables are not mentioned in *top.* 2. 10; 4. 23, 24; 10. 43; 16. 64; *de orat.* 1. 56. 237.

openly from interpretation of the code to interpretation of other provisions. Educated laymen regarded the code with general, if imprecise, approval.

It remains to mention that by the beginning of the first century B.C. at the latest, the tradition of even the modernized wording of the XII Tables was no longer secure. This is difficult to prove in detail since the surviving sources for the XII Tables do not go back beyond that time, but it emerges clearly none the less from Cicero, *de inventione*, 2. 50. 148.[1] He quotes as one clause: 'Si paterfamilias intestato moritur, familia pecuniaque eius agnatum gentiliumque esto.' But the provision must rather have run something like: 'Si intestato moritur cui suus heres nec escit, adgnatus proximus familiam habeto. Si adgnatus nec escit, gentiles familiam habento.'[2] Again, his 'Paterfamilias uti super familia pecuniaque sua legassit, ita ius esto' cannot be correct, whether one prefers Gaius'[3] 'Uti legassit suae rei, ita ius esto' or Ulpian's[4] 'Uti legassit super pecunia tutelave suae rei, ita ius esto.'

[1] Cf. *Rhet. ad Herenn.* 1. 13. 23.   [2] Cf. *FIRA* i. 38 f.
[3] G. 2. 224.   [4] *Epit. Ulp.* 11. 14.

9

INTERPRETATION

To a modern observer from the British Isles the most striking thing about Republican interpretation is how similar it is to twentieth-century interpretation. It is very difficult to find any principles for the interpretation of English statutes other than 'the mischief rule' and 'the golden rule';[1] it seems impossible to find any for Roman statutes. Rather more principles are discernible for the interpretation of wills in both English and Roman law, and these are remarkably similar in the two systems. Moreover, general standards of interpretation are very much alike in Republican Rome and modern England. Most Republican decisions occasion no surprise. The few which do, whether because they appear excessively wide or excessively narrow, can be paralleled in English law. In this chapter, of course, we are leaving aside the special case of the XII Tables, which, because the code was so old yet so fundamental, tended to be treated in a different way from other statutes and documents.

To look first at the principles of interpretation which appear in wills. By far the most important was that the presumed intention of the testator was to be followed.[2] But this could not stand unqualified. Thus Servius admitted that one should look at the notion of the testator, in which category he put the things under discussion;[3] but if he considered to be in one category things which,

---

[1] Here I am using 'principles' loosely in distinction from 'rules' of interpretation, such as that male includes female, singular includes plural.

[2] D. 33. 10. 7. 2 (Celsus, 19 *dig.*); 34. 2. 32. 1 (Paul, 2 *ad Vitellium*); 34. 2. 33 (Pomponius, 4 *ad Quintum Mucium*); 33. 7. 16. 2 (Alfenus, 2 *dig. a Paulo epit.*). See also the texts on the *causa Curiana*: Cicero, *de orat.* 1. 39. 180; 2. 32. 141; *de inven.* 2. 42. 122; *Brutus*, 52. 194–53. 198; *top.* 10. 42; *pro Caecina*, 18. 53.

[3] D. 33. 10. 7. 2: 'Servius fatetur sententiam eius qui legaverit aspici oportere, in quam rationem ea solitus sit referre.' My own comment, *Succession*, p. 86, 'Servius admitted that the intention of the testator had to be examined in order to see the category in which he placed the object in question', is rather misleading.

without doubt, belonged in another, then the things were not
included in a legacy of the first category, 'for the meaning of words
ought to be established by common usage, not by the judgments
of individuals'.[1] Hence, if a person who considered silver tableware
or woollen cloaks or togas as furniture left a legacy of 'furniture',
Servius did not consider that these things were included in the
legacy. Tubero said he was of a different opinion, 'for what is the
point of names unless they show the intention of the speaker?'[2]
Many scholars have seen in this difference of opinion between
Servius and Tubero the influence of Greek philosophical ideas.
But the dispute is easily explicable without the hypothesis of
influence from specific philosophical doctrines,[3] and, as Horak has
made clear, Servius' argument from *usus communis* is hardly that
of Greek linguistic philosophy but is untechnical and unphilo-
sophic, even if it betrays Servius' education in Stoic–eclectic
dialectic. Tubero's opinion is certainly not in accord with Stoic
philosophy, even though the jurist himself is said by Pomponius[4]
to have studied Stoicism. Horak concludes, indeed, that the jurists
were very conscious that their decisions were of practical significance.[5] That the view of Servius was widely held appears from
D. 33. 10. 10 (Iavolenus, 3 *ex post. Labeonis*). A person who was
accustomed to enter into his accounts as 'furniture' all clothing
and things of many kinds, left a legacy of 'furniture' to his wife,
and both Ofilius and Cascellius denied that clothing was included
in the legacy. The contrasting view of Tubero, however, appears
again in D. 34. 2. 32. 1 (Paul, 2 *ad Vitellium*) where the same jurist
would hold that whatever the testator considered as gold work[6]
would be included in a legacy of *aurum factum*.[7]

[1] 'Non enim ex opinionibus singulorum, sed ex communi usu nomina ex-
audiri debere.'
[2] 'Nam quorsum nomina, inquit, nisi ut demonstrarent voluntatem dicentis?'
Pace Watson, loc. cit., the following part of the text—at least as the text now
stands—is not to be attributed to Tubero but to Celsus. For the correct approach
see Horak, *Rationes*, i. 228 f., who considers something may have been cut out
after *dicentis*.
[3] Cf. already Watson, *Succession*, p. 86, n. 1.
[4] D. 1. 2. 2. 40 (*sing. enchiridii*).   [5] *Rationes*, i. 227 ff.
[6] The text here has *aurum*, not *aurum factum*, but the context makes it clear
that Tubero is thinking of *aurum factum*.
[7] It is not clear, but is unimportant, whether *alioquin* to the end also gives the

To elucidate the testator's intention, Alfenus at least was prepared to look at facts known to the testator. Thus, unlike most of
his contemporaries, he did not regard slaves or animals as *instrumentum* for a legacy of a *fundus cum instrumento*,[1] yet in a case
where a testator who lived on a farm left a legacy to his wife of the
fundus, uti instructus est, and the question arose whether the female
weavers were contained in *instrumentum*, Alfenus replied that they
were, indeed, not part of the *instrumentum fundi*, yet since the
testator had lived on that farm it could not be doubted that the
slave women and other things with which the *pater familias* was
equipped on the farm were legated. There is, of course, an illogicality here on Alfenus' part, but the emphasis on the fact that the
testator himself lived on the farm shows that Alfenus' main concern was to follow the presumed intention of the testator. This
illogicality of Alfenus is actually diminished, since his view that
slaves are not part of the *instrumentum* is a minority one: Alfenus
is attempting to discover the testator's intention and it is reasonable
for him to assume that the testator was using words in the sense
acceptable to most jurists.

Likewise one could look to facts known about the testator.
Quintus Mucius declared he knew a senator who wore women's
dinner dresses, and that if this senator left a legacy of 'women's
clothing' he could not be considered to have intended those which
he himself wore as if they were men's.[2]

When a clause was ambiguous, it was permissible to attempt to
interpret it in conjunction with other clauses of the will.[3] When
a bequest was specific, a false reason for it had no effect. Thus
a legacy of as much as the 50 coins which a wife brought her

thought of Tubero. The opinion of Gallus recorded in the text does not really
concern us.

Of course, what was regarded as falling within a specific category, such as
furniture, might vary from age to age: D. 33. 10. 3. 5 (Paul, 4 *ad Sab.*); cf., e.g.,
Watson, *Succession*, p. 141.

[1] For Alfenus, D. 33. 7. 12. 2 (Ulpian, 20 *ad Sab.*); for other jurists, D. 33. 7.
12pr., 1, 3, 5, 6; 33. 7. 4 (Iavolenus, 2 *ex post. Labeonis*).

[2] D. 34. 2. 33 (Pomponius, 4 *ad Quintum Mucium*); cf. Watson, *Succession*,
p. 88, n. 2; most recently on the text, Astolfi, 'Abiti maschili e femminili', *Labeo*,
17 (1971), 33 ff.

[3] D. 28. 5. 79 (78). 1 (Papinian, 6 *resp.*); 32. 100. 1 (Iavolenus, 2 *ex post.
Labeonis*); cf. Watson, *Succession*, pp. 89 f.

husband as dowry was valid for the 50 according to Servius, though the dowry had been only 40.[1] Likewise Ofilius, Cascellius, and the pupils of Servius held that *quanta pecunia dotis nomine pro ea quinquaginta heres dato*, was a valid legacy even when the wife had had no dowry.[2] Similarly when a husband who had not received an estate as dowry left to his wife the *fundum Cornelianum, quem illa mihi doti dedit*, Ofilius and Trebatius held the legacy was valid, 'quia cum fundus Cornelianus in rerum natura sit, demonstratio falsa legatum non peremit.'[3]

We have evidence that for both Quintus Mucius and Alfenus anything so written that it could not be understood was to be treated *pro non scripto*.[4] A legacy of something which could not exist was void; hence there could be no legacy of '100 *modii* of wheat, which weighs 100 pounds for each pound.'[5]

Despite the foregoing, it must be stressed that the best guide to the testator's intention is the wording of the will. Hence, for instance—as in English law—close attention is paid to the use of tenses. A legacy to a wife of the gold which has been procured, *paratum est*, for her, means the gold which the husband has (for her) at the time he makes the will, and subsequent alienations do not diminish the amount of the legacy. But if the legacy is of the gold which will have been acquired, *paratum erit*, for her, then this will relate only to the gold which the testator had at the time of his death.[6]

Strangely, but perhaps coincidentally, a large proportion of the cases of extremely wide interpretation concern interdicts.[7,8] Thus, the *interdictum quod vi aut clam*[9] read: 'Quod vi aut clam factum

---

[1] D. 33. 4. 6pr. (Labeo, 2 *post. a Iavoleno epit.*).   [2] D. 33. 4. 6. 1.

[3] D. 35. 1. 40. 4 (Iavolenus, 2 *ex post. Labeonis*). On the texts in nn. 1–3 see Watson, *Succession*, pp. 96 f., and the references given.

[4] D. 50. 17. 73. 3 (Quintus Mucius Scaevola, *sing.* ὅρων); 34. 8. 2 (Alfenus Varus, 5 *dig.*).

[5] D. 33. 6. 7. 1 (Iavolenus, 2 *ex post. Labeonis*).

[6] D. 34. 2. 34. 1, 2 (Pomponius, 9 *ad Quintum Mucium*); cf. Watson, *Succession*, p. 91.

[7] That is, of course, excluding the interpretation of the XII Tables; cf. *supra*, pp. 113 ff.; Watson, *Limits of Juristic Decision in the Later Roman Republic* (University of Edinburgh Inaugural Lecture no. 36, 1969).

[8] The explanation may be that interdicts are based on public policy and are not purely concerned with private rights.

[9] As reconstructed by Lenel, *EP*, pp. 482 f.

est, qua de re agitur, id, si non plus quam annus est cum experiendi potestas est, restituas.' Quintus Mucius declared that something was done by force, *vi*, when a person did it who had been told not to.[1] This would include cases where on a straightforward approach, no one would claim force had been used. Servius Sulpicius then widened the scope of *clam*, by stealth. He claimed that a person also acts *clam* who does not inform someone who he knows will object 'lest the position of fools be better than that of wise men'.[2] *Clam* normally involves deliberate secrecy, and we can presume from Servius' reason for his decision both that he was well aware of that, and that he was consciously extending the scope of the interdict. He has even changed the basis of liability: the interdict by its wording applied only to deliberate wrongdoing; Servius allows it for negligence.[3] Trebatius, in his turn, allowed the interdict even where no work had been done on the estate, where no damage had been caused and the estate had suffered no alteration: If you carried manure over my estate when I had forbidden this, you were, he said, liable to the interdict.[4]

The *interdictum de cloacis* ran:[5] 'Quo minus illi cloacam, quae ex aedibus eius in tuas pertinet, qua de agitur, purgare reficere liceat, vim fieri veto. Damni infecti quod operis vitio factum sit, caveri iubeo.' This interdict speaks of cleaning and repairing an existing sewer, but Ofilius and Trebatius interpreted it to apply also to the making of a new sewer.[6]

The damages to be awarded as a result of the *interdictum uti possidetis* were also set unexpectedly high by an interpretation of Servius. The action given by the praetor against a person who acted contrary to the interdict had a condemnation in *quanti res est*, 'whatever the matter comes to'. The classical Ulpian reasonably declares that *quanti res est* means 'the financial interest anyone

---

[1] D. 50. 17. 73. 2 (Quintus Mucius Scaevola, *sing.* ὅρων); 43. 24. 1. 5 (Ulpian, 71 *ad ed.*); cf. Watson, *Property*, pp. 222 ff.; *Juristic Decision*, p. 4; Horak, *Rationes*, i. 85, n. 4.

[2] D. 43. 24. 4 (Venuleius, 2 *interd.*).

[3] Cf. Watson, *Property*, pp. 222 ff.; *Juristic Decision*, p. 4.

[4] D. 43. 24. 22. 3 (Venuleius, 2 *interd.*); Watson, *Property*, pp. 227 f.; *Juristic Decision*, pp. 4 f.   [5] Cf. Lenel, *EP*, p. 481.

[6] D. 43. 23. 2 (Venuleius, 1 *interd.*). The text is not in perfect form: cf. Watson, *Property*, pp. 197 f.; *Juristic Decision*, p. 5; Horak, *Rationes*, i. 250.

had in retaining possession', but he also tells us that Servius held
that the value of possession was the value of the thing. Ulpian, in
fact, vigorously rejects Servius' verdict, 'for the value of a thing is
very different from the value of its possession'.[1]

Servius also in one instance at least was prepared to give a wider
interpretation of the aedilician Edict on the sale of slaves than were
other jurists. The Edict, *inter alia*, allowed the redhibition of
a slave who suffered from a *morbus* or *vitium* which was not disclosed to the buyer. Servius held that a slave who lacked a tooth
could be returned to the seller.[2]

Alfenus tells us[3] of an extremely wide interpretation of a will,
probably by Servius. The testator instituted two heirs and ordered
them to build a monument within a certain time. Then he put:
'Qui eorum non ita fecerit, omnes exheredes sunto.' One heir did
not accept the inheritance, the other built the monument, asked
about his legal position, and was told he was heir. The will was
unambiguous, and so was the intention of the testator, yet the
jurist's decision is contrary to both. The decision, moreover,
cannot be defended on legal principle. We can only conclude that
the jurist had decided what the moral verdict should be, and held
accordingly.[4]

There are, of course, also instances of unduly narrow or rigid
interpretation in the later Republic.[5] The most blatant of these is
in D. 28. 5. 70 (69) (Proculus, 2 *epist.*). A testator had written:
'Cornelius et Maevius, uter eorum volet, heres esto.' Both wished

---

[1] D. 43. 17. 3. 11 (Ulpian, 69 *ad ed.*); cf. Watson, *Property*, pp. 87 f.; *Juristic
Decision*, pp. 6 f. Rodger, who does not seem to find Servius' view extreme,
regards the violent rejection of it as an interpolation and not due to Ulpian:
'A Note on A. Cascellius', *Classical Quarterly* 22 (1972), 135 ff. at p. 136.

[2] Aulus Gellius, *N.A.* 4. 2. 12.

[3] D. 28. 5. 45 (44) (Alfenus, 5 *dig.*); cf. now Watson, 'D. 28. 5. 45 (44); an
Unprincipled Decision on a Will', *The Irish Jurist*, 3 (1968), 377 ff.; Horak,
Rationes, i. 126 f.

[4] A very wide decision, but where interpretation is kept very much in the
background, is in D. 46. 3. 67 (Marcellus, 13 *dig.*); cf. now Watson, *Juristic
Decision*, pp. 11 f. See also D. 35. 1. 40. 5 (Iavolenus, 2 *ex post. Labeonis*) and
D. 32. 30. 2 (Labeo, 2 *post. a Iavoleno epit.*); cf. Watson, *Succession*, pp. 115 f.
and 157 f.

[5] Though by no means as many as, e.g., Schulz, *Legal Science*, pp. 77 ff.,
would have us believe. See now Watson, 'Narrow, Rigid and Literal Interpretation in the Later Roman Republic', *TvR* 37 (1969), 351 ff., which also deals
with Schulz's arguments from the wording of statutes.

to be heir and Trebatius held that neither could be heir. Presumably despite the conjunctive 'Cornelius et Maevius' he was taking literally 'uter eorum volet' and 'heres esto', and so felt both could not be the heirs. Since both wanted the inheritance and a choice could not be made between them, Trebatius decided neither could be heir. This approach was not necessary, and was not followed by later jurists.[1] Another miserably narrow decision by Trebatius seems to be in D. 28. 5. 21pr. (Pomponius, 1 *ad Sab.*), where he held that 'Quisquis mihi heres erit, Stichus liber et heres esto' gave Stichus his liberty but no right to the inheritance. Presumably the testator had previously instituted an heir and then had a clause of *substitutio*, and nothing in these clauses indicated the heir was to have a coheir. Trebatius refuses to allow the present clause—appearing subsequently in the will—to restrict the right of the previously named heir to the whole estate.[2] Elsewhere the same jurist treats a legacy to a daughter of '50 until she marries' as a legacy immediately due of a single payment.[3]

Servius, in his turn, was guilty of rigid interpretation contrary to the testator's intention when he held[4] of no avail a legacy to a slave freed in the will of the '5 *aurei* which I owe him according to my account books', on the ground that a master can owe his slave nothing. *Pace* Schulz,[5] the decision does not show that *falsa demonstratio nocet*. Rather, the blatantly unjust decision simply reflects the harsh attitude towards slaves, for which we also have other evidence.[6,7]

Finally[8] we must look at the famous *causa Curiana*[9] of around 93 to 91 B.C., which is probably the case mainly responsible for the view that the Republican jurists took a rigid literal view of interpretation. A testator left a will reading something like

---

[1] Cf. on the text, Watson, *Succession*, pp. 49 f.
[2] Cf. Watson, 'Literal Interpretation', p. 363.
[3] D. 33. 1. 17pr. (Labeo, 2 *post. a Iavoleno epit.*).
[4] D. 35. 1. 40. 3 (Iavolenus, 2 *ex post. Labeonis*).   [5] *Legal Science*, p. 79.
[6] For the argument see Watson, 'Literal Interpretation', pp. 360 f.
[7] Perhaps we should include in this list the narrow interpretation of *agnatus proximus*. But here the rigid interpretation was very early, though it was not modified by the jurists: cf. Watson, 'Juristic Decision', pp. 13 f.
[8] What follows is the account of the *causa Curiana* in Watson, 'Literal Interpretation', pp. 365 f. I have nothing to add.
[9] Brutus, 39. 145.

this: 'Let my son be my heir. If my son dies before reaching puberty, let M'. Curius be my heir.' Quintus Mucius Scaevola appeared for the heirs on intestacy and argued that the will was to be interpreted literally. Curius' appointment as heir was subject to the condition 'if my son dies before puberty'. But the testator in fact never had a son, therefore, the argument goes, the son could not die before reaching puberty, so the condition failed. Quintus Mucius' opponent in court was the famous orator, Lucius Licinius Crassus (whom Cicero describes as the best jurist among the orators). He successfully based his case on the presumed intention of the testator. The testator, he claimed, wished Curius to be his heir if he had a son who died before he reached puberty, or even if he never had a son.

Much has been made by modern scholars[1] of the contrast between the liberal interpretation of the orator, Crassus, who based his case on the presumed intention of the testator, and the narrow interpretation of the jurist, Scaevola, who argued for the literal meaning of the words used. Quintus Mucius Scaevola certainly was taking a very rigid line. But the importance of this for juristic interpretation in the Republic has been seriously overestimated. First, Quintus Mucius—the greatest orator among the jurists, according to Cicero[2]—was giving his opinion in this instance not as a jurist, but as an orator. And an orator has the duty of pleading the case for his client to the best of his ability and need not be strongly convinced by the arguments he uses.[3] So Quintus Mucius' rigid interpretation in the *causa Curiana* is no sure guide to his true feelings.[4] Secondly, we do have evidence that Quintus Mucius could take a wider view and consider the intention of the testator. Thus, in D. 34. 2. 33 which has been already mentioned[5] he is undoubtedly taking into consideration the testator's presumed

---

[1] For literature and a rather atypical view see Wieacker, 'The "*causa Curiana*" and Contemporary Roman Jurisprudence', *The Irish Jurist*, 2 (1967), 151 ff.: cf. Watson, *Succession*, pp. 53 ff., 94 ff.

[2] *Brutus*, 39. 145.

[3] Cf. *Rhet. ad Herennium*, 2. 9. 13–10. 14.

[4] Gandolfi observes that some of Scaevola's statements are to be attributed to the needs of his defence rather than to his personal opinion: *Studi sull'interpretazione degli atti negoziali in diritto romano* (Milan, 1966), p. 293.

[5] See *supra*, p. 125.

intention. Again, when a legacy was left of a farm 'with its equip-
ment or with those slaves who are on it',[1] Quintus Mucius declared
that the legacy did not include a groom who had been sent to the
villa by the testator 'because he had not been sent in order to be
there'.[2,3]

Separate from interpretation in any proper sense, but akin to it
and of more fundamental importance, is the development by the
jurists of legal concepts and institutions which are not defined
or described in any *lex* or *edictum*. The process, which is also
common in other systems, is well known. The institution in
question, such as theft or the contract of sale, comes somehow
into being and will be actionable in court but its nature and
boundaries are not set out in any 'official' or binding source of law,
but what these boundaries are are known (or are presumed to be
known) by the persons engaged in the practice of the law. With
time, greater sophistication, and altered conditions, the institutions
change. It cannot surprise us that in an early code institutions are
not defined and their requirements are simply assumed: thus in
the XII Tables we are not told what constitutes *nexum*, *mancipatio*,
or *furtum*. But at Rome the same situation exists also at a much
later stage and during the period of the greatest legal sophistication. This is most clearly seen from the Praetor's Edict, and
two examples out of many will suffice.

Somehow or other the contract of sale came into existence and
became actionable without a statute and without an edict.[4] What
gave *emptio venditio* its legal standing was the model *formulae* set
out in the Praetor's Edict. For the *actio ex empto*:

Quod Aulus Agerius de Numerio Negidio hominem quo de agitur
emit, qua de re agitur, quidquid ob eam rem Numerium Negidium
Aulo Agerio dare facere oportet ex fide bona, eius iudex Numerium
Negidium Aulo Agerio condemna, si non paret, absolve.

---

[1] D. 28. 5. 35. 3 (Ulpian, 4 *disp.*).
[2] And there is also his extremely wide interpretation of the *interdictum quod
vi aut clam*: D. 50. 17. 73. 2 (*sing. ὅρων*); 43. 24. 1. 5 (Ulpian, 71 *ad ed.*).
[3] The types of argument and methods of argumentation current among the
jurists of the later Republic are not specifically dealt with in this volume. On
these matters see now above all Horak, *Rationes*, i, and the authorities he cites.
[4] Cf. *supra*, pp. 35 ff., 42 ff., 90 ff.

For the *actio ex vendito*:

Quod Aulus Agerius Numerio Negidio hominem quo de agitur vendidit, qua de re agitur, quidquid ob eam rem Numerium Negidium Aulo Agerio dare facere oportet ex fide bona, eius iudex Numerium Negidium Aulo Agerio condemna si non paret absolve.[1]

Nothing in these *formulae* discloses the radical nature of *emptio venditio* as a consensual contract; nothing shows the need for agreement, price, and a thing to be sold, and we are told nothing of the nature of these three requirements; nothing is said about the respective duties of the buyer and seller. Hence long after the introduction of the *formulae* there could be discussion by the jurists, and development of the contract without the need of any intervention of edict or statute. Hence even in the Empire there could be extended continuing debate on questions so basic as whether sale and barter could be the same contract, the effect of error on a sale, and the seller's warranties against eviction.[2]

A striking illustration of all this is afforded by the *edictum de dolo* of 66 B.C. Neither the edict itself nor the action given under it defined *dolus malus*, but the praetor responsible for the edict, Aquillius Gallus, elsewhere and presumably as a jurist, explained that he thought the *dolus* caught by it was that 'when one thing is pretended, another thing done'.[3] Gallus' contemporary, Servius, accepted this scope for the *actio de dolo*, but not much later Labeo defined *dolus* for the purpose of this action as 'any stratagem, trick, or machination used to circumvent, dupe, or ensnare another'.[4] All this means that for Gallus, the action would be available only where there had been negotiations between the parties, and hence the *actio de dolo* would be in effect a contractual action, whereas for Labeo there was no longer any need for any dealings between the parties.[5]

---

[1] These two *formulae* are Lenel's reconstruction of those in the Hadrianic Edict: *EP*, p. 299. It may well be that the *formulae* were not in that form throughout the whole of the period which interests us, but that should not affect the present issue.

[2] It is a great pity that there is no direct evidence for the Roman conception of *emptio venditio* at the time the *formulae* were introduced.

[3] Cicero, *de nat. deor.* 3. 30. 74.

[4] D. 4. 3. 1. 2 (Ulpian, 11 *ad ed.*).

[5] Cf. Watson, *Obligations*, pp. 259 f.

Many other similar instances could be given. It was this habit of drafting which leads Schulz—wrongheadedly I feel—to dismiss the Hadrianic Edict as a 'short booklet'.[1] Whether this habit also prevailed in our period (as it did earlier) in the drafting of *leges* on private law cannot really be determined, since in no case do we have the full wording of any such statute which would be informative. But I doubt very much whether the *lex Cincia* of 204 explained what counted as a gift.

---

[1] *Principles of Roman Law* (Oxford, 1936), p. 12: cf. *supra*, p. 62, n. 1.

10

BOOK PRODUCTION:
THE SECOND CENTURY B.C.

ONE of the greatest services of the jurists to legal development was the production of books which made their views, and those of their colleagues, available both to a wider circle of contemporaries and to their successors. Unfortunately none of these Republican books has survived, though fragments of some are preserved in the Digest or are cited in that compilation or in other writings. It is quite likely that some important legal books were written of whose very existence we are completely unaware.

So far as we can tell, the beginning of the period covered by this book marked the start of a new era. For earlier times we hear of only three legal books. A century before, Appius Claudius, consul of 307 and 296, is said by Pomponius to have written a book *de usurpationibus*,[1] which Pomponius tells us was not extant in his time. The very existence of such a work is doubted by some modern scholars, and its subject-matter (if it existed) cannot, I think, be established.[2] The other two early juristic works recorded are collections of the forms of the *legis actiones*: the *ius civile Flavianum* issued by Gnaeus Flavius, Claudius' *scriba*, not later than 304;[3] and the *ius Aelianum* of a few years later.[4,5] But a work

[1] D. 1. 2. 2. 36 (*sing. enchirid.*).
[2] The last extended discussion (with full citation of literature) is by Mayer-Maly, 'Roms älteste Juristenschrift', *Mnemosynon Bizoukides* (Thessalonike, 1960), pp. 221 ff.; cf. Wieacker, 'Die römischen Juristen in der politischen Gesellschaft des zweiten vorchristlichen Jahrhunderts', *Sein und Werken im Recht, Festgabe von Lübtow* (Berlin, 1970), pp. 183 ff. at p. 187 and n. 27.
[3] For the sources see *supra*, p. 3, n. 2.
[4] Cf. Watson, '*Ius Aelianum* and *tripertita*', *Labeo*, 19 (1973), 26 ff. The author was not Sextus Aelius Paetus Catus.
[5] Perhaps we should also mention the *ius civile Papirianum*, the collection of the *leges regiae* said to have been made by Gaius Papirius at the beginning of the Republic or very end of the monarchy. On this see now Watson, 'Roman Private Law and the *Leges Regiae*', *JRS* 62 (1972), 100 ff. at p. 104.

of an entirely new kind was written by Sextus Aelius Paetus Catus who was consul in 198 and censor in 194. This book was called the *tripertita* and was still extant in the time of Pomponius, who alone mentions it.[1] He describes it as containing, as it were, the *cunabula iuris*, and he declares that it received its name because the *lex duodecim tabularum* was written out, the *interpretatio* was then joined to it, and the *legis actio* was set out underneath.

The text of Pomponius does not give a very clear picture of the *tripertita*. Whether his choice of phrase *cunabula iuris* should be translated as 'the elements of law'[2] or 'the beginnings of law'[3] probably cannot be determined, but does not seem important for our understanding of the nature of the book. But Pomponius does at least show that the arrangement was by division into individual clause of the XII Tables, its interpretation and action, next clause, interpretation, action, and so on; and that the *tripertita* was not a work in three parts, first the whole of the XII Tables, then the interpretation of all the clauses, and finally all the relevant *legis actiones*. This emerges clearly from his use of the singular in 'deinde subtexitur legis actio',[4] which can only mean that the relevant form of action was given beneath the appropriate clause and its interpretation. One may perhaps doubt Pomponius' accuracy, but he does say that the *tripertita* was extant in his day. This is, moreover, by far the more practical arrangement. No argument can be drawn from the name. The word *tripertita* may be feminine singular, and if so it is presumably an adjective agreeing with *lex duodecim tabularum*, but equally well could be a neuter plural, either a noun, or an adjective qualifying some word such as *commentaria*.

The book dealt only with the XII Tables, not also with other existing statutes.[5] This, of course, emphasizes the central position held at that time in legal thought by the XII Tables. But it also

---

[1] D. 1. 2. 2. 38. The relevant part of the text is quoted, *supra*, pp. 112 f.

[2] So Schulz, *Legal Science*, p. 35, n. 9.

[3] So Bretone, *Tecniche e ideologie dei giuristi romani* (Naples, 1971), p. 126, n. 3 at p. 127.

[4] His previous singulars, *lege duodecim tabularum* and *interpretatio*, may properly be regarded as ambiguous, and so should not be relied on.

[5] Cf. *supra*, p. 113.

shows the characteristic Roman interest in their own early history.[1]

A few texts may contain references to the *tripertita*[2] but none casts further light on the book, except perhaps Cicero, *de leg.* 2. 23. 59. This tells us that for the clause, 'Mulieres genas ne radunto neve lessum funeris ergo habento', Sextus Aelius (and Lucius Acilius)[3] admitted uncertainty as to the meaning of *lessum* but suggested it was some sort of mourning garment. This shows that Aelius was prepared to comment even on obsolete clauses of the XII Tables—if the clause had been in use the meaning of *lessum* would not have been forgotten—and on clauses which were not concerned with what we would regard as private law. Thus, it is likely that Sextus Aelius passed on to later generations all that was known in his time of the provisions of the code.[4]

Sextus Aelius was a member of a plebeian *nobilis* family. He himself is the first jurist known to us who did not hold a priestly office, but his father was a *pontifex* and his brother Publius Aelius Paetus, also a jurist of distinction, was an *augur*.[5] The particular respect in which Sextus Aelius was held is shown in his nickname Catus.[6]

Cato the Censor and more particularly his son who died when

[1] Wieacker, 'Juristen', p. 192, sees in Aelius' historical and grammatical explanations of the XII Tables the result of Hellenistic education. But the choice of subject is as Roman as are *imagines* of ancestors.

[2] D. 19. 1. 38. 1 (Celsus, 8 *dig.*); 33. 9. 3. 9 (Ulpian, 22 *ad Sab.*); Cicero, *ad fam.* 7. 22; *de leg.* 2. 23. 59; Aulus Gellius, *N.A.* 4. 1. 20.

[3] That in this text Cicero names L. Acilius along with Sextus Aelius, and describes them both as 'veteres interpretes', is not proof that Acilius also wrote a commentary on the XII Tables, though, e.g., Schulz, *Legal Science*, p. 90, claims that he did. Cf. *supra*, p. 120.

[4] It is, in fact, reasonable to suppose that the *tripertita* was one of the main sources of the later Roman tradition of the wording of the clauses: cf., e.g., Wieacker, 'Die XII Tafeln in ihrem Jahrhundert', *Les Origines de la république romaine. Entretiens sur l'antiquité classique*, xiii (Fondation Hardt, Vandoeuvres-Geneva, 1967), pp. 293 ff. at p. 295.

[5] Cf., e.g., Schulz, *Legal Science*, pp. 10 f.; Kunkel, *Herkunft*, pp. 8 f.; Wieacker, 'Juristen', pp. 192 f.; D'ippolito, 'Sextus Aelius "Catus"', *Labeo* 17 (1971), 271 ff.

[6] He was also described as 'egregie cordatus homo' by Ennius. Cf. Cicero, *de re pub.* 1. 18. 30; *Tusc. disp.* 1. 9. 18; Varro, *de ling. lat.* 7. 46. The choice of 'Catus' suggests he was regarded as very Roman, and one might contrast it with 'Sophus' which was given to Sempronius; D. 1. 2. 2. 37: cf. Wieacker, 'Juristen', p. 192, n. 55.

praetor designatus in 152 both wrote legal books,[1] but the few remaining citations[2] cannot be attributed to one or the other.[3] One work extended to at least fifteen books.[4] Cicero tells us that in the books of Cato and Brutus the person, man or woman, to whom the jurist gave advice is actually named.[5] The elder Cato was an *augur* as well as being consul in 195 and censor in 184.[6]

After mentioning the two Catos, Pomponius lists a famous trio:[7]

Post hos fuerunt PUBLIUS MUCIUS et BRUTUS et MANILIUS, qui fundaverunt ius civile. ex his Publius Mucius etiam decem libellos reliquit, Brutus septem, Manilius tres: et extant volumina scripta Manilii monumenta. illi duo consulares fuerunt, Brutus praetorius, Publius autem Mucius etiam pontifex maximus.

Publius Mucius, Brutus, and Manilius are said to 'have laid the foundations of the civil law'. Pomponius' meaning here can probably never be recovered with certainty. Previously in § 5 Pomponius made it clear that although *ius civile* had a general sense he also used the term to designate juristic interpretation, and it seems most likely that *ius civile* in § 39 carries this narrower meaning.[8] Of course, juristic interpretation had existed long before, and it seems safe to say only that Pomponius regarded the trio as 'the first of the moderns'. A more precise understanding of Pomponius' meaning cannot be achieved.[9] We can, of course, ask why these

---

[1] D. 1. 2. 2. 38.

[2] See the texts collected by Bremer, *Iurisprudentiae* i. 19 ff.; Lenel, *Pal.* i. 125 f.

[3] For the elder Cato see now Wieacker, 'Juristen', pp. 193 f.

[4] D. 45. 1. 4. 1 (Paul, 12 *ad Sab.*).

[5] *de orat.* 2. 33. 142: 'Video enim in Catonis et in Bruti libris nominatim fere referri, quid alicui de iure viro aut mulieri responderit.' This, of course, does not justify Schulz's statement that Cicero tells us that the commentaries of Cato and Brutus contained their *responsa* 'word for word'.

[6] Cf. Kunkel, *Herkunft*, p. 9.   [7] D. 1. 2. 2. 39.

[8] Cf. Bretone, *Tecniche*, pp. 166 f. Since it would appear impossible that Pomponius could claim Publius Scaevola, Brutus, and Manilius had laid the foundations of Roman law!

[9] But attempts to explain Pomponius may in fact help us to understand the trio. Thus it has been suggested that they were the first who scientifically defended their opinions; or that it was their activity which furnished the basis for the *ius civile* of Quintus Mucius Scaevola: cf. references given by Krüger, *Geschichte der Quellen und Litteratur des römischen Rechts*, 2nd edit. (Munich, Leipzig, 1912), p. 60, n. 28. Karlowa suggests that they worked through the

three were grouped together, and we can attempt to discover what contribution they made to legal development.

First of all, it should be noticed how often the opinions—contrasting or not—of all three of these jurists, or of two of them, appear together in other texts. Thus, Cicero has: 'An partus ancillae sitne in fructu habendus, disseretur inter principes civitatis, P. Scae volam, M'que Manilium ab hisque M. Brutus dissentiet . . .'[1] Aulus Gellius, 'Sed Q. Scaevola patrem suum et Brutum et Manilium, viros adprime doctos, quaesisse ait dubitasseque, utrumne in post facta modo furta lex [i.e. Atinia] valeret an etiam in ante facta.'[2] Again Cicero: 'Itaque etsi domum bene potus seroque redieram, tamen id caput, ubi haec controversia est, notavi et descriptum tibi misi, ut scires id, quod tu neminem sensisse dicebas, Sex. Aelium, M'. Manilium, M. Brutum sensisse. Ego tamen Scaevolae et Testae adsentior',[3] though the Scaevola referred to here is perhaps more likely to be Quintus Mucius Scaevola, the consul of 95.[4] Ulpian reports 'Celsus quoque libro octavo digestorum refert Mucium Brutum Labeonem quod Sabinum existimare':[5] Paul has 'ceterum quod Brutus et Manilius putant . . . non est verum';[6] and Modestinus tells us, 'inter Brutum et Scaevolam varie tractatum est.'[7] Every one of these citations refers to a different legal situation or case.

In proportion to the surviving material these three jurists, or at least two of them, are cited more often together than any other

---

whole *ius civile* in a case-law manner and by means of this rich casuistic laid the foundations for later jurisprudence. For Bretone, 'fundaverunt ius civile' means that they made juristic opinion ('interpretatio') autonomous: contrast the link between the XII Tables and the *tripertita*. He says 'L'*interpretatio* si rende autonoma rispetto al dato normativo della legge, lo attrae dentro di sé e si costituisce secondo una sua intrinseca razionalità': *Tecniche*, p. 169. See now also Bretone, '*Publius Mucius et Brutus et Manilius qui fundaverunt ius civile*, (D. 1. 2. 2. 39)', *Atti del secondo congresso internazionale della società italiana di storia del diritto*, i (Florence, 1971), pp. 103 ff.

[1] *de fin.* 1. 4. 12. *M'que* seems the best reconstruction of the text.
[2] *N. A.* 17. 7. 3.   [3] *ad fam.* 7. 22.
[4] The view of Aelius, Manilius, and Brutus may represent an earlier stage of development than that of Trebatius and Scaevola.
[5] D. 18. 2. 13pr.   [6] D. 41. 2. 3. 3.
[7] D. 49. 15. 4. The case under discussion is probably that of the consul L. Hostilius Mancinus, and hence the Mucius involved would be Publius Mucius: cf., e.g., Watson, *Persons*, pp. 245 ff.; Wieacker, 'Juristen', pp. 204 ff.

group or pair of Republican jurists. They were linked in people's minds. Yet none is obviously a pupil or follower of another. Clearly they often gave their opinions on the same legal problem but—unlike the *pontifices*—as individuals and not as a team. This behaviour[1] would, of necessity, demand that they give arguments[2] for their opinions and would sharpen people's—especially other jurists'—awareness of legal reasoning.

Moreover, the surviving sources show them concerned with live issues, with problems not always too closely attached to the XII Tables or other statutes. Whatever general commentaries they may have written on *ius civile*, they are remembered most for their views on particular knotty points: whether the child of a slave girl who had been given in usufruct belonged to the usufructuary or the girl's owner;[3] the effect of a clause of *in diem addictio* where two of the sellers wished to accept a subsequent offer but the third did not;[4] whether someone who usucapted land also usucapted treasure in the land which he did not know was there;[5] whether the *lex Atinia* was of retroactive effect;[6] whether an heir could sue for a *furtum ante factum*;[7] whether a Roman who returned after having been surrendered to the enemy and who was not accepted by the Romans was a citizen;[8] the severity of the damages for *furtum*;[9] the availability of the *actio legis Aquiliae* when a slave woman was struck and aborted;[10] the proper formulation of warranties against eviction and latent defects in sale;[11] the

---

[1] Too much precision should not be demanded on how and in what circumstances they expressed these opinions.

[2] See Aulus Gellius, *N.A.* 17. 7. 3. But they would not be the first jurists to give reasons; cf. Cato in D. 45. 1. 4. 1 (Paul, 12 *ad Sab.*). Legal argument will always have been prominent in court actions, though there the possibility of true juristic differences will have been obscured by partisanship.

[3] Cicero, *de fin.* 1. 4. 12; D. 7. 1. 68 (Ulpian, 17 *ad Sab.*).

[4] D. 18. 2. 11. 2; *h.t.* 13pr. (Ulpian, 18 *ad Sab.*).

[5] D. 41. 2. 3. 3 (Paul, 54 *ad ed.*).

[6] Aulus Gellius, *N.A.* 17. 7. 3.

[7] Cicero, *ad fam.* 7. 22. The exact situation envisaged is not wholly clear: cf. now Watson, *Obligations*, pp. 228 f.

[8] D. 49. 15. 4 (Modestinus, 3 *reg.*). See also D. 50. 7. 18 (17) (Pomponius, 37 *ad Quintum Mucium*), which prima facie seems to concern a rather different but very similar situation.

[9] Aulus Gellius, *N.A.* 6. 15. 1.

[10] D. 9. 2. 27. 22 (Ulpian, 18 *ad ed.*).

[11] Varro, *de re rust.* 2. 3. 5; 2. 5. 11; 2. 7. 6; cf. also 2. 4. 5.

meaning of *ambitus*;[1] and the return of *res dotales* to Licinia.[2,3] Their reputation, therefore, was very different from that of, say, Sextus Aelius Catus, which rested on his commentary on the XII Tables.[4]

Moreover, Manilius was responsible for an exciting new kind of legal book which one might describe as generalized cautelary jurisprudence.[5] It contained a discussion of clauses in contracts of sale and would seem to have recommended the particular clause which should be demanded to fit the particular circumstances; for instance the warranty against latent defects to be taken when buying goats was to differ from that taken when buying cattle.[6] It was therefore not limited to an account of the legal effect of a clause; though it will also have explained the actions which could be brought on the clause and their consequences. The argument for this latter point is simply that Varro seems to call the book something like *actiones*.[7] Cicero apparently calls the same work the *venalium vendendorum leges*.[8,9] It continued to be used until the end of the Republic,[10] and may have provided the inspiration for other collections of forms of *stipulationes* and actions which we learn of from Cicero.[11]

Brutus is the earliest jurist of whom it is expressly said that he published books on the *ius civile*, but we cannot be certain that this was a continuous, comprehensive, and orderly commentary.

[1] Cicero, *top.* 4. 24. Though this concerned the interpretation of a clause of the XII Tables, Mucius' attitude was remote from antiquarianism; cf. *supra*, pp. 114 f.

[2] D. 24. 3. 66pr. (Iavolenus, 6 *ex post. Labeonis*).

[3] The relationship of these opinions to the books of these three jurists probably cannot be determined, but the opinions, to survive, must have been written down.

[4] Hence succeeding generations would view him with mainly antiquarian interest.

[5] Though Schulz links this type with the collections made in the archaic period: *Legal Science*, p. 90.

[6] Varro, *de re rust.* 2. 3. 5; 2. 5. 11.   [7] *de re rust.* 2. 5. 11; 2. 7. 6.

[8] *de orat.* 1. 58. 246. Given the notorious variation of book titles in the ancient world there is no reason to think Varro and Cicero are not referring to the same book.

[9] Manilius' explanation of *nexum* was also probably in this book: Varro, *de ling. lat.* 6. 105.

[10] This appears from Varro, *de re rust.* 2. 3. 5; 2. 5. 11; 2. 7. 6; Cicero, *de orat.* 1. 58. 246.   [11] *de leg.* 1. 4. 14.

Indeed, Cicero, who is our source, might seem rather to imply that the books in question were three separate works, possibly on different subjects: 'noster hic [i.e. Crassus] facetissime tris patris Bruti de iure civili libellos tribus legendos dedit';[1] and elsewhere, 'tris ipse excitavit recitatores cum singulis libellis, quos M. Brutus, pater illius accusatoris de iure civili reliquit.'[2] The opening words of each book have been preserved by Cicero: 'Forte evenit, ut ruri in Privernati essemus ego et Brutus filius'; 'In Albano eramus ego et Brutus filius'; and 'In Tiburti forte cum adsedissemus ego et Brutus filius'.[3] These openings justify the belief that the books had the form of a dialogue and hence, probably, that they were elementary in character.[4,5] They would seem to have been well known even in Cicero's time.[6] Cicero had heard from Scaevola that only these three were authentic books of Brutus.[7] This statement has cast doubt on the accuracy of D. 1. 2. 2. 39, and it has been suggested by some scholars that 'Brutus septem, Manilius tres' is a scribal error for 'Manilius septem, Brutus tres'.[8] But the passage of Cicero indicates that even in his day Brutus was credited with more than three books:[9] so we must hold *non liquet*. Nothing more can be said with confidence about the nature of the books of the trio; neither about the ten *libelli* of Publius Mucius nor the *volumina scripta monumenta*[10] of Manilius.

---

[1] *de orat.* 2. 55. 223.   [2] *pro Cluentio*, 51. 141.

[3] *pro Cluentio*, 51. 141; *de orat.* 2. 55. 224 (with minor variations).

[4] Cf. Schulz, *Legal Science*, pp. 93 f.

[5] But we cannot conclude from the similarities of structure of the volumes that they were a continuous comprehensive commentary, or formed part of the same work.

[6] *pro Cluentio*, 51. 141, 'quae vobis nota esse arbitror': cf. Schulz, *Legal Science*, p. 94.

[7] *de orat.* 2. 55. 224, 'tot enim, ut audivi Scaevolam dicere, sunt veri Bruti libri.'

[8] *Pace* Bretone, *Tecniche*, p. 163, n. 2, we can draw no argument from 'illi duo consulares fuerunt', though the phrase refers to Publius Mucius and Manilius. Where two persons who have previously been mentioned are referred to as *hic* and *ille*, *ille* does normally—but not always—refer to the first and *hic* to the second. But in a more complicated case such as that in our text there is no reason why 'illi duo' should relate to the first and second, rather than first and third. It simply means 'these two'; and which two is clear.

[9] Cf. Bremer, *Iurisprudentiae* i. 41. Schulz conjectures that the last four books were a collection of *responsa* by Brutus which was posthumously annexed to the three books of dialogue: *Legal Science*, p. 92.

[10] There have been suspicions here too of scribal error.

The blind C. Livius Drusus, son of the consul of 147 and brother of the consul of 112,[1] is also reported to have written legal books, but of what type we cannot tell.[2]

[1] Cf. Kunkel, *Herkunft*, p. 14.
[2] Valerius Maximus 8. 7. 4: cf. Bremer, *Iurisprudentiae* i. 27.

11

BOOK PRODUCTION:
QUINTUS MUCIUS SCAEVOLA

PERHAPS the most celebrated of the Republican jurists was Quintus Mucius Scaevola who was consul in 95 B.C. and also held the office of *pontifex maximus*. Of him Pomponius writes (D. 1. 2. 2. 41 (*sing. enchirid.*)): 'Post hos QUINTUS MUCIUS Publii filius pontifex maximus ius civile primus constituit generatim in libros decem et octo redigendo.' Whatever precisely this may mean, a first implication is that Mucius' arrangement was of some importance for the ordering of future accounts of the *ius civile*, and we must try to recover Quintus Mucius' scheme.

I would reconstruct the subject-matter of the 18 books as follows:

1. *De testamentis*
2. *de legatis*
3. *de legatis*
4. *de legatis*+*de legitima hereditate*
5. [   ]
6. [?   ][1]+*de servitutibus*+*de stipulationibus*+*de tutela*
7. *de pauperie et de lege Aquilia*+*de statuliberis*+[   ]
8. *de his qui alieni iuris sunt*+standards and extent of liability+*de adquirendo rerum dominio*
9. *de possessione et de usucapione*
10. *de usucapione*
11. *?de condictione?*+[?   ]
12. [   ]+*de emptione venditione*
13. *de servitutibus*+*de contractibus earum personarum quae in aliena potestate sunt*+[   ]

---

[1] The sign [   ] means that an unknown topic was dealt with; [?   ] that an unknown topic was probably but not certainly dealt with.

14. *de societate*
15. *de postliminio*
16. *de furto*
17. [   ]
18. [   ]

No fragments have survived. The factors which make feasible an attempt to reconstruct the arrangement are, first, a very few texts which tell us in which book Quintus Mucius made a particular statement: these reveal where Mucius dealt with *legata*, *societas*, and *furtum*. Secondly, there is a number of texts which refer to or even quote Mucius and which seem to be referable to his *ius civile*. These provide an indication that a topic was dealt with somewhere. Thirdly, we have over a hundred fragments from Pomponius' commentary *ad Quintum Mucium* which was in thirty-nine books. It is reasonable to suppose—in the absence of counter-indications—that the order follows that of Quintus Mucius himself. There is even some positive support for this in the placing in Pomponius of the accounts of *legata*, *societas*, and *furtum*. But it would be unreasonable to assume that the same relative proportion of space would necessarily be devoted to each topic in Pomponius' thirty-nine books as in Quintus Mucius' eighteen. Obsolescence of some subjects, the growing importance and development of others in the two and a half centuries which separate these jurists, and, possibly, Pomponius' own interests, might lead to some distortion in our picture from Pomponius of the length of discussion in Quintus Mucius. From this commentary, considered in conjunction with the other texts which refer to Mucius, we can also form some idea of topics which were not discussed in Mucius' *ius civile*.[1] Fourthly, we can to a large extent reconstruct the arrangement of Sabinus' commentary on the *ius civile*, especially from Pomponius *ad Sabinum*. Though the arrangement is by no means identical with that of Quintus Mucius, Sabinus was certainly influenced to some extent by Mucius, and the ordering of topics in Sabinus may at times provide a useful check. Moreover, if

[1] For the need for caution in arguing from Pomponius *ad Quintum Mucium* see Lenel, 'Das Sabinussystem', *Festgabe für Ihering* (Strassburg, 1892), pp. 1 ff. at pp. 11 f.

topics which seem to have been omitted from Quintus Mucius
are omitted from Sabinus we have some confirmation that the
topics were, indeed, not dealt with by Quintus Mucius in his
18 books.[1]

I have stressed that we may discover topics not dealt with by
Quintus Mucius. Where such can be established we shall be spared
the mistake of finding a place for them in the eighteen books.
Moreover, we may be able to explain why they were not discussed,
and this can help to explain the inclusion of other topics, to confirm
the apparent arrangement, and to uncover the thought behind the
arrangement.

The first fixed point is that Quintus Mucius dealt with *legata*
in book 2.[2] We can therefore be sure that book 1 was concerned
with *testamenta*,[3] especially since in Pomponius *ad Quintum Mucium*
books 1, 2, and part of 3 related to testaments. Pomponius *ad
Quintum Mucium* devotes the rest of book 3, and books 4 to 9,
to legacies. Hence, since we also know that the Republican jurists
were particularly interested in questions of testate succession, we
can be confident that Quintus Mucius' own book 3 and (at least)
part of book 4 further dealt with *legata*. Pomponius' book 10 seems
to discuss the *legitima hereditas*,[4] and it is very reasonable to think
that Quintus Mucius also dealt with this subject after *legata*,
hence most likely in book 4 or possibly at the beginning of book 5.

The second fixed point is *societas*, which was dealt with by
Quintus Mucius in book 14.[5] This corresponds to books 35 and 36
in Pomponius.[6] Pomponius dealt with *emptio venditio* in book 31,
so it is reasonable to fix Quintus Mucius' treatment of sale around
book 12. Immediately after book 31 Pomponius dealt either with
servitutes or *aqua*—exactly which need not concern us at this

---

[1] For two other possible, but minor, sources of information see *infra*, p. 158
and n. 1.

[2] D. 32. 55pr. (Ulpian, 25 *ad Sab.*); 33. 9. 3pr. (Ulpian, 22 *ad Sab.*); 34. 2.
27pr. (Ulpian, 44 *ad Sab.*): cf. Lenel, *Pal.* i. 757 f.

[3] There is no reason why one topic must finish neatly at the end of a book, and
the next begin the following book, but for the sake of clarity and simplicity such
an assumption will usually be made here.

[4] There is room for some doubt: cf. Lenel, *Pal.* ii. 69.

[5] D. 17. 2. 30 (Paul, 6 *ad Sab.*).

[6] Though again there may be some doubt: cf. Lenel, *Pal.* ii. 76 f.

moment—not with the remaining two consensual contracts, *locatio conductio* and *mandatum*. Indeed, it seems that Pomponius *ad Quintum Mucium* (and hence Quintus Mucius' *ius civile*) did not deal with *locatio conductio* or *mandatum* at all. The argument for this is that there is not the slightest sign of a discussion of either of these consensual contracts anywhere in Pomponius *ad Quintum Mucium* and that it is extremely difficult to see where he could have placed any such discussion. Confirmation is to be found in the well-known fact that Sabinus' *ius civile* also did not deal with *locatio conductio* or *mandatum*. If a jurist of Sabinus' stature omitted such important contracts[1] from a commentary on the *ius civile* which was greatly influenced by Quintus Mucius' *ius civile*, then in the absence of contrary evidence it becomes very unlikely that Quintus Mucius, writing about a century earlier, included them.[2] Lenel thought, on the basis of D. 17. 1. 48 (Celsus, 7 *dig*.), that Quintus Mucius did deal somewhere with *mandatum*,[3] and it was presumably this text which led Schulz rather to the same conclusion. But the text is concerned with personal security[4] and hence would be at least as appropriate—and probably more appropriate—in the context of verbal obligations. In the great commentaries of Pomponius, Paul, and Ulpian *ad Sabinum*, personal security is discussed under the heading of verbal obligations.[5]

---

[1] The reason for the omission is discussed *infra*, pp. 147, 152 ff.

[2] A fine example of the difficulties which arise if one thinks Quintus Mucius did deal with *mandatum* appears in Schulz, *Legal Science*. He suggests (p. 95) that Mucius dealt with *locatio conductio* after sale, and that *mandatum* may have been discussed after *societas*. He accepts that Sabinus did not deal with *locatio* or *mandatum* (p. 158) and he says (pp. 156 f.): 'But he (i.e. Sabinus) left un-examined important topics which a comprehensive treatise of the time of Tiberius ought not to have passed over. Of the real contracts none, of the consensual only sale and partnership, were dealt with. No rational explanation of these omissions can be given, and it is out of the question that Sabinus him-self should have published as a systematic work anything so fragmentary. Obviously what we are dealing with is not such a work, but a collection of lecture-notes made by the famous professor for his pupils and first published after his death. It may be that he had not yet worked out his scheme in all its parts, or again, that many of his notes were not forthcoming, when the posthumous publication was prepared.'   [3] *Pal.* i. 762.

[4] The verb in the text as it now stands is *fideiubere*, but this would be originally *spondere* or *fidepromittere*: cf., e.g., Watson, *Obligations*, pp. 152 f.

[5] Cf. Lenel, *Pal.* i. 1283; *Pal.* ii. 136, 1183 ff.

This omission from Quintus Mucius of *locatio conductio* and *mandatum* plus the separation between the book dealing with *emptio* and that dealing with *societas* is very significant, because it indicates that these last two institutions were dealt with not simply because they existed as consensual contracts. *Societas* appears because of the old *ercto non cito*, *emptio* because of its strong connection with *mancipatio*. This explains why *emptio* in Pomponius, 31 *ad Quintum Mucium* is followed in book 32 by a discussion either on *aqua* or more generally on *servitutes*. Which it is is not wholly clear. Lenel suggests with some hesitation that the book was *de aqua*,[1] which would fit at least three of the four texts. I would rather hold that the subject-matter was servitudes, since this would fit these three texts and also the fourth, D. 8. 2. 29. But whether *de aqua* or *de servitutibus*, the subject is dealt with there because of the importance of *mancipatio* in the creation of these rights. In Quintus Mucius' *ius civile*, therefore, *emptio* in book 12 would be followed by *servitutes* in book 13. But since *servitutes* takes up only one book in Pomponius *ad Quintum Mucium* and there are two further books before *societas* is discussed in that work, only part of Quintus Mucius' book 13 would relate to servitudes.

The third fixed point is that Quintus Mucius discussed *furtum* in book 16,[2] which corresponds to book 38 of Pomponius *ad Quintum Mucium*. Since in that work Pomponius dealt with *postliminium* in book 37 immediately after *societas* in book 36, and before *furtum*, we are entitled to conclude that *postliminium*— which we know was discussed by Quintus Mucius[3]—was treated in book 15.

According to Lenel,[4] Pomponius dealt in book 23 with *possessio* and *usucapio*, and in books 24 to 27 with *usucapio*. We would not be far wrong in arguing from this that Quintus Mucius' *ius civile* devoted book 9 to *possessio* and *usucapio*

---

[1] *Pal.* ii. 76.

[2] Aulus Gellius, *N.A.* 6. 15. 2.

[3] D. 50. 7. 18 (17) (Pomponius, 37 *ad Quintum Mucium*); 49. 15. 4 (Modestinus, 3 *reg.*); Cicero, *top.* 8. 37. Oddly, Schulz uses the first of these texts to argue that Quintus Mucius dealt with *iniuria* immediately before *furtum*.

[4] *Pal.* ii. 72 ff.

and book 10 to *usucapio*: this is the place corresponding to Pomponius' books 23 to 27, the complexities of *possessio* and *usucapio* require fairly extensive treatment, and we have confirmation from four texts that Quintus Mucius did discuss these subjects.[1]

Though Lenel comes to no conclusion as to the subject-matter of the immediately preceding book, 22, of Pomponius, and suggests hesitatingly that it may have been on *dos* or *operae servorum et libertorum*, we can be reasonably confident that it was in fact on the acquisition of ownership. To begin with, Sabinus in his commentary on the *ius civile* dealt with *de adquirendo rerum dominio* just before *possessio* and *usucapio* (with possibly the *rei vindicatio* coming between).[2] Secondly, of the three texts which have survived from book 22, one relates to *fructuum perceptio* (after a gift between husband and wife),[3] another to acquisition of ownership through a slave given in usufruct and through a slave *nobis bona fide serviens*.[4] The third text, on the *deminutio et augmentum et mutatio* of *obligationes operarum*,[5] could easily find its way—by attraction or as an explanation or comparison—into a book on acquisition of ownership. Pomponius' book 22 would correspond not to a whole book but to the final part of Quintus Mucius' book 8.

Lenel states that he would not dare make any conjecture as to the subject-matter of Pomponius, 21 *ad Quintum Mucium*,[6] but it seems to be the same as that of the part of Pomponius, 29 *ad Sabinum* which Lenel hesitatingly heads *de iudiciis*.[7] And in their respective works both these books occupy the same position, coming immediately before *de adquirendo rerum dominio*. The subject-matter, I submit, is not a particular legal institution but standards and extent of liability. This is obviously both the main point of interest and the connecting link between four[8] of the five texts in Pomponius, 21 *ad Quintum Mucium*. The remaining text, D. 47. 2. 76, tells us that the *actio furti* does not lie against a *falsus*

---

[1] D. 8. 2. 7 (Pomponius, 26 *ad Quintum Mucium*); 41. 2. 3. 23 (Paul, 54 *ad ed.*); 41. 2. 25. 2 (Pomponius, 23 *ad Quintum Mucium*); Aulus Gellius, *N.A.* 17. 7. 1–3.

[2] Cf. Lenel, *Pal.* i. 1287 f.; ii. 138 ff.   [3] D. 22. 1. 45.
[4] D. 45. 3. 39.   [5] D. 38. 1. 34.   [6] *Pal.* ii. 71.
[7] *Pal.* ii. 137.   [8] D. 3. 5. 10; 13. 6. 23; 6. 1. 29; 42. 1. 22.

procurator who persuaded someone to promise by *stipulatio* to himself or another person delegated by him. Jolowicz rightly explains the situation:

> *A* owes money to *X*, and *Y*, pretending to be *X*'s authorized agent, induces *A* to promise to pay what he owes *X* either to himself, *Y*, or to some other person whom *Y* mentions. If *Y* really were *X*'s agent such promise, made at the creditor's request, would release *A* by novation (Buckland, 570), but here clearly there is no release, and *A* is burdened by an additional debt. If sued on this debt *A* could of course in classical times plead *exceptio doli* so that he would not suffer, but this was probably not possible in the time of Quintus Mucius on whose work Pomponius was commenting, and it had perhaps been suggested as a way out of the difficulty that such trickery could be construed as theft.[1]

With this background it is easy to see how the fragment would fit into a book concerned with standards and extent of liability. Again, four of the five texts from Pomponius, 29 *ad Sabinum* which Lenel places under the heading *de iudiciis* are directly concerned with standards and extent of liability, and the fifth, D. 6. 1. 70, is capable of such explanation. To Pomponius, 21 *ad Quintum Mucium* would correspond the middle part of book 8 of Quintus Mucius' *ius civile*. To this book and subject-matter I would assign D. 13. 6. 5. 3.

Pomponius, 18 *ad Quintum Mucium* discussed *statuliberi*,[2] a topic which we know from D. 40. 7. 29. 1 (Pomponius 18 *ad Quintum Mucium*) and 40. 7. 39pr. (Iavolenus, 4 *post. Labeonis*) was also dealt with by Quintus Mucius. The part of Quintus Mucius' *ius civile* which corresponds to Pomponius' book 18 would seem to be the middle section of book 7.

Book 17 of Pomponius *ad Quintum Mucium* was probably concerned with the *lex Aquilia*.[3] This topic, too, we can be sure from D. 9. 2. 31 (Paul, 10 *ad Sab.*) and 9. 2. 39 (Pomponius, 17 *ad Quintum Mucium*), was dealt with in Mucius' *ius civile*. Mucius, we know from D. 9. 1. 1. 11 (Ulpian, 18 *ad ed.*), also discussed the *actio de pauperie* and it seems reasonable to think that these two

---

[1] *Digest XLVII. 2, de furtis* (Cambridge, 1940), p. 112.
[2] Cf. Lenel, *Pal.* ii. 70.
[3] Cf. Lenel, loc. cit., who has some hesitation.

topics were treated one after the other,[1] therefore in the first part of book 7 of the *ius civile*.

Quintus Mucius dealt with *tutela* somewhere, as D. 26. 1. 3pr. (Ulpian, 37 *ad Sab.*) and G. 1. 188 testify, and it seems likely that this was the subject of Pomponius' book 16.[2] Hence we would probably be justified in placing Mucius' treatment around the end of his book 6.

Pomponius' book 15 would seem to have dealt with *stipulationes*, but there is only one fragment, D. 45. 1. 112pr. There is, however, an indication in D. 17. 1. 48 (Celsus, 7 *dig.*), that Quintus Mucius discussed the subject in his *ius civile*,[3] and we may with some hesitation suggest that it occupied the middle part of Mucius' book 6 immediately before *tutela*. In sharp contrast to the apparent paucity of treatment in Mucius, it seems that Sabinus devoted considerable attention to the subject: thus, of the thirty-six books of Pomponius *ad Sabinum* four are devoted to *verborum obligationes*.

It may be that a few further conjectures as to the order of topics may reasonably be made, but each positive hypothesis from this point on is for one reason or another more open to question than those dealt with earlier.

Three texts survive from Pomponius' book 14. Two of them, D. 8. 1. 13 and D. 39. 3. 19, have servitudes as their main subject and the third, D. 41. 1. 53, would be easily understandable in that context. But Lenel hesitates to assign this book to servitudes and water rights because he attributes the discussion of water to book 32.[4] None the less, despite the fault of arrangement which it would imply, it seems right to hold that book 14 concerned servitudes. Hence Quintus Mucius will have treated this subject in book 6 of his *ius civile*, immediately before *stipulationes*.

The subject-matter of Pomponius' books 11, 12, and 13 cannot be discovered from the few surviving texts; hence we cannot recover the topics discussed in Quintus Mucius' book 5 and perhaps also at the beginning of book 6. There is no information

[1] As was commonly the case later.
[2] But certainty is impossible: cf. Lenel, *Pal.* ii. 70.
[3] Cf. *supra*, p. 146.   [4] *Pal.* ii. 69, n. 4.

on the contents of Pomponius' book 19, and so we must also leave a gap in our reconstruction of Mucius at the end of book 7.

Though there can be no certainty, the two surviving texts from Pomponius' book 20, D. 1. 7. 43 and 44. 7. 56, seem to indicate that the book was concerned with persons who are *alieni iuris*,[1] and we may conjecture that that was the subject treated at the beginning of Quintus Mucius' book 8 (or perhaps at the end of 7).

The subject of Pomponius' books 27 to 30 cannot be discovered, though perhaps 27 dealt with the *condictio*.[2] Hence we must leave blank the subject-matter of Quintus Mucius' book 11 and the beginning of 12, or with the expression of some hesitation place the treatment of *condictio* in book 11.

Pomponius' book 33 was apparently[3] devoted to contracts by persons *in aliena potestate*, so we are probably justified in supposing that this subject was treated by Quintus Mucius immediately after servitudes in book 13. There is no clue as to the contents of Pomponius' book 34, so we must allow space for an unknown subject about the end of Mucius' book 13.

The subject-matter of Pomponius' book 39 is not at all clear,[4] and the contents of Mucius' two final books, 17 and 18, are a complete mystery.[5]

The most striking feature of the topics which we know were discussed in Quintus Mucius' *ius civile* is their antiquity. Thus, we know the XII Tables had specific clauses on *testamenta*,[6] *legata*,[7] *legitima hereditas*,[8] *servitutes*,[9] *stipulatio*,[10] *tutela*,[11] *pauperies*,[12] *statuliberi*,[13] *hi qui alieni iuris sunt*,[14] acquisition of ownership,[15] *usucapio*,[16] *emptio*,[17] and *furtum*.[18] *Societas* appears in Quintus

---

[1] Cf. Lenel, *Pal.* ii. 71.
[2] Suggested by the sole surviving text, D. 12. 6. 52.
[3] Cf. Lenel, *Pal.* ii. 76.
[4] Lenel suggests doubtfully *de iure praediatorio*: *Pal.* ii. 78.
[5] De Francisci's argument from Cicero, *ad fam.* 7. 22, that Scaevola's *ius civile* was divided into *capita* is not persuasive: '*Cic. ad fam.* 7. 22 e i *libri iuris civilis* di Q. Mucio Scevola', *BIDR* 5 (1963) 93 f.

[6] V. 3; VIII. 22. [7] V. 3. [8] V. 4, 5, 6, 8.
[9] VII. 1, 6, 7. [10] II. 1b. [11] V. 1, 2, 6; VIII. 20.
[12] VIII. 6. [13] VII. 12. [14] IV. 1, 2; XII. 2.
[15] VI. 6. [16] V. 2; VII. 6.

[17] In the framework of *mancipatio*, which is the reason for the positioning of *emptio*, VI. 1, 2, 3, 4, 6; VII. 11.
[18] I. 10; VIII. 12, 13, 14, 15, 16, 17.

Mucius because of *ercto non cito* which is very ancient; *possessio* because by this time there could be no proper treatment of *usucapio* without a discussion of possession. The *lex Aquilia*[1] dates from 287 B.C., and the legal concept of *postliminium* is certainly very old.[2] This leaves as known topics in Mucius, standards and extent of liability and the contracts of persons *in aliena potestate*. Both these subjects, in one context or another, would be important from the earliest times.

Some topics of private law are not evidenced at all, and we may single out as the most striking *mandatum*, *locatio conductio*, marriage, divorce, dowry, *cura*, slavery, *donatio*, *actio finium regundorum*, *damnum infectum*, *iniuria*, *actio de pastu*, *actio de arboribus succisis*, and *tignum iunctum*.[3] Some of these will have been dealt with somewhere in the *ius civile* of Mucius; others, as I have already maintained in the case of *mandatum* and *locatio*, were omitted.

At times these omissions can be established. Thus, marriage, divorce, and *cura* were not dealt with. The main argument here, apart from the silence of the sources, is again that these subjects were not discussed in Sabinus' *ius civile*,[4] which owes so much to Mucius. This is extraordinary in Sabinus, especially for marriage and divorce after the legislation of Augustus, and the explanation, at least in part, must be Sabinus' reliance on his Republican model. The reason for the exclusion is not easy to find. All three subjects were dealt with in the XII Tables.[5] It cannot be suggested that they were omitted because they had little legal significance;[6] thus apart even from other considerations, marriage still usually involved

---

[1] Which may have replaced clauses of the XII Tables: D. 9. 2. 1pr. (Ulpian, 18 *ad ed.*).

[2] Cicero, *de orat.* 1. 40. 181, shows that if a *pater familias* sold his son abroad *postliminium* did not apply. All the indications are that the right of a *pater familias* to sell his sons abroad was obsolete from a fairly early date.

[3] I have not included *aqua pluvia* in this list since there is probably enough evidence in the texts to justify the belief that it was dealt with beside *servitutes*, as in Sabinus' *ius civile*.

[4] Evidenced from the absence of these topics in the commentaries of Pomponius, Paul, and Ulpian *ad Sabinum*.

[5] Marriage in VI. 5, divorce in IV. 3, and *cura* in V. 7.

[6] Though apart from dowry—which also was not dealt with—divorce had not much legal importance.

manus,[1] the nature of *cura* was fascinating and unique and of practical importance.[2] One factor which may have had some relevance is that no specific action descending from the XII Tables was available for marriage, divorce, or *cura*. No private law action was directly given at all for marriage or divorce: the civil law action against a misbehaving *curator*, the *actio negotiorum gestorum*,[3] if it existed at all, would have been a recent innovation. That this is not the full explanation for the omission is indicated by the treatment in Quintus Mucius of *postliminium* (of early date), which also lacked a specific action.[4]

Slavery, as a particular institution, was also omitted. Again, the main argument is its absence from Sabinus' *ius civile*, as shown by the three great commentaries on that work. This time the explanation is more easily found: though slavery existed from very early times, the institution in the Republic generated very little law that was peculiar to it.[5] There is no trace of specific clauses on slavery as an institution in the XII Tables.

Totally unexpected, though, is the complete omission of *dos*. *Dos* was dealt with by Sabinus and, of the 36 books of Pomponius *ad Sabinum*, two, and a large part of a third, were dedicated to the subject. The importance and complexity of dowry were such that if Quintus Mucius had dealt with it he would presumably have had to devote considerable attention to it and some evidence is almost bound to have survived. Moreover, we can find confirmation that *dos* was not treated in its surprising omission from another work whose organization of material was also greatly influenced by Quintus Mucius' arrangement, namely Gaius' Institutes.[6]

---

[1] For the argument see Watson, *Persons*, pp. 19 ff.

[2] The interest in it is perhaps best seen in the humorous references to it in Varro, *de re rust*. 1. 2. 8, and Catullus, XLI. 5 ff. See further Watson, *Persons*, pp. 155 ff.

[3] The *bonae fidei actio negotiorum gestorum* existed by the time of Cicero: *top*. 10. 42; 17. 66. But the problems of the origins of this, and its relationship with the *edictum* and the *actio in factum*, seem insuperable. There is, in fact, no evidence for the Republic that the *actio negotiorum gestorum* could be brought against the *curator*.

[4] We must also bear in mind the apparent reluctance to reform marriage and divorce by *lex* or *edictum*, which may suggest they were not thought of as proper matters for law to deal with: cf. *supra*, pp. 95 ff., especially at pp. 99 f.

[5] Cf. Watson, *Private Law*, pp. 50 f.

[6] Schulz explains this omission, too, on the ground that either Gaius for some

The reason for Quintus Mucius' failure to discuss dowry is, I suggest, that there was no specific law on the subject until the introduction of the *actio rei uxoriae* some time after the divorce of Spurius Carvilius Ruga which was around 230 B.C.[1] Dowry as a social institution did exist, we can be sure, from early times,[2] but before the *actio rei uxoriae* any claim for its return would have been based on a *stipulatio* which was taken from the husband or his *pater familias*. There is no evidence for any clause on dowry in the XII Tables. The explanation, I submit, was that there was none!

A different reason might be suggested for some of the omissions so far observed. It might be maintained that the *actio rei uxoriae* with its condemnation in *quod eius melius aequius erit*, and the actions with a condemnation in *quidquid . . . dare facere oportet ex fide bona* for mandate, hire, and *cura*, were not yet regarded as civil law actions and hence the relevant subject-matter was appropriately excluded. But this idea—which perhaps has some weight —would not explain or justify Quintus Mucius' treatment. To begin with, he does deal with *emptio venditio* and *societas*. Though this is because the former can be tied to *mancipatio* and the latter descends from *ercto non cito*, both were in his day nothing but consensual contracts actionable by *bonae fidei iudicia* and in these respects indistinguishable from *locatio conductio* and *mandatum*. Secondly, the legal aspects of *cura* went far beyond the limits of the action against the *curator*. Thirdly, *dos recepticia*, which one might suspect to have been the most common form of dowry, in practice was independent of the *actio rei uxoriae*, and actionable because of the *stipulatio* which had been taken, and this kind of dowry could have formed the basis for discussion.

---

reason had not written up the topic in his manuscript or that this part of his lecture could not be found when it came to posthumous publication: *Legal Science*, p. 162.

Though the matter is not directly relevant to the present book (and will not be discussed), it should by now have become obvious that the whole strange problem of omissions from Sabinus' *ius civile* and Gaius' *Institutiones* cannot be properly explained without an examination of Quintus Mucius' *ius civile*, which first arranged the civil law *generatim*.

[1] Cf. now Watson, *Private Law*, pp. 26 f., and the references cited.

[2] Dionysius of Halicarnassus 2. 10. 2 implies the existence of dowry in the time of Romulus.

Which of the remaining topics of private law which are not
evidenced for Quintus Mucius were dealt with by him or were not
dealt with cannot be determined. I would, however, suggest that
either *iniuria* was not discussed at all or it received very short
treatment. This was the case in Sabinus' *ius civile*: *iniuria* does not
appear in the remaining fragments of Pomponius *ad Sabinum*, and
it occupies only a small part of Paul's book 10 *ad Sabinum* and of
Ulpian's 42 *ad Sabinum*. The reason is that although *iniuria* was
specifically treated in the XII Tables,[1] it came to be considered
part of edictal law after the *edictum generale* was issued in the last
quarter of the third century B.C. Though this was not intended to
alter substantive law, the new form of proceedings would quickly
wipe out the XII Tables' distinctions between *membrum ruptum, os
fractum*, and *iniuria*.[2]

There is no indication that Quintus Mucius' *ius civile* dealt
anywhere with actions, or with the aspects of procedure covered by
the XII Tables such as summoning to court, the time at which
actions may be heard, and execution of judgment. Likewise there
is no trace of the elements in the XII Tables concerning matters
other than private law, such as the provisions on death and mourning placed in Table X. It would be tempting to hold that Mucius'
system was sophisticated enough to exclude from discussion the
non-private law topics, but the evidence we have would not
justify such an opinion. There remain the last two books of the
ius civile, whose contents are completely unknown. What is certain
is that Pomponius, 39 *ad Quintum Mucium*—which alone seems
to correspond to Mucius' books 17 and 18—does not give a full
treatment of these books on the same scale as that of the previous
books. Presumably, for one reason or another he did not regard it
as necessary or appropriate to give proper treatment to the contents of these books.

Quintus Mucius deserves the highest praise for being the first to
arrange the civil law *generatim*. To our eyes, the organization of
material may seem imperfect, but we must remember the enormous

[1] VIII. 2, 3, 4, 5. We may treat *membrum ruptum, os fractum*, and *iniuria*
together for our purposes.
[2] Cf. Watson, *Private Law*, pp. 154 ff.

difficulty of the task and, without doubt, we are at times unaware
of the factors which determined the order of topics.[1] But some
faults must be noted. Thus, it is hard to imagine that there was
a logical rationale for the order around books 6 and 7 of servitudes,
stipulations, *tutela*, *pauperies* and the *lex Aquilia*, and *statuliberi*.
Then, servitudes do seem to have been discussed both around
book 6 and again in book 13. The consensual contracts of *emptio
venditio* and *societas* owe their presence and their positioning in
the work to their old non-contractual forerunners. In fact we
cannot free Quintus Mucius from the accusation of being very
backward-looking in his *ius civile*: subjects are dealt with which are
very old; matters not older than the later third century B.C. or not
then provided with a proper action are omitted. We may sometimes
suspect that Mucius, instead of writing a systematic treatise on law,
was constructing a handbook for persons appearing in the ordinary
courts on private law matters, hence the omission of subjects like
matrimonium and *cura*; but this view cannot explain the presence
of *postliminium*. Perhaps in some ways the underlying rationale
was not wholly worked out.[2,3]

Interestingly, it must be recorded that Quintus Mucius was well
aware of the legal importance of some of the subjects he omitted.
Thus his pupil Cicero records[4] that Quintus Mucius used to say
('dicebat') that the greatest force resided in all the actions in which
were added the words *ex fide bona*; and that he listed as such actions,
'in tutelis, societatibus, fiduciis, mandatis, rebus emptis venditis,
conductis locatis'. Aulus Gellius relates[5] that he read that Mucius
was accustomed to say ('dicere solitum legi') that a woman did not

---

[1] And some of our reconstructions may be inexact.

[2] More criticism may be levelled against subsequent writers like Sabinus and
Gaius who did not undertake a thorough revision of Mucius' arrangement for
their own works, and who consequently were in turn equally guilty of crimes of
omission.

[3] The reconstruction and arrangement of Quintus Mucius' *ius civile* which is
proposed here differs in several respects from those of Schulz, *Legal Science*,
p. 95; and of Lepointe, *Quintus Mucius Scaevola* (Paris, 1926), pp. 53 ff.,
especially at pp. 69 f. The earlier reconstruction of Voigt, *Über Aelius- und
Sabinussystem* (Königlich. sächs. Gesellsch. der Wissenschaften, VII, 1879), has
not found favour: cf., e.g., Lenel, 'Das Sabinussystem', at, e.g., pp. 12 ff.;
Krüger, *Geschichte der Quellen und Litteratur des römischen Rechts*, 2nd edit.
(Munich, Leipzig, 1912), p. 64, n. 6 (at p. 65); Lepointe, *Mucius*, pp. 64 ff.

[4] *de off.* 3. 17. 70.   [5] *N.A.* 3. 2. 12, 13.

enter the *manus* of her husband in circumstances in which the *trinoctium* was not completed. From the language of both Cicero and Gellius it is apparent that they are reporting what Mucius said on more than one occasion, and not what (so far as they knew) he anywhere put in writing.

A further literary production, the *liber singularis* ὅρων, is attributed to Quintus Mucius in the Digest but, following other scholars,[1] I would reject this as a genuine book of that jurist. The convincing arguments are not those so far adduced,[2] but that the contents of three of the surviving eight texts concern specific and complex matters, and that these texts are not at all suitable for definitions or aphorisms.[3] They have acquired their aphoristic appearance only as a result of being removed from their original context, whether this was in Mucius' *ius civile* or Pomponius' *ad Quintum Mucium*.[4] One has to say then either that Quintus Mucius extracted these texts from his own earlier work for the *liber singularis* and failed to notice that they were not fit for the function he was giving them; or that some later jurist extracted them from Quintus Mucius with the same lack of attention. The second hypothesis seems very much the more likely.

If it is accepted that the *liber singularis* is derived from Mucius' *ius civile*,[5] then the texts from it may throw further light on the *ius*

---

[1] Lenel cautiously expressed doubt as to whether it was a book by Quintus Mucius or a compilation by another from Mucius' *libri iuris civilis*: *Pal.* i. 762, n. 7. H. Krüger considered it a post-classical compilation from Pomponius *ad Quintum Mucium*: 'Römische Juristen und ihre Werke', *Studi Bonfante* ii (Milan, 1930), pp. 301 ff. at p. 336; cf. Schulz, *Legal Science*, p. 94; Guarino, *Storia di diritto romano*, 4th edit. (Milan, 1969), pp. 321 f. Scherillo argues for the genuineness of the book: 'Note critiche su opere della giurisprudenza romana', *IURA* 3 (1952), 180 ff.; and its authenticity is assumed by Stein, *Regulae Iuris* (Edinburgh, 1966), pp. 36 ff.; 'The Relations between Grammar and Law in the Early Principate: the Beginnings of Analogy, *Atti del II congresso internazionale della società italiana di storia del diritto* (Florence, 1971), pp. 757 ff. at p. 760: followed by Jolowicz and Nicholas, *Introduction*, p. 93. Neither Martini, *Le definizioni dei giuristi romani* (Milan, 1966), pp. 90 ff., nor Rodger, 'Roman Rain-Water' *TvR* 38 (1970), 417 ff. at p. 426 expresses any firm opinion.

[2] Scherillo's counter-arguments, loc. cit., have considerable strength.

[3] D. 50. 17. 73pr.; cf. for the meaning, Watson, *Persons*, pp. 118 ff.: D.41. 1. 64; cf. Watson, *Property*, p. 61: D. 43. 20. 8; cf. Watson, *Property*, pp. 188 ff.

[4] So far as I am aware, no one has ever doubted that the texts in the *liber singularis* ὅρων do go back to Quintus Mucius.

[5] Whether the texts were excerpted by Mucius or another.

civile. In this connection the only text helpful to us is D. 41. 1. 64, which would give some confirmation that the *ius civile* dealt with the acquisition of ownership (and not just with *mancipatio* and *usucapio*).[1]

---

[1] If we could be sure that all the texts which we have referring to a difference of opinion between Mucius and Servius have Servius' *reprehensa Scaevolae capita* (*infra*, pp. 159 ff.) as their source of information, then these texts, too, would provide some confirmation of the contents of Mucius' *ius civile*. But they would tell us nothing new since they concern legacies, *tutela*, partnership, ownership (D. 50. 16. 25. 1 (Paul, 21 *ad ed.*)), and theft.

12

BOOK PRODUCTION: TO THE END
OF THE REPUBLIC

TANTALIZING scraps of information disclose that many books of private law were written by other jurists in the first century, but usually we are unable to discover their subject and often even their author.

It would probably be fair, though, to think that no other book approached Quintus Mucius' *ius civile* in importance. So great was the standing of that work that during the remainder of the Republic no other comprehensive commentary was written on the *ius civile*.[1] But Servius Sulpicius Rufus, consul of 51 B.C., of a patrician noble[2] family, did write on Mucius' *ius civile* itself, a book which is named by Aulus Gellius as *reprehensa Scaevolae capita*[3] and by Paul as *notata Mucii*.[4] From these names[5] we might surmise that Servius' work was a commentary on Quintus Mucius, in which he showed his disagreement with individual legal propositions of Mucius, not a work proposing a different structure for commentaries on *ius civile*. But what, then, are we to make of Cicero, *Brutus*, 41. 151 ff.? Cicero claims that Servius was easily supreme in the civil law, not only over those of his own time, but also over those who had gone before; that Quintus Scaevola and many others had great practical skill in the civil law, but only Servius made it an art; that this Servius could not have done had he not also learned the art of dialectic which teaches how to divide a whole thing into its parts, how to bring out what is hidden by defining and explain

---

[1] At least we hear of none.

[2] Cicero, *pro Murena*, 7. 15 f. *Pace* Kunkel, *Herkunft*, p. 25, the nobility was not doubtful though the family had been in eclipse for several generations.

[3] *N.A.* 4. 1. 20.

[4] D. 17. 2. 30 (Paul, 6 *ad Sab.*).

[5] And see, too, the surviving citations collected by Bremer, *Iurisprudentiae* i. 220 ff. and Lenel, *Pal.* ii. 323.

the obscure by interpreting, first to see what is ambiguous and then distinguish.[1] Schulz is thoroughly cynical and writes:

If we had only Cicero to guide us, we should be obliged to accept Servius as the earliest systematizer and to regard Mucius' treatise as a disorderly assemblage of materials in the old style. But here, as always where his sympathies are affected, Cicero is untrustworthy. The fact that Servius was his friend and had written a polemic against Mucius sufficed to make him cheapen Mucius' work, with which his acquaintance was clearly only superficial, and to hail Servius as the true Prometheus. No doubt it is true that Servius employed the dialectical method, but he wrote no systematic work like Mucius.[2]

But this analysis of Schulz is not satisfactory at all points. To begin with, Cicero had been a pupil of Quintus Mucius[3] and had such a high opinion of him that he could describe him as 'the outstanding man of our state both in ability and justice'.[4] Again, if we can assume—as I think we can—that Cicero was acquainted with Quintus Mucius' *ius civile*, then he cannot have had a very high opinion of its arrangement since he himself intended to write, or actually did write a book *de iure civili in artem redigendo*,[5] which implies that he did not consider that the civil law as a system had already been raised to an art. Cicero's praise of Servius is, I submit, directed towards his handling of individual legal cases, and nothing in Cicero's words need suggest that he was thinking of anything more. A very good case can be made out from the surviving texts

---

[1] 'Atque haud scio an par principibus esse potuisset; sed fortasse maluit, id quod est adeptus, longe omnium non eiusdem modo aetatis sed eorum etiam qui fuissent in iure civili esse princeps. 152. Hic Brutus: Ain tu? inquit. Etiamne Q. Scaevolae Servium nostrum anteponis? Sic enim, inquam, Brute, existimo, iuris civilis magnum usum et apud Scaevolam et apud multos fuisse, artem in hoc uno; quod numquam effecisset ipsius iuris scientia, nisi eam praeterea didicisset artem quae doceret rem universam tribuere in partis, latentem explicare definiendo, obscuram explanare interpretando, ambigua primum videre, deinde distinguere, postremo habere regulam qua vera et falsa iudicarentur et quae quibus propositis essent quaeque non essent consequentia. 153. Hic enim adtulit hanc artem omnium artium maximam quasi lucem ad ea quae confuse ab aliis aut respondebantur aut agebantur.'

[2] *Legal Science*, p. 96.   [3] *Brutus*, 89. 306.

[4] *de amic.* 1. 1; cf. his 'vir sanctissimus atque ornatissimus huius civitatis': *pro Rosc. Amer.* 12. 33.

[5] *de orat.* 1. 42. 190; Quintilian, *inst. orat.* 12. 3. 10; Aulus Gellius, *N.A.* 1. 22. 7; cf. Schanz–Hosius, *Geschichte der römischen Literatur* i, 4th edit. (Munich, 1927), pp. 526 f.

concerning Quintus Mucius and Servius for the view that the latter's analysis of individual legal situations is much more acute and subtle. At the moment, however, it is enough for us to notice that the passage from Cicero's *Brutus* provides no argument either that Servius' *reprehensa Scaevolae capita* propounded a new systematic arrangement of the *ius civile* or that Servius was responsible elsewhere for a new arrangement.[1]

But Servius was the first jurist to write a commentary on the Edict, a very short one in two books entitled *ad Brutum*, according to Pomponius.[2] His pupil Ofilius, who remained always an *eques*, in turn was the first to write a thorough commentary on the Edict.[3] We know little of the nature of these works, though presumably they followed the order of the praetor's Edict.

Perhaps a commentary on a very different subject-matter should also be attributed to Ofilius. He was a close friend of Julius Caesar,[4] and is credited by Pomponius with having left many books on the civil law, which were intended to lay the foundations of all branches of the subject; 'nam de legibus vicensimae primus conscribit.'[5] The import of this last clause probably cannot be determined. As it stands it should mean that Ofilius was the first jurist to write about the laws on the 5 per cent tax. But the only known statute imposing such a tax before the Augustan *lex Julia* of about A.D. 5 on inheritances and legacies—and it is not known if Ofilius was still alive then—was the *lex Manlia* of 357 B.C. on manumissions.[6] Even if we were to assume that Ofilius' work was written after A.D. 5, it would still be difficult to believe that the statutes were complex enough to merit a treatise or that this book of Ofilius was important enough to be singled out by Pomponius for special mention in the context. One possibility which has been suggested is that instead of *vicensimae primus* the text should read something like *xx libros*,[7]

---

[1] On collections of Servius' *responsa*, see *infra*, pp. 162 ff.
[2] D. 1. 2. 2. 44 (*sing. enchirid.*).
[3] D. 1. 2. 2. 44. Texts which may derive from these two commentaries are collected by Bremer, *Iurisprudentiae* i. 232 ff., 341 ff.; and Lenel, *Pal.* ii. 322; i. 795; but as Schulz says, *Legal Science*, p. 91, n. 4, it is not certain that the citations refer to the commentaries. [4] Cf. Münzer, *RE* 17. 2040 f.
[5] D. 1. 2. 2. 44. [6] Livy 7. 16. 7: Cicero, *ad Att.* 2. 16. 1.
[7] Huschke, 'Pomponius über die Aelier und Catonen und über A. Ofilius', *Zeitschrift f. geschichtliche Rechtswissenschaft* 15 (1850), 177 ff. at p. 188; Lenel, *Pal.* i. 798, n. 3.

and it has been further conjectured that these twenty books *de legibus* were connected with Caesar's plan to codify statute law.[1]

Servius wrote at least two monographs, the earliest recorded since the mysterious *de usurpationibus* of Appius Claudius. One of these was in at least two books on *detestatio sacrorum*,[2] the other was a single book on dowries[3] which was used even in the second century A.D.[4] The significance of the last work will be recognized when it is remembered that the XII Tables contained no provision on the law of dowry, that Quintus Mucius did not deal with the subject in his *ius civile*, but Sabinus appears to have devoted considerable space to the topic in his commentary on the *ius civile*.[5] It can be shown that Servius' work on dowry had a considerable influence on Sabinus.[6]

No textbook for students is known from this period, though Q. Aelius Tubero produced a work on the duty of a judge[7] which was presumably meant to instruct the lay *iudices*.[8]

Practical collections of forms continued to be made,[9] though perhaps not by jurists of note.

I have left to the end the most exciting type of legal book of this period, collections of *responsa*. Of these the most important was the *digesta* in forty books of Alfenus Varus, a pupil of Servius, who was *consul suffectus* in 39 B.C. The *digesta* itself does not appear to have survived to the time of Justinian—since

---

[1] Huschke, 'Pomponius', p. 195; *contra*, most recently, Pólay, 'Der Kodifizierungsplan des Julius Caesar', *Iura*, 16 (1965), 27 ff. at pp. 49 f.

[2] Aulus Gellius, *N.A.* 7. 12. 1.

[3] D. 12. 4. 8 (Neratius, 2 *membran.*); Gellius 4. 3. 2; 4. 4.

[4] Cf. Schulz, *Legal Science*, p. 93.

[5] In Pomponius *ad Sabinum* books 14 and 15 and part of 16 concern *dos*.

[6] See *infra*, p. 164.   [7] Aulus Gellius, *N.A.* 14. 2. 20.

[8] Cf. Schulz, *Legal Science*, p. 94.

[9] This appears from Cicero, *de leg.* 1. 4. 14. Varro, *de re rust.* 2. 3. 5; 2. 4. 5; 2. 5. 11, show that modifications were made to the forms of guarantees taken when buying animals, which were published by Manilius; but *pace* Schulz, *Legal Science*, p. 90, these texts do not confirm that Varro made use of later collections. Schulz, loc. cit., claims, apparently on the basis of 'sunt humiliora' in *de leg.* 1. 4. 14, that very eminent jurisconsults thought the making of collections of formulae beneath their dignity. But Cicero is talking of what might be considered beneath *his* dignity and he includes in that category treatises on servitudes, that is, presumably, works on private law generally. Kenter misunderstands the import of Cicero's 'formulas': *M. Tullius Cicero, de legibus; a Commentary on book 1* (Amsterdam, 1971), p. 71.

no fragments from it were extracted—but two epitomes did survive, one by Paul, the other by an unknown jurist. The arrangement of the latter, as is well known, follows that of the Edict; the epitome of Paul, it is said,[1] follows neither the arrangement of the Edict nor any other arrangement found in the writings of the jurists. But it seems in fact that Paul's epitome—which we will look at first—does have an order which is recognizable in its historical setting. Lenel gives the following headings to the subjects treated:

1. ??
2. *de testamentis et legatis*
   de usu fructu legato
   de servitute legata?
   de instrumento legato
3. *de hereditatis petitione*
   de rei vindicatione
   pro socio
   de emptione et venditione
   de locatione et conductione
   de in factum actionibus?
   de dotibus
4. *de legibus mancipi aut venditionis*
   de aqua pluvia arcenda
   de fluminibus publicis
5. *de servitutibus?*
   de furtis et onere averso
6. ??
7. ??
8. *de legatis*

It should be noted that within each book the suggested arrangement derives from external factors and not from any information in the texts themselves. Lenel suggests that legacies were dealt with a second time in book 8 perhaps because the author inserted matters which had been overlooked.[2] This seems plausible

[1] Cf. Lenel, *Pal.* i. 37, n. 1; Jörs, *RE* i. 1474; De Sarlo, *Alfeno Varo e i suoi Digesta* (Milan, 1940), pp. 1 ff.   [2] *Pal.* i. 53, n. 1.

enough, and we should accept for the time being at least that book 8 should be ignored when looking for the scheme of arrangement. Likewise we shall leave aside for the moment books 1, 6, and 7, of whose subject-matter Lenel is very doubtful.

What then emerges from the remaining books is a scheme, midway in character between Quintus Mucius' *ius civile* and Sabinus' *ius civile*.

Thus, book 2 on wills and legacies corresponds to Quintus Mucius' books 1, 2, 3, and part of 4 and to books 1, 2, 3, 5, 6, and 7 of Pomponius *ad Sabinum*.

Among the topics treated in book 3 were partnership, sale, hire, and dowry. Hire was not dealt with by Sabinus or by Quintus Mucius, but in Pomponius *ad Sabinum* sale was the subject of books 9, 10, and 11, partnership of books 12 and 13, and dowry of 14, 15, and part of 16. The correspondence between Alfenus' *digesta* and Sabinus' *ius civile* is obvious, and I would submit first that in the former the order of treatment here was sale, hire, partnership, dowry; secondly that Sabinus was influenced by this in his own arrangement, and thirdly that dowry which was not treated by Quintus Mucius owes its existence in Sabinus, at least in part, to the *digesta*. In Quintus Mucius, of course, the order was very different: sale appeared in book 12 and partnership in book 14.

But after these insertions into the Mucian scheme, the influence of Quintus Mucius' *ius civile* reasserts itself. The first topic which we know about in that work[1] after the treatment of succession was servitudes and/or water rights, which were discussed in book 6. And, it will be remembered, Quintus Mucius reverted to these matters in book 13 and I have argued[2] that servitudes and/or water rights were treated there because of their connection with *mancipatio*; that this is their connection with sale—the immediately preceding subject—which actually owes its existence in Quintus Mucius to its historical relation with *mancipatio*. Alfenus at this point begins to treat the same subjects—as one might expect on the present hypothesis—but he improves on the Mucian scheme by avoiding the unfortunate dispersal of material. Thus in book 4 he treats problems concerning the terms in *mancipationes*,

[1] There is a gap in our knowledge: cf. *supra*, p. 143.   [2] *Supra*, p. 147.

then water rights (*aqua pluvia* and *flumina publica*) and, in book 5, servitudes. The arrangement would have been neater still if servitudes had come before water rights, and this we actually find in Sabinus where servitudes appear in Pomponius *ad Sabinum* at book 33 and water rights at book 34. Interestingly, in Sabinus the placing of servitudes and water rights results from following Quintus Mucius' second treatment of these subjects.

When we continue with the scheme of Mucius' *ius civile* we find that the next topic treated there, which also appears in Paul's epitome of the *Digesta*, is *furtum*,[1] which is the subject of Mucius' book 16. It is also the next subject of which we have evidence in the epitome in book 5.[2] In Sabinus' *ius civile furtum* occupied a very different position.

The subject-matter of the last two books—apart from the appendix on legacies—of Paul's epitome is not discoverable, just as we cannot determine the contents of the last two books of Mucius' *ius civile*. In both works, that is, the subject-matter after the treatment of *furtum* is not known.

The only subjects which are evidenced in books 2 to 5 of Paul's epitome which we have not yet discussed are the *hereditatis petitio* and the *vindicatio*, both of which were treated in book 3. Their position at the beginning of that book is thoroughly reasonable. There is no place more suitable for the action claiming an inheritance than immediately after the treatment of wills or succession in general. And it cannot surprise us that this action, which even in Cicero's time could give rise to a *legis actio sacramento in rem*,[3] should be followed by the *vindicatio* which had always been the prime instance of a *legis actio sacramento in rem*. It is not known where these subjects were dealt with by Quintus Mucius or Sabinus.[4]

It emerges from this analysis of Paul's epitome that that work

---

[1] Apart, that is, from *societas* which has already been explained.

[2] Lenel suggests as the heading here *de furtis et onere averso*. Whatever *onus aversum* was it was undoubtedly a variety of theft. D. 19. 2. 31 from this book is the only text which mentions the *actio oneris aversi*, and Alfenus declares it superfluous.

[3] Cicero, *in Verrem* II, 1. 45. 115: cf. Watson, *Succession*, pp. 195 f.

[4] Lenel tentatively assigns the *vindicatio* to book 31 of Pomponius *ad Sabinum*: *Pal.* ii. 139. But there is no confirmation in Paul or Ulpian *ad Sabinum*.

follows in general the arrangement of Quintus Mucius' *ius civile*, but with some variations; that some, but not all, of these variations correspond to alterations from Mucius' order also to be found in Sabinus' *ius civile*. This last work, in its turn, has alterations from the arrangement of Quintus Mucius, which are not to be found in Paul's epitome. Thus, the arrangement of the epitome is intermediate between Quintus Mucius' *ius civile* and Sabinus' work of the same name. From all this, I think we can conclude first that the arrangement in Paul's epitome is an arrangement which was to be found in Alfenus' *digesta*;[1] secondly that for the arrangement of his *ius civile* Sabinus used both Quintus Mucius' *ius civile* and Alfenus' *digesta*, sometimes accepting the latter's changes, sometimes not, sometimes making further alterations of his own.

Book 1 of Paul's epitome has so far been left out of account, and it must be admitted that its subject-matter cannot be recovered. There seems no obvious connection between the matters dealt with in the three surviving texts.[2] From D. 28. 1. 25 (Iavolenus, 5 *post. Labeonis*), which refers to book 1 of the original *digesta* of Alfenus, it might appear that wills were treated in that book, but without doubt Paul's epitome book 1 had wider subject-matter.[3]

The other epitome of Alfenus' *digesta* is in at least seven books and is, this time, the work of an unknown jurist. As has been already mentioned, the arrangement follows the order of the praetor's Edict.[4] The most plausible explanation of the difference in arrangement of the two epitomes was given long ago by Lenel,[5] that 'Anonymous' changed the order of Alfenus to the well-known order of the Edict because of its usefulness in practice.[6]

---

[1] This was also Lenel's conclusion, but for the reason that the arrangement corresponded to that of no other work whereas the anonymous epitome followed the order of the Edict: *Pal.* ii. 37, n. 1.

[2] D. 8. 4. 15; 41. 3. 34; 48. 22. 3.

[3] No help in discovering the arrangement of Alfenus' *digesta* is to be found in Aulus Gellius, *N.A.* 7. 5. 1 or D. 3. 5. 20(21)pr. (Paul, 9 *ad ed.*), the only other texts which refer to the original Republican work.

[4] Cf., e.g., Lenel, *Pal.* i. 37, n. 1; Schulz, *Legal Science*, p. 206.

[5] Loc. cit.

[6] But I should like to mention another possibility, namely that Alfenus' *digesta* were originally two collections of *responsa*, one of which was arranged in the order of the Edict. If convincing arguments could be found for this view, we would then have direct evidence—which is otherwise totally lacking—that in the Republic the Edict was arranged in the same order as under Hadrian.

The great worth of Alfenus' *digesta* is shown both by the making of two epitomes[1] and by the presence in Justinian's Digest of so many fragments from the epitomes.[2] A number of the *responsa* in the *digesta* was the work of Servius,[3] but some were undoubtedly the opinions of Alfenus himself.[4] Which jurist was responsible for the *responsum* in a particular case is usually not discoverable since most texts have *respondit* without an expressed subject, and in the epitome by 'Anonymous' all references to Servius have been excised. But since Pomponius tells us that Servius left almost 180 books[5] and we have direct evidence of very few of these, it seems reasonable to hold[6] that most of them were unpublished books of *responsa* which were later edited and published by his pupils, above all by Alfenus, and that a very large proportion of the *responsa* in the *digesta* were given by Servius. Not all the juristic replies in this work should be regarded as a *responsum* in the narrow sense of a legal opinion given on a real case by a jurist to a client, judge, or orator who consulted him. Some texts concern hypothetical situations.[7] Thus, in one a reply is given to explain the meaning of words in a treaty between Rome and Carthage, and this treaty can hardly still have given rise to practical problems.[8] In another we find an *institutio* of an heir, 'If my mother Maevia and my daughter Fulvia are alive then be Lucius Titius my heir' where the testator never had a daughter but his mother survived him.[9] It is very difficult to believe such a case could ever have arisen in practice.

There were also many other books of which we know nothing or virtually nothing. For instance, Pomponius tells us[10] that of

[1] Presumably the epitomes contained only the *responsa* which were thought to have continuing value.

[2] Collected in Lenel, *Pal.* i. 38 ff.

[3] e.g. D. 28. 1. 25; 3. 5. 20(21)pr.; 33. 7. 16.

[4] This emerges most clearly from D. 33. 7. 16. 2 (Alfenus, 2 *dig. a Paulo epit.*) since the reply corresponds to what we know from D. 33. 7. 12. 2 (Ulpian, 20 *ad Sab.*) was the opinion of Alfenus, which was different from that of Servius; D. 33. 7. 12pr.: cf. Watson, *Succession*, pp. 144 ff.

[5] D. 1. 2. 2. 43 (*sing. enchirid.*).

[6] Cf. Schulz, *Legal Science*, p. 92.   [7] Cf. Schulz, *Legal Science*, p. 91.

[8] Aulus Gellius, *N.A.* 7. 5. 1; cf. Schulz, *Legal Science*, p. 91, n. 8. In introducing the matter Gellius terms Alfenus 'rerum antiquarum non incuriosus'.

[9] D. 28. 5. 46(45) (2 *dig. a Paulo epit.*); cf. Schulz, loc. cit.

[10] D. 1. 2. 2. 44.

the ten pupils of Servius whom he lists eight wrote books, and that Aufidius Namusa, himself one of them, made a digest of all these writings in 140 books.[1] And references to the writings of other jurists such as Cascellius[2] and Trebatius[3] also survive.

[1] The *centum* has been doubted: add to the references in the *Index Itp.*, Schulz, *Legal Science*, p. 92. Strangely, Schulz takes the text as meaning that Aufidius published the *responsa* of Servius in forty books.

[2] Collected by Lenel, *Pal.* i. 107 f.

[3] Collected by Lenel, *Pal.* ii. 343 ff.

13

MOS AND *RES IUDICATAE*

In his definition of civil law by enumeration of parts, Cicero gives among the parts of the civil law both custom and previous court decisions.[1] Likewise the *Rhetorica ad Herennium* lists these two matters among the *partes* of law.[2] Hence we must ask whether custom and precedent can be regarded as important factors in the development of law in the later Republic.

But first we should notice that the author of *ad Herennium*[3] lists *pactum* as a part of law; and by *pactum* he clearly means[4] an agreement between individuals which is recognized by law as having legal effectiveness. The idea seems to be that the parties, having made an agreement which will be enforced by the court, have made their own law.[5] This *pars* which is not concerned with the development of general legal rules need not detain us further.

Mos[6] can properly be regarded as making law in the later Republic though it was not one of the major factors in development.[7] Thus the prohibition of gifts between husband and wife was introduced *moribus*, even though the *lex Cincia* of 204 B.C. which imposed restrictions on gifts expressly excluded husband and wife from the restrictions.[8] Probably also from this period but

---

[1] *top.* 5. 28: cf. *supra*, pp. 3 ff. [2] 2. 13. 19.

[3] Cf. Cicero, *de inven.* 2. 22. 67. [4] Shown by 2. 13. 20.

[5] Perhaps the same idea is relevant to the medieval English rule that the King's court would not enforce or take note of private agreements: cf. Glanvill, *Tractatus de legibus et consuetudinibus regni Anglie*, 10. 8; 10. 18.

[6] *Mos* in Cicero, *top.* 5. 28 is the exact equivalent of *consuetudo* in the *Rhetorica ad Herennium* and must be translated as 'custom', not 'morality'. In what follows I intend to ignore the possible distinction between 'legal custom' and 'customary law' which need not be drawn for our period, and has been overemphasized by some scholars: cf. Thomas, 'Custom and Roman Law', *TvR* 31 (1963), 39 f. at p. 41. Bove, *La consuetudine in diritto romano* i (Naples, 1971) reached me too late for consideration.

[7] Though presumably many major institutions, like *mancipatio*, are ultimately of customary origin.

[8] For the argument that the prohibition was introduced by custom in the later Republic see now Watson, *Property*, pp. 209 f. The main texts are D. 24. 1. 1

perhaps earlier is the rule expressed in *Rhetorica ad Herennium* 2. 13. 19, 'id quod argentario tuleris expensum, ab socio eius recte petere possis.' The precise scope of this rule, whether or not the author was thinking of the literal contract, need not detain us, but it should be noticed that the right was restricted to persons transacting with bankers.[1] Probably but not certainly earlier is the soldier's right to the *legis actio per pignoris capionem* for his pay, for the money for buying his horse and for the money for buying barley for his horse.[2] Other instances,[3] for example pupillary substitution,[4] seem to be older.

It has been noticed, and properly stressed, that the Roman jurists never list custom among the sources of law.[5] These juristic lists, of course, date from the Empire and it is in relation to the Empire, I think, that Thomas, reasonably, says 'In Roman law itself, *mores* are known to the world through, and depend for their recognition on their being expounded by the jurists.'[6] But we are, none the less, left with a problem. Why do jurists (and other writers) attribute a few—but only a few—rules to custom? In each case there must be some reason why it was not appropriate simply to rely on the authority of the jurists for the introduction of the rule.

Thus in banking—I suggest in the absence of any evidence—the practice developed of one partner's paying debts incurred by the others. The practice was so regular that in time it became formalized and an action based on it became acceptable to the courts. It is thus a true example of a business custom becoming law. Its

(Ulpian, 32 *ad Sab.*); 24. 1. 38 (Alfenus, 3 *dig. a Paulo epit.*); 41. 6. 3 (Pomponius, 24 *ad Quintum Mucium*).

[1] Cf. for a later period D. 2. 14. 25pr. (Paul, 3 *ad ed.*); *h.t.* 27pr. (idem).

[2] G. 4. 26.

[3] See the lists of texts in Schiller, 'Custom in Classical Roman Law', now in *An American Experience in Roman Law* (Göttingen, 1971), p. 48; Thomas, 'Custom', pp. 40 f.

[4] D. 28. 6. 2pr. (Ulpian, 6 *ad Sab.*).

[5] Cf., e.g., Schiller, 'Custom', pp. 41 ff. at p. 44; Thomas, 'Custom', pp. 42 ff. Nörr argues attractively that the juristic theory of customary law developed in the second century A.D., though what modern jurists would regard as customary law did, of course, exist earlier: 'Zur Entstehung der gewohnheitsrechtlichen Theorie', *Festschrift Felgentraeger* (Göttingen, 1969), pp. 353 ff.; most recently, *Divisio und Partitio* (Berlin, 1972), pp. 1 ff.

[6] Loc. cit.

development first as business practice then as law can be envisaged without the hypothesis of juristic intervention. Though jurists might have urged the recognition of the rule by the courts, they could not have taken an active part in its formation. Its restriction to bankers' arrangements means that it had to be derived from what people did rather than from juristic theory. Similarly the extension to soldiers of the right to a *legis actio per pignoris capionem* probably followed seizures by soldiers under a claim of right. Since the circumstances in which the *legis actio* was available were set out by statute, it was difficult to make extensions to completely new situations rest upon the authority of jurists, and much easier to ascribe them to custom. Above all, in view of the *lex Cincia* it would have been impossible to ascribe to the jurists the prohibition of gifts between husband and wife: juristic *auctoritas* cannot prevail against a statute. Of course there are also difficulties, though lesser ones, in ascribing the prohibition to custom. How these difficulties—especially the relationship of statute to custom,[1] and the length of time a custom must have existed before it became law—were solved cannot be known in the absence of a theory of custom in the Republic.[2] The nearest thing we have to a theory is in Cicero, *de inven.* 2. 22. 67, where we are told that by custom that is thought to be law which, by the consent of everyone, lapse of time has approved without the aid of statute. And he adds that there are rules of law which are certain because of lapse of time.[3]

The role of precedent cannot be determined with precision. As a *pars iuris* or a source of law, precedent appears nowhere other than in these lists of Cicero and the *Rhetorica ad Herennium*. A difficulty

---

[1] Since the *lex Cincia* continued in force, it is hard to think in terms of desuetude of the relevant clause.

[2] Also for *consuetudo* see the *lex Antonia de Termessibus* (of 71 B.C.), II. 18–23.

[3] 'consuetudine autem ius esse putatur id, quod voluntate omnium sine lege vetustas comprobarit. In ea autem quaedam sunt iura ipsa iam certa propter vetustatem. Quo in genere et alia sunt multa et eorum multo maxima pars, quae praetores edicere consuerunt. Quaedam autem genera iuris iam certa consuetudine facta sunt; quod genus pactum, par, iudicatum. 68. Pactum est, quod inter quos convenit ita iustum putatur, ut iure praestare dicatur; par, quod in omnes aequabile est; iudicatum, de quo iam ante sententia alicuius aut aliquorum constitutum est.'

with it, displayed in the *Rhetorica*,[1] is the frequent conflict between one decision and another. None the less, previous decisions were a weapon in the orators' armoury, and probably they made collections of precedents.[2] It is easy to imagine that cases in court were sometimes won because of previous decisions. Yet that does not entitle us to treat precedent as a factor in the development of legal rules. Precedent would have that status only if decided cases were regularly persuasive or if judicial decisions influenced interpretation by the jurists.

---

[1] 2. 13. 19 f.
[2] See on all this Schulz, *Legal Science*, pp. 92 f. He points out that Galba the orator was ready with many *similitudines*, which in the context cannot mean *responsa*: Cicero, *de orat.* 1. 56. 240. And he suggests that the reports given by Valerius Maximus would derive from such collections: see the instances of striking decisions in Valerius Maximus 8. 2.

14

AEQUITAS

BOTH Cicero[1] and the unknown author of the *Rhetorica ad Herennium*[2] include *aequitas* among the 'parts of the civil law'. But *aequitas* stands apart from the other items listed by Cicero.[3] In the first place, *aequitas* does not provide a rule of thumb for finding the law; a diligent orator, even one lacking in imagination, can find out the objectively relevant statutes, edicts, precedents, and so on, for his case, but *aequitas* is a vaguer concept. Secondly, all law should be based on *aequitas*,[4] but the essence of positive law is its separation from 'fairness'. A legal rule should be followed as law irrespective of its justness.

As a first result, although it may be easy for an orator to urge from the floor of the court that his client's case is well founded in *aequitas*, it will be difficult for a judge or jurist to justify his opinion on that basis. In none of the surviving sources does a Republican jurist give *aequitas* or any similar idea as an argument for his decision. But two cases come close to it, and they both strongly reinforce the point of view maintained here. One is D. 3. 5. 20(21)pr. (Paul, 9 *ad ed.*), where Servius replies that it would be *aequum* for the praetor to give a *iudicium (in factum)*; the other D. 44. 1. 14 (Alfenus Varus, 2 *dig.*) where Alfenus declares it would be *aequum* to give an *exceptio in factum*. Now it was the whole function of praetorian decretal *actiones in factum* and *exceptiones in factum* to fill a gap in the existing law as revealed by the particular case, hence it is exactly appropriate to declare that it would be *aequum* for the praetor to grant a remedy. More significantly still, these two decisions stand right at the beginning of the

---

[1] *top.* 5. 28. The text is quoted, *supra*, p. 25.

[2] 2. 13. 19. The text is quoted, *supra* p. 4.

[3] For *natura* in the list in the *ad Herenn.* see *infra*, pp. 177 f.

[4] Indeed, Cicero, *top.* 2. 9, defines *ius civile* in terms of *aequitas*: 'Ius civile est aequitas constituta eis qui eiusdem civitatis sunt ad res suas obtinendas.'

development of the decretal *actio in factum* and *exceptio in factum*,
and the cautious form of expression, 'it would be fair for the
praetor to grant a remedy', reflects uncertainty as to whether the
praetor will in fact grant the remedy.[1] Juristic opinions later in
the Republic disclose neither hesitation over the praetorian
decision to give a remedy *in factum*, nor reliance on *aequitas* as the
ground for praetorian intervention. Once the granting of praetorian
decretal actions becomes standardized in set circumstances,
aequitas as an expressed reason for the grant disappears.

A second result of the facts set out in the first paragraph is that
many legal developments, especially those resulting from distinctions drawn by jurists, are based on the notion of what is just or
fair, though this basis is left unexpressed. Of the straightforward
instances nothing need be said, though one might call attention to
examples such as *remissio mercedis* in hire,[2] and to Quintus Mucius
Scaevola's view that it was contrary to the nature of partnership
for one partner to have a greater share in profits than in losses.[3] Of
more interest are the cases where legal logic is twisted, where
a decision is given different from what could be expected on strict
legal reasoning in order to achieve a result which was presumably
considered fair. This is why a slave freed *censu* or *vindicta* is the
libertus of his former owner;[4] and why Servius decided as he did
in the situation in D. 21. 2. 69. 3 (Scaevola, 2 *quaest.*). In that text
a person sold a *statuliber* and declared he was to be free under the
will when he paid twenty. In fact the *statuliber* was to be free
when he paid ten. Servius' opinion that the action against the
seller was the *actio ex empto* and not the *actio auctoritatis* cannot
be defended on legal grounds and must be because the measure of
damages in the latter—twice the price stated in the *mancipatio*—
seemed much too high to Servius, who thought that the damages
in the *actio ex empto*—whatever ought to be given in accordance
with good faith—was sufficient.[5]

[1] Cf. *supra*, pp. 92 f.

[2] For this see now Watson, *Obligations*, pp. 110 ff.; Seager, 'Of *vis* and weeds:
D. 19. 2. 15. 2 and 19. 2. 19. 1', *SDHI* 31 (1965), 330 ff.

[3] G. 3. 149.

[4] Cf. *supra*, p. 89 and Watson, 'Illogicality and Roman Law', *Israel Law
Review* 7 (1972), 14 ff. at pp. 16 f.

[5] For the argument see Watson, *Obligations*, pp. 76 f.; *Limits of Juristic*

A third result is the contrast which inevitably comes to be drawn at times between *aequitas* and *ius*, perhaps first by outsiders but then occasionally in the law itself. The classic contrast in the Republic is between *aequum atque bonum* on the one hand and *ius* on the other. The clearest instance from literature is in Terence, *Heauton Timorumenos*, 642, where Chremes asks rhetorically, what can one do with people (i.e. women) who 'neque ius neque bonum atque aequum sciunt'.[1] More important, the same contrast is found in magisterial measures even from the very beginning of our period. Thus, the praetor seems to have issued an *edictum* on *iniuria* in the late third century B.C., which did not change the substantive law but had the function of providing more satisfactory damages.[2] If we can argue from the evidence for a later period, the measure of damages to be awarded according to the *formula* for this *edictum* was as much money as seemed *bonum aequum* to the judges.[3,4] This flexible measure of damages in *bonum aequum* contrasts with the fixed penalties of the XII Tables which constitute the *ius*. Again, the *actio rei uxoriae*, which is certainly Republican and probably not very much later than 200 B.C., runs as follows:[5] 'Si paret Numerium Negidium Aulae Ageriae dotem partemve eius reddere oportere, quod eius melius aequius erit, eius iudex Nm Nm Aae

---

Decision in the Later Roman Republic (University of Edinburgh Inaugural Lecture, 1969), pp. 9 f.

[1] Earlier, Plautus had drawn a similar contrast between *leges* and *aequum bonum*; *Men.* 580. One must also cite Sallust, *Jugurtha*, 35. 7: 'Fit reus magis ex aequo bonoque quam ex iure gentium Bomilcar.'

[2] Cf. *supra*, pp. 48 f.

[3] Cf. Lenel, *Edictum*, p. 399.

[4] If, as is often done, we take the ἀδικήματα referred to in the famous *senatusconsultum* on the dispute between Priene and Magnesia (Dittenberger, *Sylloge Inscriptionum Graecarum* ii, 3rd edit. (Leipzig, 1917), no. 679, II. b) as wrongs in the sense of the Roman delict of *iniuria*, then the inscription's ὅσον ἂν καλὸν καὶ δίκαιον φαίνηται διατιμησάσθω would be the equivalent of the clause with *bonum aequum* in the action under the *edictum* for *iniuria*. The date of the *senatusconsultum* is not known but is generally considered to be around the middle of the second century B.C., hence later than the *edictum* on *iniuria*. If the ἀδικήματα are some other kind of wrong then the *senatusconsultum* probably tells us nothing relevant for Roman private law. For the inscription see now Sherk, *Roman Documents from the Greek East* (Baltimore, 1969), pp. 44 ff., and the references he gives.

[5] At least in the time of Hadrian: cf. Lenel, *Edictum*, p. 305. The phrase 'quod eius melius aequius', which most concerns us, certainly existed in the time of Cicero: *top.* 17. 66.

Aae condemna, si non paret, absolve.' The judge, therefore, has to proceed in two stages: first he has to decide whether the dowry or part of it should be returned according to the *ius civile*;[1] secondly, if his answer is affirmative, he has to condemn the defendant to return to the plaintiff whatever portion of that is *melius aequius*. This time the contrast between what is due according to *ius* and the amount to be awarded, whatever is *melius aequius*, is virtually explicit. Probably, though not certainly,[2] the words *bonum aequum* occurred in at least a third magisterial formulation, in the curule aediles' *edictum de feris:* 'si nocitum homini libero esse dicetur, quanti bonum aequum iudici videbitur, condemnatur.' Here, however, as in many instances of non-legal usage,[3] there is apparently no contrast intended between *bonum aequum* and *ius*.

The importance of the idea of fairness[4] in legal development will thus usually be hidden, though occasionally it will appear in one form or another, as when a judge is ordered in the *formula* to condemn a defendant in whatever is *aequum*[5] or *aequum bonum*, or whatever ought to be given or done *ex fide bona*,[6] or to award the plaintiff his interest if the defendant had not acted 'ut inter bonos bene agier oportet et sine fraudatione';[7] or where the parties to a contract refer a clause or dispute to the *arbitrium boni viri*.[8] One may also mention that in the (accurate) report in Livy in indirect

---

[1] This emerges from the 'dotem partemve eius reddere oportere'. For the significance of *oportere* in this type of context see Daube, *Forms*, pp. 8 ff.

[2] Cf. *supra*, pp. 85 f.

[3] e.g. Plautus, *Curc.* 65; *Most.* 682; *Pers.* 399. On the whole subject see above all Pringsheim, *'Bonum et aequum'*, now in *Gesammelte Abhandlungen* i (Heidelberg, 1961), pp. 173 ff.; cf. Kaser, 'Zum Ediktsstil', *Festschrift Schulz*, ii (Weimar, 1951), pp. 21 ff. at pp. 42 f. Pringsheim thinks that some other actions were also originally *in bonum et aequum conceptae*: pp. 190 ff.

[4] *Aequitas* in this context means any appeal to morality. It is, indeed, possible to distinguish *aequitas, bona fides, iustitia*, and so on, but for the orator's *pars iuris*, and likewise here, there is no compelling need to separate them.

[5] As under the edictal clauses *si iudex litem suam fecerit; de his qui deiecerint vel effuderint; de sumptibus funerum;* and *de sepulchro violato*. It may be, as Pringsheim suggests, that the actions originally spoke of *bonum aequum*.

[6] As in the *actio tutelae* and the actions on the four consensual contracts of *emptio venditio, locatio conductio, societas*, and *mandatum*.

[7] As in the action on *fiducia*.

[8] Cato, *de agri cult.* 146, 148, 149; D. 18. 1. 7pr. (Ulpian, 28 *ad Sab.*): cf. Watson, *Obligations*, pp. 98 f.

speech of the Senate's decree in 186 B.C., asking for rewards to be given to Hispala Faecenia and Publius Aebutius for their services in uncovering the Bacchanalia, we have the words, 'Id senatum velle et aequum censere, ut ita fieret'.[1]

More striking are the cases where there is a failure, at least for a considerable time, of fairness, justice, or morality. Thus, originally and for a very long time, a person could usucapt property belonging to another if he exercised the requisite degree of control over the thing, even if his control was not the result of a legally recognized transaction such as sale,[2] and even if the control had begun in bad faith.[3] At some time during the later Republic the requirements of both *iustus titulus* and *bona fides* came into being, but neither can be discerned earlier than the first century B.C.[4] Again, fraud on the part of the creditor in the *stipulatio* and other *stricti iuris* contracts did not adversely affect his rights under the contract until the *edictum de dolo* around 66 B.C. Even then, if he sued the defendant on the contract he would win his action unless the defendant expressly pleaded the *exceptio doli*.[5] Further, more surprising still, right into the time of Gaius in the second century A.D., a plaintiff who even accidentally over-claimed (in the part of the *formula* known as the *intentio*) lost his case entirely, including the part to which he could justify his claim, and he was not restored to his original position by the praetor.[6]

The *Rhetorica ad Herennium*, 2. 13. 19, also includes *natura* among the *partes iuris*, and explains: 'Natura ius est quod cognationis aut pietatis causa observatur, quo iure parentes a liberis et a parentibus liberi coluntur.' *Pietas* is best translated here as 'family loyalty',[7] as the examples given show. Hence, the unknown orator is

---

[1] Livy 39. 19. 6.
[2] That is, even if he had no *iustus titulus*.
[3] See above all, Yaron, 'Reflections on *usucapio*', *TvR* 35 (1967), 191 ff.
[4] For the texts see Watson, *Property*, pp. 48 ff.
[5] Cf. on all this, Watson, *Obligations*, pp. 258 ff.
[6] G. 4. 53–60.
[7] As Caplan translates it: *Rhetorica ad Herennium* (London and Cambridge, Mass.), p. 93. On a denarius, *c.* 101 B.C., of the moneyer M. Herennius, the obverse has the head of *Pietas*, the reverse portrays either Amphinomus or Anapius carrying on his shoulder their father, thus saving him from an eruption of Mount Etna: Sydenham, *Roman Republican Coinage*, revised by Haines (London, 1952), p. 77.

concerned with nature in the sense of blood relationship, etc., and not with any abstract, philosophical concept of 'The Law of Nature'.[1] Obviously this argument from nature could be used by an orator in other contexts: for succession rights, for the impossibility of a marriage within certain degrees, and so on. But as a factor in legal development (after the very earliest period), *natura* would be of very limited worth.

[1] For 'The Law of Nature' see, above all, Levy, 'Natural Law in Roman Thought', now in *Gesammelte Schriften* i (Cologne and Graz, 1963), pp. 3 ff.; G. Watson, 'The Natural Law and Stoicism', *Problems in Stoicism* (London, 1971), edited by Long, pp. 216 ff.

15

CLASSIFICATION AND DEFINITION

ONE of the greatest Roman achievements is the organization and classification of legal matters, especially as set out in Gaius' *Institutes* in the second century A.D.[1] Some of the major steps towards this arrangement had been taken before the end of the Republic. Thus, in what is probably the most fundamental legal distinction, private law came to be separated from public and sacral law, a feat which was not paralleled in, for instance, Attic or Jewish law.

The stages in this particular development cannot be traced with precision. At one end of the time-scale the XII Tables show no sign of the division; most of the provisions concern private law, but a number clearly deals with criminal law,[2] and some have a religious sanction.[3] The provisions on mourning and the disposal of bodies[4] cannot be thought of as part of private law. At the other end of the scale, Quintus Mucius Scaevola's *ius civile* written near the beginning of the first century B.C. seems to be rigorously concerned with private law alone.[5] Admittedly we do not have knowledge of all the contents of Mucius' *ius civile* and in particular not of the last two books. But even if it were suggested—in the absence of all evidence—that these last two books were concerned with non-private law matters, it would still clearly emerge that Mucius sharply separated private law from public and sacral law. Likewise, Alfenus' *Digesta* seems to have been concerned only with private law, though here, too, the subject-matter of books 6 and 7 of Paul's epitome—the last books, apart from book 8, which seems to be an appendix on legacies—is not discoverable.

---

[1] This arrangement was very largely followed in Justinian's *Institutes* and became the basis of legal arrangement in most of Western Europe.
[2] e.g. VIII. 23.
[3] e.g. VIII. 9; VIII. 21; VIII. 24.
[4] Now collected in Tab. X.
[5] Cf. *supra*, pp. 143 ff.

We are, of course, not here comparing like with like. The XII Tables were a legal code, Quintus Mucius' *ius civile* a treatise where he could himself fix the boundaries of his work. But two points stand out and should be stressed. The first is that the earliest Roman legal treatise which was general in nature and whose structure can be determined, that is Mucius' *ius civile*, did clearly distinguish private law from other branches of law. The second is that between the time of the XII Tables and the beginning of the first century B.C., law itself had undergone a change. Whereas much of the private law at the earlier date was also sacral law, religion had virtually ceased to have any role in private law by the time of Quintus Mucius. It was involved in only four matters: in the form of adoption of a male *sui iuris*, known as *adrogatio*, the approval of the *pontifices* was needed; the creation of marriage by *confarreatio* was a religious ceremony which required the presence of the *pontifex maximus* and the *flamen dialis*; certain beneficiaries on a death were responsible for the *sacra* of the deceased;[1] and *ius-iurandum liberti* involved an oath.[2] But *adrogatio* can never have been common even though Servius wrote at least two books on *detestatio sacrorum*.[3] *Confarreatio*, which had always been restricted to the small circle of the upper classes, cannot have been performed during the Republic after 87 B.C., since from the suicide of the *flamen dialis* in that year until the time of Augustus no *flamen dialis* was appointed.[4] Performance of the *sacra* was regarded as burdensome, and Quintus Mucius himself and his father, Publius Mucius, both of them *pontifices maximi*, gave advice on how to take the profit from the death but avoid the *sacra*.[5] The *iusiurandum liberti* was a verbal contract which gave rise to an *actio stricti iuris*,[6] and it survived into the time of Justinian.[7] How common it was we cannot tell, since it was equally open for the *libertus* to promise his services by *stipulatio*; only one text mentions the *iusiurandum* in

---

[1] For the details see now Watson, *Succession*, pp. 4 ff.
[2] For this see Buckland, *Textbook*, pp. 458 f.
[3] Aulus Gellius, *N.A.* 7. 12. 1.
[4] Tacitus, *Ann.* 3. 58; Cassius Dio 54. 36. 1.
[5] To Cicero's disgust: *de leg.* 2. 20. 50 ff.
[6] For the action see Lenel, *Edictum*, pp. 338 ff.
[7] Cf., e.g., D. 38. 1. 7pr. (Ulpian, 28 *ad Sab.*).

the Republic.[1] The surprising thing is not that the *iusiurandum liberti* gave rise to a private law action, but that it was the one case of an obligation created by oath.[2] Thus private law had become secularized.[3]

Sextus Aelius' *tripertita* throws no light of any kind on the development of classification. This work on the XII Tables seems to have dealt with all the known provisions of the code, on non-private law and private law, on obsolete law and enduring law alike.[4]

The organization and arrangement of private law itself was primarily the work of Quintus Mucius who, according to Pomponius, first arranged the civil law *generatim*.[5] The order of topics in his *ius civile* has already been set out[6] and criticisms have been expressed.[7] Here we are concerned with what can be learned from the arrangement about classification.

To begin with, it emerges that there was no concept of what we can call 'obligations'. Thus *stipulatio* was discussed in book 6, *pauperies* and the *lex Aquilia* in book 7, *emptio venditio* in book 12, *societas* in book 14, and *furtum* in book 16. The positioning of these topics also shows that there was as yet no classification of 'contracts' and none of 'delicts'. The concept of 'property' seems to have been rather more developed. Thus, acquisition of ownership appears in book 8 and is reasonably followed by *possessio* and *usucapio* in book 9, and the latter is again the subject of book 10. *Emptio venditio* and *servitutes* are dealt with one after another—the latter in book 13—because of their connection with *mancipatio*. But one must wonder why these topics are apparently separated from the rest of acquisition of ownership by *condictio* in book 11;[8] and why servitudes were also dealt with in book 6. 'Succession', however, was treated as a unit in the first four books. The law of 'persons' had not yet been so clearly isolated: *tutela* is in book 6,

---

[1] Cicero, *ad Att.* 7. 2. 8.   [2] As Gaius tells us in the Empire: G. 3. 96.
[3] Mainly before our period.
[4] Cf. *supra*, p. 136. It would, of course, have been extremely significant if the *tripertita* had dealt only with the private law provisions of the XII Tables.
[5] D. 1. 2. 2. 41 (Pomponius, *sing. enchirid.*).
[6] *Supra*, pp. 143 ff.   [7] *Supra*, pp. 155 f.
[8] Other topics were also treated in between, though the surviving sources do not disclose what these were.

but is separated from *statuliberi* in book 7 by *pauperies* and the *lex Aquilia*. After the treatment of *statuliberi* there is a gap in our knowledge, but persons *alieni iuris* were the first topic treated in book 8.[1] Lastly for our present purposes we should observe that it is very difficult to give a rational justification for *postliminium*'s appearing between *societas* and *furtum*.

Alfenus' *digesta*, in so far as it can be reconstructed from Paul's epitome, shows a marked advance in arrangement. The structure is much more logical and rigorous. To a modern eye the most important changes would be the grouping together of all the contracts—or at least of the consensual contracts since only *emptio venditio*, *locatio conductio*, and *societas* were treated[2]—in book 3 of the epitome, and of all the law of property in book 4 and the beginning of book 5. But to say no more would be seriously to underestimate the thought behind Alfenus' scheme. Thus wills and legacies lead on to the real action claiming an inheritance, and this in turn to the real action in general. The next group is of the consensual contracts to which dowry is appended. The link here is the nature of the actions: the contracts give rise to *bonae fidei iudicia* with a *condemnatio* in 'quidquid ob eam rem Numerium Negidium dare facere oportet ex fide bona, eius iudex Numerium Negidium Aulo Agerio condemna'; the action for the return of dowry, the *actio rei uxoriae*, has the unique *condemnatio* in 'quod eius melius aequius erit', which also demands that the judge looks to what is fair.[3] The third group comprises property rights: the terms in *mancipationes*, water rights in book 4, servitudes in book 5.[4] Lastly in book 5 we have *furtum*.[5]

During the course of the second century B.C. the *edictum perpetuum* was gradually being formed, even though, as I have argued, it was not until around 100 B.C. that *edicta* were being issued which in effect changed the substance of the law.[6] We have

---

[1] We should also remember that neither marriage nor slavery was dealt with in Mucius' *ius civile*.   [2] So far as we know.

[3] It may be, as Lenel hesitatingly suggests, *Pal.* i. 49, that Alfenus dealt somewhere in this group with decretal *actiones in factum*.

[4] As already mentioned, *supra*, p. 165, the arrangement would have been neater if servitudes had come before water rights.

[5] There is no way of knowing whether the other delicts were treated along with *furtum*.   [6] Cf. *supra*, pp. 35 ff.

no direct evidence for the arrangement of the Edict in the Republic[1] and I therefore propose to say little about it.[2] But I would suggest with some degree of confidence that the broad outline was similar to that in Hadrian's Edict,[3] since the general arrangement in the latter is less systematic than one would expect if it had undergone full revision.[4] It is also reasonable to think that the clauses on procedure always came first in the Edict.[5]

Each legal institution such as *emptio venditio* and *furtum* would itself raise continuing questions of classification in juristic discussions on the essential nature and the boundaries of each. Does sale require a price in coined money? Can there be a sale in which the vendor retains an interest in the thing to be sold? For theft to be committed must the thief intend to make a gain? Can land be stolen? And so on. The high achievement of the Republican jurists here is best seen in the large extent to which the boundary lines which they set between one institution and another can still clearly be recognized in the laws of the modern Western world.

Further classification and subdivision might be required within the boundaries of an institution. Quintus Mucius distinguished five *genera* of *tutela*[6] and different *genera* of possession.[7] Servius distinguished three *genera* of *tutela*[8] and four *genera* of *furtum*.[9] But however great the conceptual advance implicit in the recognition of *genera*, it is incomplete without the further subdivision into *species*, and of the idea of *species* as a subdivision of *genus* there is not the slightest trace in juristic thinking in the Republic. The point is considered more fully in the next chapter, and here it is enough to note that for modern scholars the division of *genera* into *species* is so essential for conceptual thinking that it does not seem to have been noticed that there is no sign of *species* in

---

[1] But see *supra*, p. 166, n. 6.

[2] And to draw no conclusions from it.

[3] For this see above all Lenel, *Edictum*.

[4] A further argument, which also indicates that the detailed arrangement remained unchanged at times, can be drawn from the appending of the *actio Serviana* to the *interdictum Salvianum*: cf. *supra*, p. 41, n. 2.

[5] Probably, too, one would not go far wrong in thinking there was some mutual influence of the Edict and of Quintus Mucius' *ius civile* in the arrangement of provisions relating to substantive law.

[6] G. 1. 188.   [7] D. 41. 2. 3. 23 (Paul, 54 *ad ed.*).

[8] G. 1. 188.   [9] G. 3. 183.

Republican legal thought. Indeed, modern writers often give the impression that the evidence does exist.[1] The subdivision of *genera* into *species* was, of course, well known to the Republican rhetoricians.[2]

The process of distinguishing and classifying leads naturally, but not inevitably, to definition, and it seems indeed that the Republican jurists were not very ready to give definitions.[3] A few Republican definitions, however, have survived, and they can be subdivided into three main types. First, there are definitions not of legal concepts but of things whose extent has to be measured for the interpretation of a will or contract. In this class are Quintus Mucius' definition of *penus*[4] and Servius' of *silva caedua*.[5] Secondly there are definitions of what are true legal concepts but where the definition seems to have been made with the ulterior motive of establishing excessively narrow or extremely wide boundaries: Publius Mucius' definition of *ambitus*,[6] Quintus Mucius' of *vis*,[7] Servius' of *clam*.[8] Thirdly, there are definitions which seem to be objective attempts to set out the essentials of a legal concept. This is the type which should interest us most in the present context, but it must be admitted that the surviving specimens cannot command unqualified admiration. Servius' definition of *tutela*, 'vis ac potestas in capite libero ad tuendum eum, qui propter aetatem se defendere nequit, iure civili data ac permissa',[9] reveals very little of the essential nature of that institution. Cicero objected[10] that Aquillius Gallus' definition of *litus*,[11] 'qua fluctus eludit', did not

---

[1] Cf., e.g., Schulz, *Legal Science*, p. 64; Stein, *Regulae Iuris* (Edinburgh, 1966), p. 36; explicitly, Kaser, 'Die Gliederung der Rechtsbegriffe in *genera* und *species* wird uns bei den republikanischen Juristen nur für einzelne Begriffe bezeugt', *Zur Methode der römischen Rechtsfindung* (Nachrichten der Akademie der Wissenschaften in Göttingen, i, philologisch-historische Klasse, 1962), pp. 49 ff. at p. 69; and Mette, 'Im einzelnen ist kenntlich, dass Q. Mucius dem γένος 'Vormundschaft', fünf εἴδη zuwies usw.', *Ius civile in artem redactum* (Göttingen, 1954), p. 7.   [2] Cf. *infra*, pp. 191 f.

[3] Cf., e.g., Schulz, *Legal Science*, p. 67.   [4] Aulus Gellius, *N.A.* 4. 1. 17.

[5] D. 50. 16. 30pr. (Gaius, 7 *ad ed. prov.*).

[6] Cicero, *top.* 4. 24; cf. *supra*, pp. 114 f.

[7] D. 50. 17. 73. 2 (Quintus Mucius, *sing.* ὅρων); cf. *supra*, p. 127.

[8] D. 43. 24. 4 (Venuleius, 2 *interd.*); cf. *supra*, p. 127.

[9] D. 26. 1. 1pr. (Paul, 38 *ad ed.*); J. 1. 13. 1: cf. Watson, *Persons*, pp. 102 ff.

[10] *top.* 7. 32.

[11] The word *litus* means the sea-shore, but in the context of the law of property it is right to consider it a legal concept.

use words appropriate to the thing and the jurist. But also the definition lacks precision and leaves considerable doubt as to the extent of the sea-shore. The only satisfactory juristic definition is of *dolus*, again by Aquilius Gallus, 'cum aliud sit simulatum, aliud actum',[1] which does show the scope of fraud for the *actio de dolo*.[2,3] Perhaps we should add to these definitions two which emerge from Cicero, *top*. 6. 29. First, 'hereditas est pecunia quae morte alicuius ad quempiam pervenit iure nec ea aut legata testamento aut possessione retenta.' It is striking that *hereditas* is defined as the part which comes to the heir, not as the whole property left by the deceased.[4] We do not know that a jurist was responsible for this definition. Secondly, 'Gentiles sunt inter se qui eodem nomine sunt quorum maiorum nemo servitutem servivit qui capite non sunt deminuti.' This definition may, but need not, be the work of Scaevola, since Cicero claims 'Nihil enim video Scaevolam pontificem ad hanc definitionem addidisse.' We know so little of the *gentiles* that we cannot tell whether the definition was fully satisfactory.[5]

Thus, the Republican contribution to juristic definition is slight.[6] I have not specifically dealt with the *liber singularis* ὅρων since (with many others) I cannot accept that it is a book written by Quintus Mucius.[7] In any event it does not provide us with any further instances of definitions.[8,9]

---

[1] Cicero, *de nat. deor.* 3. 30. 74.

[2] The definition was accepted by Servius, but the scope of the *actio de dolo* was widened and a new definition was given by Labeo; D. 4. 3. 1. 2 (Ulpian, 11 *ad ed.*).

[3] We know too little to be able to classify Manilius' definition of *nexum*: Varro, *de ling. lat.* 7. 105. On the normal understanding of the term, *nexum* had long been obsolete.   [4] Cf. Watson, *Succession*, p. 1.

[5] Coing espies a rather larger list of Republican definitions: 'Zur Methodik der republikanischen Jurisprudenz', *Studi Arangio-Ruiz* i (Naples, n.d.), 365 ff. at pp. 368 ff.

[6] It may very well be that not all the instances listed in this chapter were originally intended as definitions.   [7] Cf. *supra*, pp. 157 f.

[8] The surviving texts can be examined in Lenel, *Pal.* i. 762 f.

[9] I see no justification for the statement of Stein: 'The early jurists concentrated their writings on definition of the law and their efforts culminated in Q. Mucius Scaevola's great work significantly entitled *liber horon*'; 'The Relations between Grammar and Law in the Early Principate: The Beginnings of Analogy', *Atti del II congresso internazionale della società italiana di storia del diritto* (Florence, 1971), 757 ff. at p. 760.

16

GREEK INFLUENCE

THE two centuries covered by this book were the period of greatest Greek influence on Roman life. Rome started in 200 B.C. what eventually became—though was not planned that way—the conquest of Greece. Roman literature can be said to have begun with Livius Andronicus' (284?–204? B.C.) translation of the *Odyssey*. The major work of the succeeding generation was the comedies of Plautus (255?–184 B.C.) which are adaptations of Greek originals, as are the elegant plays of Terence (190?–159? B.C.). At the other end of the period, the poetry of Catullus—as well as of the slightly later Virgil and Horace—has clear roots in Greek verse. In philosophy Lucretius (94?–55? B.C.) is a disciple of Epicurus, and the philosophical writings of Cicero, the best-known Republican exponent, are mainly derivative. The art of rhetoric, whether exemplified by Cicero or the unknown author of the *Rhetorica ad Herennium*, came almost entirely from the Greeks. The same is true of the visual arts. The style of Roman silver coinage, for instance, from the beginning (around 290 B.C.)[1] to the time of Augustus owes much to Greek coins, and for many designs Greek artists must have been employed. In the first century B.C. Roman copies of Greek marble statues were abundant. It has also been estimated that by the late second century B.C. most educated Romans were probably bilingual.[2]

Inevitably some of this Grecizing would spill over into law and it is not surprising that these two centuries have been described as 'The Hellenistic Period of Roman Jurisprudence'.[3] But foreign

---

[1] Cf. Crawford, *Roman Republican Coin Hoards* (London, 1969), p. 4, the references he cites, and his Table 1.

[2] Scullard, *From the Gracchi to Nero*, 3rd edit. (London, 1970), p. 10.

[3] Schulz, *Legal Science*, pp. 38 ff. For the view that Greek philosophy had a

influence, no matter how strong, will not penetrate all parts of a civilization with equal vigour, and a strong native culture which is regarded with pride, as law was at Rome, may prove resistant.[1] In an attempt to determine the extent of Greek influence on Roman law we shall first look for traces in the substance of the law, then in its arrangement and classification.

Greek thought might, in theory at least, affect the substance of Roman law in various ways. To begin with, the Romans might have taken over or adapted a rule of Greek law. But here the influence, at most, was negligible. No principle, no detail of law seems to have developed from a Greek example unless it is true, as some scholars assert, that the praetorian *actiones iniuriarum* (which at first covered physical assault and, later, defamation)[2] owe something, whether in the substantive law or in the flexible pecuniary condemnation, to the Attic δίκη αἰκίας[3] or the Alexandrian ὕβρις. There are certain similarities between the Greek and Roman law in this area, but also serious divergences, and I doubt whether a case has been, or can be, established in favour of Greek influence.[4] But even if one accepts that the praetorian *actiones iniuriarum*—as opposed to the older civil law remedies—were subject to Greek influence this would still not mean that the

considerable influence on Roman law in general see also Villey, *Leçons d'histoire de la philosophie du droit*, 2nd edit. (Paris, 1962), pp. 23 ff.

[1] Cf. Pringsheim, 'Griechischer Einfluss auf das römische Recht', *BIDR* 2 (1960), 1 ff. especially at pp. 1 f.

[2] Cf. *supra*, pp. 45 ff. The Praetor's *edictum generale* was not intended to change the substantive law.

[3] Lipsius, *Das attische Recht und Rechtsverfahren* (reprinted Darmstadt, 1966), p. 643 and n. 25 maintains that αἰκείας, not αἰκίας, is the correct form.

[4] Cf., for Greek influence of one kind or another, e.g., Hitzig, *Iniuria, Beiträge zur Geschichte der 'iniuria' im griechischen und römischen Recht* (Munich, 1899); Partsch, 'Die alexandrinischen Dikaiomata', *Archiv für Papyrusforschung*, 6 (1913), 551 ff.; Lenel, *Edictum*, p. 398, n. 5; Pringsheim, '*Bonum et aequum*', now in *Gesammelte Abhandlungen*, i (Heidelberg, 1961), pp. 173 ff. at pp. 178 ff. In general against, Pugliese, *Studi sull' 'iniuria'* i (Milan, 1941), pp. 39 ff.; Schulz, *Classical Roman Law* (Oxford, 1951), p. 598; Bongert, 'Recherches sur les récupérateurs', in *Varia, études de droit romain* (Paris, 1952), pp. 99 ff. at pp. 136 ff.; Schmidlin, *Das Rekuperatorenverfahren* (Fribourg, 1963), p. 32, n. 3 (at pp. 32 ff.). Very reasonably Raber deliberately expresses no opinion: *Grundlagen klassischer Injurienansprüche* (Vienna, 1969), p. 1; and Kaser, *RPR* i. 624, n. 11.

substance of Roman law in the late Republic was much influenced by the Greeks.[1]

Again, Greek thought might affect the substance of Roman law if a philosophical opinion was the basis of a legal rule or principle. There is remarkably little evidence for this happening and only two instances can be brought forward for consideration. The first is in D. 33. 10. 7. 2 (Celsus, 19 *dig.*), which has already been discussed.[2] The dispute recorded in the text between Servius and Tubero can be explained without recourse to any specific philosophical doctrines, and it betrays little reliance on philosophical ideas. The second is in D. 50. 16. 25. 1 (Paul, 21 *ad ed.*): 'Quintus Mucius ait partis appellatione rem pro indiviso significari: nam quod pro diviso nostrum sit, id non partem, sed totum esse. Servius non ineleganter partis appellatione utrumque significari.' It is probably not fanciful to think that somewhere behind Quintus Mucius' idea of *pars* lurks Greek philosophical discussion of the relationship between part and whole and between the divisible and the indivisible. But further than that one cannot reasonably go. It does not seem possible to find any forerunner, direct or even indirect, for Mucius' idea.[3] I would suggest, indeed, that an idea akin to Mucius' never existed in Greek philosophical writings: the situation which concerned the jurists was of little interest to the philosophers. A *pro indiviso* share (which Mucius considers a *pars*) can, of course, normally be converted into a *pro diviso* share (which Mucius considers a *totum*),[4] though the steps to do so have not been taken. In most cases whether a share is construed as *pro diviso* or *pro indiviso* will depend entirely upon the wording of the

---

[1] Though *arra* was part of Greek law, and the giving of *arra* was known at Rome as early as Plautus, there is no indication that the early Roman law of sale was influenced by Greek law: cf., for the argument, Watson, *Obligations*, pp. 46 ff. A different view of the role of *arra* in Plautus' plays has since been taken by MacCormack, 'A Note on *Arra* in Plautus', *Irish Jurist*, 6 (1971), 361 ff. Whether his opinion is correct or not does not affect us here.

[2] *Supra*, pp. 123 f.: the best treatment of the text is by Horak, *Rationes decidendi* i (Aalen, 1969), pp. 224 ff.

[3] Sokolowski claims that Mucius' definition is the same as that of Theophrastus, *Historia Plantarum*, i. 1: *Die Philosophie im Privatrecht* i (reprinted Aalen, 1959), p. 442. This is incorrect: cf. Horak, *Rationes* i. 230.

[4] That one can think of *pro indiviso* shares which cannot be made *pro diviso* is not relevant to the argument.

conveyance or will, and not at all upon the subject-matter involved. This is a world away from Greek discussions of the smallest possible unit and of its indivisibility.[1] I submit that at the most the influence of Greek philosophy on this idea of Mucius was the recollection that what was separable from a whole might itself be considered a whole.

Closely related to the foregoing is the situation where a legal decision is supported by an argument from Greek philosophy and where, in fact, the decision could have been suggested by the philosophical theory. There is only one instance but, as it happens, it provides the clearest evidence of the jurists' acquaintance with philosophy.

D. 5. 1. 76 (Alfenus, 6 *dig.*): Proponebatur ex his iudicibus, qui in eandem rem dati essent, nonnullos causa audita excusatos esse inque eorum locum alios esse sumptos, et quaerebatur, singulorum iudicum mutatio eandem rem an aliud iudicium fecisset. respondi, non modo si unus aut alter, sed et si omnes iudices mutati essent, tamen et rem eandem et iudicium idem quod antea fuisset permanere: neque in hoc solum evenire, ut partibus commutatis eadem res esse existimaretur, sed et in multis ceteris rebus: nam et legionem eandem haberi, ex qua multi decessissent, quorum in locum alii subiecti essent: et populum eundem hoc tempore putari qui abhinc centum annis fuisse(n)t, cum ex illis nemo nunc viveret: itemque navem, si adeo saepe refecta esset, ut nulla tabula eadem permaneret quae non nova fuisset, nihilo minus eandem navem esse existimari. quod si quis putaret partibus commutatis aliam rem fieri, fore ut ex eius ratione nos ipsi non idem essemus qui abhinc anno fuissemus, propterea quod, ut philosophi dicerent, ex quibus particulis minimis consisteremus, hae cottidie ex nostro corpore decederent aliaeque extrinsecus in earum locum accederent. quapropter cuius rei species eadem consisteret, rem quoque eandem esse existimari.[2]

Alfenus holds that a case remains the same case if one or all the judges appointed to it are changed, and he supports his decision by claiming that, for instance, a legion remains the same though

---

[1] For an account of various views held see, e.g., Aristotle, *de generatione et corruptione*, 324^b ff.; and among modern writings, Stokes, *One and Many in Presocratic Philosophy* (Washington, D.C., 1971).

[2] Schulz regards the text as interpolated from 'neque in hoc solum', hence the text could not be evidence for the influence of Greek philosophy or rhetoric: *Legal Science*, pp. 84 f. But see on this and other suggested interpolations, Horak, *Rationes* i. 231 ff.

many of the individual soldiers have been changed, a people is
regarded as the same people as it was a century before, a ship is the
same ship even if it has been so often repaired that no single
timber remains unreplaced, and he ends by a *reductio ad absurdum*:

But if anyone thinks that a thing becomes different when its parts are
changed, it would be the case, on that reasoning, that we ourselves are
not the same persons as we were a year ago because, as the philosophers
say, we are made of certain very small particles which daily withdraw
from our body and others from elsewhere take their place.

The ship example, as has been recognized, comes from the thirty-
oared galley of Theseus which was preserved at Athens until the
very late fourth century B.C. and whose timbers were replaced
from time to time, and which was, as Plutarch relates,[1] a standing
illustration for the philosophers in the question of growth. But
as Horak reminds us,[2] Plutarch makes it clear that while some
philosophers regarded the often-repaired ship as the same ship,
others did not. Alfenus for his own purposes has given only one
view as if it were accepted dogma. The question involved is of the
kind which interested both the Stoics and the Peripatetics, whose
doctrines cannot be sharply distinguished.[3] In Alfenus' *reductio
ad absurdum* there is probably a reference to the atomic theory
both in the idea that the human body (like other things) is com-
posed of numerous minute parts and also that these are in constant
motion. We cannot, however, be certain that Alfenus is referring
to the atomic theory. The change of matter in a living body is an
obvious fact for everybody, not only for atomists. And for everyone it is due to the addition and subtraction of 'very small particles':
only the atomists would say that these were the 'smallest possible
particles'. Alfenus' words 'particulis minimis' might mean 'atoms',
but equally need mean only 'very small particles'.[4] The atomic
theory, though properly associated with Epicurus and his school,[5]

[1] *Theseus*, 23. 1.   [2] *Rationes* i. 232.
[3] Horak claims that here in Alfenus there is only 'Vulgärphilosophie' in
which Stoic and Peripatetic ideas are commingled: *Rationes* i. 232. For the views
of other scholars see the references given by Horak, *Rationes* i. 232, n. 24.
[4] I owe this point, along with others, to the kindness of Professor F. H.
Sandbach.
[5] For a Roman view see Lucretius, *de rerum natura*, 2. 62 ff.

also goes back to Democritus and Leucippus.[1] According to Servius, *in Verg. Eclog.* 6. 13, and the *scholia veronensia in Verg. Eclog.* 7. 9, Alfenus had been a pupil of the Epicurean, Siron. The statement that we are not the same person we were a year ago seems to be Alfenus' own contribution for the purpose of making the *reductio* even more striking. What some philosophers seem to have said is that a man is not the same today as he was yesterday.[2] Such a view used in legal argument would have received little sympathy from the Republican lawyers, and Alfenus rightly prefers to talk of a year, whether he knew of the philosophers' similar argument about a day or not. From the arguments from the ship and from the apparent use made of the atomic theory the conclusion is unavoidable that Alfenus was more concerned with having his opinion on the legal case accepted than he was with the purity of his philosophical position, and, further, that he reached his conclusion not on philosophical considerations but on common-sense grounds, and that philosophy merely provided him with subsequent justifications. If this view is correct, the text would demonstrate the jurist's knowledge of general philosophical learning but not that this learning contributed to the development of the substance of the law.

Less directly Greek thought could have helped in the development of the substance of the law if, as a result of proper understanding of the dialectical method, institutions were placed in *genera*, *species* were observed, and the proper distinctions within an institution were drawn and applied. Organization and ordering of concepts is, to some extent, natural to the human mind and is not specifically Greek. The Code of Hammurabi provides one example of what had been achieved in the organization of legal material without the help of Greece. But the Greek contribution was the double invention of γένος, genus and εἶδος, species. A genus contains classes of items possessing common structural characters and it is divided into species where the classes are

---

[1] Apparently there is no evidence that the theory goes back to Heracleitus, as was once thought.

[2] Plutarch, *Moralia* 392D; 559B. The idea seems to go back to Epicharmus: fr. 2 in Diels, *Die Fragmente der Vorsokratiker* i, 6th edit. by Kranz (Berlin, 1951), p. 196.

marked off from each other by the differences existing between them.[1] The conception of genus and species does appear very clearly in Cicero,[2] but it cannot be emphasized too strongly that there is no sign of species in this context[3] in Republican juristic thought.[4] Certainly we are told that Quintus Mucius distinguished five *genera* of *tutela*[5] and different *genera* of possession,[6] and Servius three *genera* of *tutela*[7] and four *genera* of *furtum*.[8, 9] But the drawing of these distinctions could easily have occurred without the influence of Greek dialectics; and without the further division of a genus into its species the essential Greek contribution is lacking. It is not indicative of strong Greek influence on Quintus Mucius and Servius that they use the word *genus* in this connection,[10] since that word had been used to mean 'kind' since at least the time of Terence.[11]

Again it has been argued that the Stoic theory of etymology— that the word shows the reality of the thing named—influenced the Republican jurists.[12] And indeed we do find the jurists concerned with etymology: Quintus Mucius with *postliminium*[13] and *penus*;[14] Servius also with *postliminium*,[15] with *testamentum*[16] and *vindicia*;[17] Alfenus with *urbs*;[18] Ofilius with *tugurium*;[19] and Trebatius with *sacellum*.[20] But in Greece itself, long before the Stoics and any Hellenistic theory of language, attempts were being made—as early as Homer—to use etymology to clarify the meaning of

---

[1] What constitutes a genus or species is a relative matter.

[2] e.g. *top.* 3. 13, 14; 7. 30, 31; 9. 39, 40. Cicero prefers to translate εἶδος by *forma* rather than *species*.

[3] D. 33. 10. 7. 1 (Celsus, 19 *dig.*) has Tubero using the word *species*, but not referring to the subdivision of a *genus*.   [4] Cf. also *supra*, pp. 153 f.

[5] G. 1. 188.   [6] D. 41. 2. 3. 23 (Paul, 54 *ad ed.*).

[7] G. 1. 188.   [8] G. 3. 183.

[9] D. 33. 10. 6pr. (Alfenus, 3 *dig. a Paulo epit.*) is not relevant.

[10] In fact it is not absolutely certain, though it is probable, that they did use the word *genus*.

[11] *Hec.* 198; Cato, *de agri cult.* 46. 1; Accius, fr. 15; Lucilius 1100.

[12] Coing, 'Zur Methodik der republicanischen Jurisprudenz', *Studi Arangio-Ruiz* i (Naples, n.d.), 365 ff. at pp. 372 ff.

[13] Cicero, *top.* 8. 37.   [14] Aulus Gellius, *N.A.* 4. 1. 17.

[15] Cicero, *top.* 8. 37.   [16] Aulus Gellius, *N.A.* 7. 12. 2.

[17] Festus s.v. *vindiciae*; but not, I think, with *noxia*: Festus s.h.v.

[18] D. 50. 16. 239. 6 (Pomponius, *sing. enchirid.*).

[19] D. 50. 16. 180. 1 (Pomponius, 30 *ad Sab.*).

[20] Aulus Gellius, *N.A.* 7. 12. 5, 6.

obscure words.[1] And in the Republican jurists' attempts to use etymology to show the meaning of a word there is nothing which points specifically to Stoic doctrine[2] or to the teachings of any other school. Proof of Greek philosophical influence is accordingly non-existent.[3] The very most that might be legitimately claimed is that the Roman jurists[4] learned from the Greeks (directly or indirectly) that to know the etymology of a word might help in elucidating its meaning.[5]

To sum up: there would appear to be remarkably little evidence to support a hypothesis that Greek philosophical thought had much influence on the development of the substance of the law in the later Republic.

Schulz, who claims that Quintus Mucius Scaevola's *ius civile* was the most considerable work of the period, writes of it: 'A product of the dialectical method, which Mucius was the first to employ systematically, it was the first dialectical system of law in the grand manner and long remained fundamental.'[6] But such a statement raises a question to which I think no proper answer can be given, namely what does legal arrangement and classification in the late Republic owe to Greek thought? Certainly there was no model in Greek law codes or legal or philosophical writings for any Republican arrangement, whether of Quintus Mucius or Alfenus or of the Edict.[7] The question relates, therefore, to the general issue whether Greek thought suggested the desirability of classification and arrangement, and whether without the dialectical method the arrangement and classification would have been less

---

[1] Cf., e.g., Reitzenstein, *RE* 6. 807 ff. at 807 f., s.v. *Etymologika*; Pfeiffer, *History of Classical Scholarship* (Oxford, 1968), pp. 4, 12.

[2] For a brief account of the Stoic doctrine see Reitzenstein, *RE* 6. 808 ff.

[3] Philosophical dependence is too easily claimed by modern scholars; cf. the demonstration by Pfeiffer that Philetas, Callimachus, and their followers were *not* Peripatetics: *Classical Scholarship*, p. 95.

[4] Jurists; we are not here concerned with the Roman grammarians.

[5] Again nothing relevant here should be argued from the fact that the jurists were aware that a word might have more than one meaning; or that Servius observed that a *lex* which uses two negatives permits rather than prohibits. D. 50. 16. 237 (Gaius, 5 *ad leg. XII tab.*).

[6] *Legal Science*, p. 94. Elsewhere Schulz claims that 'the importation of the dialectical method from Greece worked a far-reaching change': *Legal Science*, p. 62.

[7] So far as I know the existence of such a model has never been suggested.

satisfactory than it was. A thoroughly ambiguous answer must be returned. On the one hand by the time of Quintus Mucius the Romans were well acquainted with the dialectical method and it is difficult to believe that the jurists would be immune from its influence. Indeed, Cicero praises Servius for his skill in the art of dialectic.[1] On the other hand, as the example of the Code of Hammurabi shows, legal classification and arrangement did not need Greek dialectics to develop. Moreover, Schulz consistently exaggerates the extent and quality of arrangement and classification in Republican juristic writings. His reconstruction of the arrangement of Quintus Mucius' *ius civile*[2]—which he claims is 'a true dialectical system'—is much too neat and is at variance with the evidence;[3] and he can also maintain without real evidence that the adoption of dialectic by jurisprudence 'led to a systematic study of legal genera and species'.[4,5]

So far nothing has been said about the influence of Greek rhetoric, though some scholars believe that it 'was not so much Greek philosophical thought as it was Greek rhetoric which gave Roman legal thought the decisive impulse'.[6] Once again we are faced with an impossible problem of evidence and proof. It is certain that rhetoric was a matter of very serious study at Rome in the later Republic, that Roman rhetoric derived almost entirely (though with its own emphasis)[7] from Greek rhetoric, and that the Roman jurists would be well acquainted with the art of rhetoric. It can be confidently assumed that the jurists' knowledge of the kinds and forms of argument would help them to frame their own arguments with greater precision, and we can presume that in turn this would at times lead to the drawing of legal distinctions.[8] But

---

[1] *Brutus*, 41. 151 ff.; cf. *supra*, pp. 159 f.   [2] *Legal Science*, p. 95.

[3] Cf. *supra*, pp. 143 ff.   [4] *Legal Science*, p. 63.

[5] Nothing will be said of the arrangement of the Edict since this cannot be reconstructed for the Republic. But the arrangement of Hadrian's Edict is far from being satisfactory.

[6] So Kunkel, 'Legal Thought in Greece and Rome', *Juridical Review*, 65 (1953), 1 ff. at p. 14: cf. Stroux, *Römische Rechtswissenschaft und Rhetorik* (Potsdam, 1949).

[7] Cf. Marrou, *A History of Education in Antiquity* (London, 1956), pp. 252 f.

[8] Yet to judge from Cicero, *top.* 1. 1 f., Trebatius (and a learned teacher of oratory, who is not named) had been unaware of the existence of Aristotle's *Topica*, and the jurist did not understand the system of τόποι.

it would be unjustified, in the absence of concrete evidence,[1] to make a greater claim for the influence of Greek rhetoric on Roman law. Different types of argument can be and have been used in debate without a formal science of rhetoric.[2] It should also be stressed that there was a sharp division of labour at Rome between the *oratores* and the *iuris consulti*[3] and that the training of the latter remained thoroughly Roman and was not visibly affected by Hellenistic educational methods.[4,5] There is, however, one institution, the *querella inofficiosi testamenti*, where it is plausible to assert that rhetoric played a role in its evolution.[6]

It would seem, therefore, that there is very little concrete evidence which would support an opinion that there was considerable Greek influence on the development of Roman law in the last two centuries of the Republic.[7]

[1] For the absence of evidence see Wesel, *Rhetorische Statuslehre und Gesetzesauslegung der römischen Juristen* (Cologne, 1967), especially at pp. 137 f. Even the standard vocabulary of rhetoric for the types of argument arising from the issue was not taken over by the Republican jurists: Wesel, who concludes that the influence of rhetoric on Roman law was very small, finds only one of the five rhetorical *status*, the *status scriptum et sententia* in the jurists, and even that only in a changed form and in the Empire: *Statuslehre*, pp. 138 ff. On *verba et voluntas* cf. already *supra*, pp. 123 ff. and pp. 129 ff.

[2] Cf., e.g., on the *reductio ad absurdum*, Daube, *Roman Law, Linguistic, Social and Philosophical Aspects* (Edinburgh, 1969), pp. 176 ff.

[3] Cf. *supra*, pp. 106 ff.   [4] Cf. *supra*, pp. 108 f.

[5] On the problems discussed in this chapter see most recently Nörr, *Divisio und Partitio* (Berlin, 1972), especially at pp. 2 f. Nothing has been said in the chapter about the vaguer matter of Hellenistic cultural attitudes which might affect the approach to law. No doubt these attitudes could be of importance—for instance, it can reasonably be suggested that Sextus Aelius' historical and grammatical explanations of the XII Tables owe something to Hellenistic education (cf. *supra*, p. 136, n. 1)—but how can their significance be assessed?

[6] But the early development, including the part played by the *color insaniae*, is the subject of much controversy: cf. Watson, *Succession*, pp. 62 ff. and the authorities there cited.

[7] Of the aristocratic *Weltanschauung* of the same period, Badian writes: 'As for the Greek influence it seems to me that—here as elsewhere—Roman aristocrats merely acquired a certain skill at formulating Roman ideas in Greek language'; *Roman Imperialism in the Late Republic* (Pretoria, 1967), p. 15, n. 1.

INDEX OF TEXTS

I. LEGAL SOURCES

II. NON-LEGAL SOURCES

INDEX OF TEXTS

|---|---|
II, 1. 47. 123	93, n. 3; 93, n. 5
	42, n. 9
II, 1. 47. 123–4	93, n. 1
II, 1. 47. 124	42, n. 9
II, 1. 48. 125–6	39, n. 7; 55, n. 3
II, 1. 60. 155	17, n. 4
II, 3. 65. 152	32, n. 3; 39, n. 2

Philosophica

de amicitia

1. 1	108, n. 3; 160, n. 4
2. 6	113, n. 4; 120, n. 3

de finibus

1. 4. 12	51, n. 11; 138, n. 1; 139, n. 3

de legibus

1. 4. 13	109, n. 2
1. 4. 14	140, n. 11; 162, n. 9
1. 5. 17	31; 31, n. 2; 61, n. 5; 120, n. 4
1. 21. 55	121, n. 4
1. 22. 57	121, n. 5
2. 7. 18	117, n. 2
2. 20. 50	52, n. 1; 105, n. 9
2. 20. 50 ff.	180, n. 5
2. 21. 53	52, n. 1; 105, n. 9
2. 23. 58–25. 64	121, n. 5
2. 23. 59	51, n. 4; 120; 136; 136, n. 2
2. 23. 59–25. 62	121, n. 1
2. 24. 61	121, n. 1
3. 3. 8	69
3. 8. 19	121, n. 5
3. 9. 22	17, n. 4
3. 19. 44	121, n. 2

de natura deorum

3. 30. 74	32, n. 1; 32, n. 2; 39, n. 4; 72; 132, n. 3; 185, n. 1

de officiis

1. 12. 37	121, n. 5
2. 13. 47	56, n. 1; 56, n. 2
3. 14. 60	32, n. 1; 32, n. 2; 39, n. 4; 72 f.; 104, n. 12
3. 15. 61	121, n. 5
3. 16. 66	51, n. 9
3. 17. 70	156, n. 4
3. 17. 71	86, n. 6

de re publica

1. 13. 20	41, n. 3
1. 18. 30	104, n. 4; 136, n. 6
2. 36. 61	16, n. 4

2. 37. 63	8, n. 3; 18, n. 4
4. 10. 12	121, n. 2

de senectute

4. 10	8, n. 5

Tusculanae disputationes

1. 9. 18	136, n. 6
2. 23. 55	121, n. 5
3. 5. 11	121, n. 5
4. 2. 4	121, n. 5

Rhetorica

Brutus

7. 26 ff.	106, n. 3
14. 53	106, n. 3
17. 65 ff.	106, n. 4
26. 98	104, n. 7
28. 108	106, n. 5
29. 110	106, n. 6
30. 113	104, n. 9
30. 113–14	56, n. 1
30. 113 ff.	106, n. 6
30. 115	107, n. 2
39. 145	107, n. 1; 129, n. 9; 130, n. 2
41. 151	107, n. 3; 107, n. 4
41. 151 ff.	159; 160, n. 1; 194, n. 1
42. 154	104, n. 12
42. 155	107, n. 2; 107, n. 4
52. 194 ff.	106, n. 7
52. 194–53. 198	123, n. 2
89. 306	108; 108, n. 4; 160, n. 3

de inventione

2. 22. 65	3, n. 9
2. 22. 65 ff.	4, n. 5
2. 22. 67	40, n. 8; 169, n. 3; 171; 171, n. 3
2. 22. 68	171, n. 3
2. 42. 122	106, n. 7; 123, n. 2
2. 50. 148	122

de oratore

1. 37. 168	102, n. 2
1. 39. 180	106, n. 7; 123, n. 2
1. 40. 181	152, n. 2
1. 41. 186	3, n. 2
1. 42. 190	160, n. 5
1. 44. 195	111, n. 2; 120; 120, n. 5
1. 45. 200	104, n. 10
1. 48. 212	105, n. 5
1. 56. 237	121, n. 5
1. 56. 239	104, n. 7

GENERAL INDEX